The Intel Safer Computing Initiative

Building Blocks for Trusted Computing

David Grawrock

Intel
PRESS

ISBN 0-9764832-6-2

This book is printed on acid-free paper. ∞

Publisher: Richard Bowles

Content Architect: Stuart Goldstein

Editor: David B. Spencer

Text Design & Composition: Wasser Studios

Graphic Art: Wasser Studios (illustrations), Ted Cyrek (cover)

Library of Congress Cataloging in Publication Data:

Printed in the United States of America

10 9 8 7 6 5 4 3 2 1

First printing, March 2006

To my wife, Sherrill, who has put up with my travels and long hours working on LT. To my children, Matthew, Jared, Steven, Evan, Christopher, Braden, and Alina, who have loved their father through thick and thin—even though he does work on computers. And finally, to my parents who are very surprised that their son is an author.

Contents

Foreword   xv

Preface   xix

Part I   Background Information   1

Chapter 1   Trusted Computing   3
The Basic Problem of Trust   4
The Trusted Computer and LaGrande Technology   5
Basic Definitions   6
    Our Definition of Trust   6
    The Trust Decision   7
    The Platform   8
    The Client   8
    Owner, User, and Operator   9
The Weakest Link   10
    Protection in the Enclave   12
    Effect of Providing More Protections   12
Basic Cryptography   13
    Symmetric Encryption   13
    Asymmetric Encryption   13
    Combination   14
    Cryptographic Hash   14

Trusted Channel and Trusted Path   15
   Trusted Channel   15
   Trusted Path   15
   Combination   15
What is LaGrande Technology (LT)?   16

Chapter 2   **History of Trusted Computing   17**
Early Papers   18
   1970 Task Force   18
   Bell-LaPadula   20
   The Rainbow Series   20
   Industry Response   21
The Future through the Past   22
Personal Computers   23
CPU Internals   25
   Protected Mode   25
   Memory Management   26
   Front-side Bus   28
   Multiple CPU Systems   28
MCH   28
   Memory   28
   Display Adapter   28
ICH   29
   Keyboard   29
   USB   29
   LPC Bus   29
Current Intel® Architecture Security Support   30
   Rings   30
   Protected Mode   30
   Paging   31
Security Properties   31

Part II   **What Is Happening Today?   33**

Chapter 3   **The Current Environment   35**
Platform   36
Hardware   36
Operating System   37
   Ring Use   37
   Drivers   38
   Configuration   39

Applications   39
  Installation   39
  Drivers   39
  Configuration   39
Malware   40
  Malware Components   40
  Break Once, Run Everywhere   41
Configurations   42
Finding Bad Platforms   42

Chapter 4   Anatomy of an Attack   43

Programmer versus Attacker   45
Application Today   46
  Application Components   47
  Display Windows   48
  Reading Keystrokes   48
  Password Processing   49
  Program Decision   49
Malware Attack Points   50
  Manipulate Memory   50
  Manipulate Input   52
  Manipulate Output   53
Attack Overview   55
Mitigating Attacks   56
  Hardware Mitigations   56

Part III   LaGrande Technology Design   57

Chapter 5   LaGrande Technology Objectives   59

The Basic Questions   60
  What is Being Protected?   60
  Who is the Attacker?   60
  What Resources Does the Attacker Have?   61
Previous Platform Objectives   62
  Ease of Use   63
  Manageability   63
  Privacy   63
  Performance   64
  Versatility   64
  Backwards Compatibility   65

Protection and Attack Matrix 66
   Attack Type 66
   User Intent 70
   Application Suitability 72
The Features 76
   Protected Execution 76
   Protected Memory Pages 77
   Sealed Storage 77
   Protected Input 77
   Protected Graphics 78
   Attestation 78

Chapter 6   LaGrande Technology Design Principles 79
Security Principles 80
   Least Privilege 80
   Economy of Mechanism 81
   Complete Mediation 81
   Open Design 82
   Separation of Privilege 82
   Least Common Mechanism 83
   Psychological Acceptability 83
Design Principles 84
   High-level Requirements 84
   Environment Requirements 84
   User Assumptions 85
   Attackers 85
   Protection Requirements 86
   Upgrade Requirements 86
   LT Non-requirements 86
LT Protection Boundary 87
   Page Protections 88
   Paging Mechanism 90
   NoDMA 91
   TGTT 92
   STM 93
   VMM 93

VMM Measurement   94
    Description of Measurement and Identity   94
    Obtaining the VMM Identity   94
    SMX Measurement Instructions   95
    Chipset Hardware   96
    Storing VMM Measurement in TPM   96
Other CPU Resources   97
Keyboard and Mouse   98
Overt Channels   98
Boundary Summary   100
Requirements and Boundary Comparison   101

Chapter 7   Protected Execution   103
VMX Operation   104
VM Control Structure   106
VMM Launch and VM Creation   107
Protected Virtual Machines   109
    VMM with No Services   112
    VMM with Kernel Features   112
Measured VMM   113
    Measuring the VMM   114
    Launching the VMM   115
Protecting Secrets   116
Establishing Secrets   117
Boundary Conditions   118

Chapter 8   Attestation   119
TPM Design   120
TPM Basic Components   121
    Input and Output   121
    Execution Engine   123
    Program Code   123
    Non-Volatile (NV) Storage   124
    Volatile Storage   126
    Secure Hash Algorithm 1 (SHA-1)   126
    Platform Configuration Register (PCR)   129
    Random Number Generator (RNG)   131
    RSA Engine   131
    Opt-in   133
    Attestation Identity Key   134
    Authorization   134

TPM Functionality   135
   Transitive Trust   135
   Sealed Storage   136
   Transport Session   138
Locality   139
Attesting To Information   141
   Measurement Agent   142
Use of the TPM   142

Chapter 9   **Protected Input and Output   143**

Trusted Channel and Trusted Path   144
Why a Trusted Channel?   145
Trusted Channel Basics   146
   Hardware Trusted Channels   147
   Cryptographic Trusted Channels   147
   Trusted Channel Device Focus   149
Device Support   149
Secured Discrete Graphics   150
Secured Integrated Graphics   151
   Trusted Sprite Model   151
   Resource Management   152
   Panic Blue Screen   154
Human Interface Design   155
Trusted Input   155
   Peripheral or Bus   156
   Trusted Input Driver Endpoint   157
Trusted USB Peripheral   157
   Verification of Session Key Creation   159
Trusted USB Controller   159
Trusted USB Operation   160
   Trusted USB Teardown   161
Trusted Mobile Keyboard Controller   161
   TMKBC Overview   163
   TMKBC Initialization   163
   TMKBC Operation   163
   TMKBC Teardown   164
Trusted I/O and LT   164

Part IV   **LaGrande Technology Architecture   165**

Chapter 10 LaGrande Technology Architecture   167
Actual Use   169
Measured Virtual Machine Monitor   170
  Memory Arbitration   170
  Resource Assignment   171
  Communication Channel   171
  Partition Lifecycle   171
Standard Partition   172
  Operating System   172
  Application   172
Protected Partition   173
  Kernel   173
  Applet   174
  Application   175
Partition Communication   175
  IPC   176
  RPC   176
  Other Mechanisms   176
The OS, MVMM, and Kernel Interaction   177
  OS, MVMM, and Kernel from Same Vendor   177
  MVMM and Kernel from Same Vendor   177
  OS and MVMM from Same Vendor   178
  OS and Kernel from Same Vendor   178
  All Three Components from Different Vendors   179
Application Design Options   180
  Unaware Applications   180
  Protected Component   181
  Contained Application   184
Application Use   184

Chapter 11 Late Launch   185
Launching the Protected Partition   186
  A History of SENTER   187
  Initiate the Protections at Any Time   188
  Ensure that All CPUs Participate   189
  Be Sure that the Launch Can Detect Any Tampering   191
  Knowing the Identity of the Launched Environment   191
  Ensure Properly Configured Hardware   191

The GETSEC [SENTER] Sequence   192
   Loading the Modules   193
   Executing GETSEC [SENTER]   194
   Issuing SENTER-ACK   195
   ILP Processing   196
SINIT Processing   198
   SINIT Load   198
Storing SINIT Measurement   200
   TPM Bus Considerations   200
   Setting the PCR   200
   TPM Response to TPM.HASH.START   201
   ILP Measurement Transmission   202
Initialize ILP State   202
   Unlocking the Chipset   203
GETSEC [SENTER] Completion   203
SINIT Execution   203
   Initialize SMM Handling   204
   Enable NoDMA   205
   SCLEAN Validation   205
   MVMM Loading   206
   Passing Control to the MVMM   207
MVMM Execution   207
   Enabling Interrupts   207
   Enabling SMI   208
Secure Launch Recap   208
GETSEC [SEXIT] Processing   209
   GETSEC [SEXIT] Initiation   210
   GETSEC [SEXIT] Validation   211
   GETSEC [SEXIT] Rendezvous   211
   MVMM Shutdown   211
LT-Shutdown   212

Chapter 12   Configuration Concerns   213
LT Chipset   213
Memory Folding   214
   Trusting Memory   215
   Locking the Memory Configuration   216
   Testing the Configuration   216

GART/Graphics Aliasing   216
   Ensure GART Properties   217
   System Memory Overlap   218
Power and Frequency   218
   Overclocking   219
SCHECK   220
Additional Platform Configurations   220
New Issues   220

Chapter 13   Hardware Attacks   221

Rogue CPU   222
   Not Joining the Protected Environment   222
   Not Exiting the Protected Environment   223
   Results of Suspending the CPU   223
RESET Protection   223
   Reset Definition   224
   System Memory Properties   224
   What to Protect?   225
   Who Determines Prior State?   225
   Protection Sequence   226
   Setting the ICH Flag   227
   Adding the TPM   227
   State Table   228
SCLEAN AC Module   228
   Running SCLEAN   229
   Registering SCLEAN   231
INIT Protection   234
S2/S3/S4 Sleep Protection   234
SMI Handling   236
   SMM Transfer Module   237
   SMM Loading   238
   STM MVMM Negotiation   240
Bus Attacks   241
   Front Side Bus   241
   Hublink   241
   Low Pin Count Bus   242

Part V   The Bottom Line   243

Chapter 14 Defending the Platform Against Attacks   245
Vulnerabilities 246
The Example Application 246
   The Attacker's Goal 247
   Application Functionality 247
   Application Design 247
   Vulnerabilities 249
Underlying V4 Vulnerabilities 251
   Memory Access 251
   Driver Manipulation 252
   Uncontrolled Program Access 253
What Remains 253
   Isolation 253
   Hardware Attacks 254
Matching Requirements 255

Chapter 15 The Future   257
New Attacks 257
   Changing the Protection Boundary 258
   Devious Attackers 258
   Being Perfect 258
New Features 259
   Chipset Topologies 259
   SEXIT ACM 260
   Additional Hardware Protections 260
Following the Principles 261

Glossary   263

References   269

Index   271

Foreword

As I write this foreword in early 2006, we are facing a growing crisis in cyber security. Computers are nearly ubiquitous in modern society, with new uses being found continuously. At the same time, the number and variety of attacks against our computing infrastructure is also increasing. Our systems and underlying infrastructure are threatened by spam, phishing, identity theft, viruses, rootkits, botnets, spyware, and more. Antivirus vendors report that they are receiving an average of 50 new viruses and variants a day from around the world. For 2005, the CERT[†] Coordination Center (CERT/CC) reported receiving almost 6,000 new security flaws in widely used software—over 115 per week, on average. Last year, some experts estimated losses from fraud, downtime, and outright damage of data to be in excess of $100,000,000,000 worldwide. All of these numbers have been growing each year, as has the online population: the estimated world online population stands at over 1 billion, with a second billion expected to come online over the next decade. Some of those people will join the ranks of the vandals and criminals attacking our systems. Most of them, however, simply become additional victims.

Mark Twain once wrote that to boil a frog, you don't drop it in a pot of boiling water because it will jump right out again. Instead, you put the frog in a pot of water and slowly bring it to a boil. The frog doesn't notice the gradual change until it meets its demise.

That's an apt analogy for what we are seeing in computing. Most people regularly install new patches, update their defenses, and clean up after incidents, all the while largely oblivious to the alarming growth of the threat to our infrastructure, finances, and livelihoods. A clear and present danger is simply not being recognized or addressed. Consumers are unwilling to pay extra for security or hold vendors accountable for flawed products, and neither industry nor government are investing sufficiently in long-term research and education to address the issues. The cyber world is coming to a boil, and its potential demise isn't sufficiently recognized.

For those of us who have been working in information security research for any length of time, this situation is terribly frustrating. Some principles for building and deploying more secure systems are well-known, and more are yet to be discovered, but the vast majority of people don't seem to listen . . . or care. End-users want flashy new features more than they seem to want safer computing. Software vendors want to sell more products to the customers, so they roll out new, larger systems that invariably incorporate new vulnerabilities. Meanwhile, the big customers, commercial and government alike, continue to buy the bloated, buggy software whose flaws and defects they view as unavoidable and tolerable. It is no wonder there is a booming business in add-on defenses to address flaws that really shouldn't be in the systems in the first place.

Albert Einstein is alleged to have said "Insanity is doing the same thing over and over, and expecting it to produce different results." By that definition, the majority of computer users—no matter whether they are found at home, in companies, or in government—may be considered insane. They are caught up in a cycle of buy-patch-upgrade that is getting continually more expensive and less safe. But they continue to do the same things, thinking that the next release or the next set of products will make everything better. Those of us who try to effect fundamental changes are often labeled as eccentrics or "cranks." We end up gaining a deeper appreciation of Apollo's curse on Cassandra in Greek mythology: she was given the power to see the future, but never able to persuade anyone of what she foresaw.

Into this arena steps David Grawrock and his colleagues at Intel. They also see the dangerous trends, and given Intel's history with modern computing perhaps they believe they can help make a difference. But how do they get vendors to write safer software and end-users to adopt better practices? Perhaps the best way is by breaking the cycle of insanity (as defined by Einstein) and doing something different.

LaGrande Technology (LT) has been years in the making. What you will read about in this book has occupied years of development effort and deep thought by many engineers and scientists. It is a combination of features that can be built into a computing platform to provide greater confidence in the software by enforcing certain behaviors in hardware. LT can be used to separate sensitive computations from other processes, can protect physical memory from snooping, and can help ensure that only trusted code can execute certain operations. LT can also provide strong evidence (attestation) about what software is running. And along with all of this, LT is backwards-compatible with current platforms, and enabling it is optional.

David Grawrock has been intimately involved in the development of LT. As someone with long experience in information security, he knows how the LT platform can help make a difference. But to make that difference, it is necessary for people to understand what LT is, and why it is designed the way it is. That understanding should help people recognize the capabilities of an LT-enabled system, which might help create market demand. As a different way of doing things, perhaps it is a partial cure for the insanity of non-secure computing.

LT is complex, with many interacting parts. In this book, David has explained what those parts are, why they are present, and how they interact. Don't be disappointed, though, if you get lost while reading this book—the complexity can be overwhelming after awhile. I've been to LT briefings at Intel, read design documents, spoken with the engineers, and I still got lost the first time I read this book because it is rich in detail and keeping all the acronyms and interrelationships sorted out isn't easy. But as with unraveling a knot, or traversing a maze, once you've gotten an overview of the whole thing, you can understand it more easily when you revisit it a second and third time. There is much more to the LT design than is immediately obvious, and David has attempted to strike a balance, being complete and informative, yet not burying the reader in minutiae.

Intel has taken a bold step forward with LT. As David notes in the text, security is about reducing risk and building trust. Deploying LT does involve risks. The market may not accept it. A hidden flaw in the design might not be discovered for some time, and unlike software, chipsets can't undergo periodic patching. Or the technology is used in some untoward way and LT is blamed. David and his colleagues have already been vilified by some people who believe that anything similar to the LT initiative is simply a means to enable big corporate entities to enforce their rapacious intellectual property policies. However, after reading this book, it should be clear that the goals for LT are different.

The biggest threat is that consumers don't understand what LT is about, and when they deploy buggy, poorly designed software on an LT platform that fails to support security, LT gets blamed. That is why Intel calls this the "Safer Computing Initiative." It is neither safe nor secure simply because LT is present. As a society, we need to also address the issues of software quality, legal response to online crime, and user expectations, if we want to have more secure systems. That means we need to kick our habit of accepting flaws and attacks as "business as usual" and actually invest in cyber security. LT is simply one building block in the process.

Whatever happens with LT, it is an interesting and important contribution to the body of cyber security design. This book is an excellent way to learn about LT and what it can do. After reading this book, maybe more than once, you won't be in a position to write software to take advantage of LT. But maybe you'll better appreciate why you might want to do so, and what LT can and can't do for you. With that appreciation, perhaps more people than just the "cranks" can see some safer computing in our future.

Eugene H. Spafford

Professor, Purdue University CERIAS

January 2006

Preface

Why write a book about an Intel security initiative codenamed LaGrande Technology (LT)? One major answer is to keep the peace in the author's home. Over the last few years, my frequent flyer account has soared, and while it's always nice to find new places on earth to visit, sometimes one needs to be at home.[1]

Mostly, the content for this book comes from a presentation known amongst Intel security wonks as the "six-hour LT presentation." The author never really gave it in six hours: it took anywhere from one hour to three days. Certainly, the days spent on the three-day seminar were long and the conversations very deep. With the release of LT comes a need for many more companies to understand the background of LT and the problems that LT can solve. So I've written this book to give you all the information you need without having to add your workplace to the destinations in my frequent flyer account.

---

[1] Although the last family vacation took advantage of all of those frequent flyer miles and flew the kids to our destination.

Geographic Primer

One of my favorite slides in the LT presentation is the slide explaining where the name LaGrande comes from. Intel picks code names from geographical features. One of the early members of the LT team, Richard Trinh, picked LaGrande as the code name from the next names on the list. As the project was working on a "technology" instead of a product, the full name of LaGrande Technology quickly became LT. LaGrande is a lovely place that I enjoy visiting. It has fly fishing in the area and, at least to me, it has some lovely scenery.

Book Structure

I would like to give the reader a roadmap to the subsequent chapters in this book. Before I do I would like to explain a "guilty pleasure" that I had in writing the book. The chapter template shows a quote that illustrates some theme about the chapter. I found it fun to search the Internet using phrases from the chapter and finding various quotes that matched, or somewhat matched, the theme. I ended up with more quotes than I could rationally use, but here in the preface, and especially here in the book structure section, I am going to use a few more of them. Enjoy the quotes and play the game of trying to see how the quote matches the section under discussion.

Background Information

> One's mind has a way of making itself up in the background, and it suddenly becomes clear what one means to do.
>
> —A.C. Benson

The first two chapters cover the background of trusted computing. LaGrande Technology is not the first use of the security concepts; rather it is the next product in a long line of research and products. The chapters provide you with an understanding of what research came before and how some products used the research.

Chapter 1: Trusted Computing

One always needs to define terms. Especially when one deals with security and trust issues, a precise definition of terms is critical. Chapter 1 starts with basic definitions that are used throughout the book. Understanding the definition of a trusted platform is mandatory before reading any additional chapters. The chapter also covers some basic cryptography terms and if the reader is familiar with those terms, the reader can skip these sections.

Chapter 2: History of Trusted Computing

Chapter 2 is a history lesson. Many of the design features of LaGrande Technology are not new but designs that have been in use for years. The chapter covers some of the early research in trusted computing and the application of the research. The history lesson is important, as with the knowledge of history the reader will understand that LaGrande Technology builds on previous research and applications.

Another part of the history lesson is to understand the personal computer platform. An understanding of the basic parts of the personal computer is mandatory for understanding what LaGrande Technology provides.

The first components under discussion are the Central Processing Unit (CPU), Memory Controller Hub (MCH) and Input Output Controller Hub (ICH). The history lesson shows you how the CPU changed over time.

The inner workings of the CPU, with a special emphasis on page tables and ring structures, provide a basis for understanding the LaGrande Technology enhancements.

A description of major platform busses explains how information moves between the various components.

What Is Happening Today?

> *The problems that exist in the world today, cannot*
> *be solved by the level of thinking that created them.*
> —Albert Einstein

Moving from the past to the present, the next two chapters discuss what platforms look like today and what vulnerabilities are present in the current platforms.

Chapter 3: The Current Environment

Many users and program designers are unfamiliar with the width and breadth of attacks that are in the "wild." The wild is where attacks are roaming, not just in a lab, but they are actual attacks that land on an individual's platform.

Understanding that changes to a platform, where change relates to manipulating software, can cause problems to applications. Manipulating software would include installing new software, applying patches or changing the configuration options of executing software.

One should understand what a "bad" platform is. How does one find a bad platform and what does one do with a bad platform?

Chapter 4: Anatomy of an Attack

The best way to understand what to protect is to attack it. Chapter 4 defines an application and then attacks the application. To understand an attack, you need a definition of who the attacker is and what resources the attacker has available. Since LaGrande Technology provides protection from software attacks, the attacks described in Chapter 4 use software mechanisms. Tying all of the attack mechanisms together reveals a common underlying vulnerability.

LaGrande Technology Design

> *When you travel, remember that a foreign country is not designed to make you comfortable. It is designed to make its own people comfortable.*
>
> —Clifton Fadiman

Chapter 5: LaGrande Technology Objectives

You get a description of what LT does, and what LT does not do. LT does not provide 100-percent security—nothing does. The trick is to understand what has protection and where no protection is available. You have no way to understand what has protection unless you understand the attacker and the resources of the attacker.

Chapter 6: LaGrande Technology Design Principles

Chapter 6 describes the design principles that led the LT design team. The principles have been around for many years and have guided many security products.

Chapter 7: Protected Execution

A basic component of LT is the use of Intel® Virtualization Technology. Virtualization technology provides the foundation for protected execution. This chapter provides a basic understanding of the technology.

Chapter 8: Attestation

A critical building block for an LT system is the use of the Trusted Platform Module (TPM). The TPM provides the ability to store, report, and use measurement values, and an LT system provides the critical measurement of the VMM controlling the system. One needs a basic understanding of the TPM to understand the architecture of the LT platform.

Chapter 9: Protected Input and Output

Communicating with a user is one of the top jobs for a personal computer. The actual communication path to move information from the input devices and out through display devices requires trusted channels. How to create trusted channels and display the presence of the trusted channel through trusted paths provides another building block of the LT architecture.

LaGrande Technology Architecture

> *The secret temple of the Piranha women. Their architecture is surprisingly advanced.*
> —Dr. Margo Hunt. *Cannibal Women in the Avocado Jungle of Death* (1989)[2]

Chapter 10: LaGrande Technology Architecture

Chapter 10 is a real "rubber hitting the road" chapter. How software uses LaGrande Technology dominates the explanations. Chapter 10 introduces the standard partition, the protected partition, and the domain manager. The three components together provide the framework for applications that use LT features.

How the components communicate provides some insight into the mechanisms that each component must provide to make the architecture work. An interesting discussion is what entities can provide the components. Who provides what gives some interesting results.

---

[2] I've never seen the movie and have no clue what it is about, but one has to admit it is a great architecture quote. The movie title alone makes it worth including.

Chapter 11: Late Launch

Chapter 11 is one of the author's favorite LT features. Late launch is one of the cruxes of the entire LT architecture. If one does not understand late launch, one does not understand what LT does.

The idea is that a platform user wants to start and stop the LaGrande Technology protections. Starting and stopping LT is very exciting as the protections are deep in the CPU and other motherboard components. Ensuring that only the authorized operations enable these protections drives many of the hardware changes required by a LaGrande Technology platform.

Chapter 12: Configuration Concerns

Chapter 12 describes how certain hardware configurations can allow software to breach the LT protections. The configurations that cause the problems are detectable so the architecture must provide the detection and mitigation mechanisms.

The major issue is how the platform handles system memory. Ensuring an evaluation of the memory configuration during the LT launch mitigates the configuration concern.

Our issues revolve around the loss of the memory configuration when the actual memory location could still contain some LT-protected information.

Chapter 13: Hardware Attacks

The LaGrande Technology design principle is to protect from software attack. Most of the features provide protection solely from software and do not contemplate hardware attacks. Hardware attacks can occur and the LT system can defend against some of them. Chapter 13 describes the hardware attacks where current system provides protection.

The Bottom Line

> *I do not participate in a sport with ambulances at the bottom of the hill.*
>
> —Erma Bombeck (1927–1996)

The last couple of chapters are the bottom of the hill for this book. I hope that if you arrive here, you do not need an ambulance. By now, an understanding of LaGrande Technology should lead one to anticipate the types of attacks that LT mitigates.

Chapter 14: Defending Against Attacks

Chapter 4 was all about describing an application and the attacks on the application. Chapter 14 describes how LaGrande Technology mitigates those attacks. From accessing memory to manipulating input and output, Chapter 14 uses the LT features and shows how the attackers do not gain access to protected information.

Chapter 15: The Future

Chapter 15 is for gazing into the future. A product that provides security is never complete. Attackers learn new techniques; users require new protections. LaGrande Technology must respond to these events and change over time. One obvious change would be for the LT objectives to change regarding hardware attacks.

Acknowledgements

Some might believe that this entire book is the sole responsibility of a single author. They would be wrong. Jim Sutton created the original six-hour presentation. Jim is the author's silent partner. As much as I travel, Jim stays home. Jim is a great friend, a security architect without peer, and he comes up with as many crazy ideas as I do. One of the great pleasures of working with Jim is having either him or me say "What about this attack?" and realizing that the whole architecture under creation just fell down.[3] If either of us got a penny for each invocation of that phrase over the past few years, we both would be retired. Luckily for me Jim is not retired and continues to provide ideas that further the work in Trusted Computing.

I would like to thank those members of the Trusted Computing Group Technical Committee and the Trusted Platform Module Workgroup (TPM WG). These two groups of people have influenced me in so many ways. The many discussions over the years have focused my thoughts on what is and is not possible. To the TPM WG, I make the comment that you can never have any ambiguities, just context-sensitive interpretations.

---

[3] One crazy history lesson is that when one of the two of us uses an attack to invalidate a mechanism, when the person who successfully attacked the previous design creates a new design, it will not mitigate the previous attack, and the other person will point that out.

Inside of Intel I would like to thank Monty Wiseman, Ned Smith, Ernie Brickell, Baiju Patel, David Doughty, amongst others.

A specific thanks to those who made comments on early versions of this book including Graeme Proudler, Greg Kazmierczak, Simon Johnson, Dave Challener, and Paul England.

Thanks for Reading

Well, before you launch into the book. I would like to thank you for giving me the opportunity to explain the Intel safer computing initiative. Hopefully, you will gain an understanding of why LT is built the way it is, what attacks LT can mitigate, what attacks LT cannot mitigate, and why LT will change in the future.

LT represents a change in the basic nature of the PC platform. Providing mechanisms to create a trust boundary, enforce the trust boundary, and report the trust boundary creates the ability to use the PC in new ways. The underlying fundamental ways software stacks take advantage of these new capabilities leads to a perception change as to what the PC platform can accomplish.

As you know, I like to go fly fishing. If you are interested in talking about security while watching an Orange Bomber float down the Trask River, drop me an e-mail and we will see what happens.

Background Information

One's mind has a way of making itself up in the background,
and it suddenly becomes clear what one means to do.

—A.C. Benson

Part I covers the background of trusted computing. LaGrande Technology is not the first use of the security concepts; rather it is the next product in a long line of research and products. The chapters provide an understanding of what research came before and how some products used the research.

Chapter 1: Trusted Computing

One always needs to define terms. Especially when one deals with security and trust issues, a precise definition of terms is critical. Chapter 1 starts with basic definitions that are in use throughout the book.

An understanding of the definition of a trusted platform is mandatory before reading any additional chapters.

The chapter also covers some basic cryptography terms and if the reader if familiar with those terms, the reader can skip these sections.

Chapter 2: History of Trusted Computing

Chapter 2 is a history lesson. Many of the design features of LaGrande Technology are not new but designs that have been in use for years. The chapter covers some of the early research in trusted computing and the application of the research. The history lesson is important, as with the knowledge of history the reader will understand that LaGrande Technology builds on previous research and applications.

Chapter 1

Trusted Computing

So in war, the way is to avoid what is strong and to strike at what is weak.

—Sun Tzu

What is trusted computing? What is trust? Don't users trust their platforms today? If the user encounters any problems, can the current platform architecture support the improvements to alleviate those problems? In this book, you should find the answers to these questions. To start the learning process by making the first set of questions personal, consider the following two questions:

- Do you trust your computer to properly protect an online purchase of a book?

- Do you trust your computer to protect an online purchase of a million dollar home properly?

The answers to these two questions are likely to vary according to the individual. Some say yes to one but not the other; some say yes to both, and finally, some say no to both.[1] Creating a system that provides the flexibility and trustworthiness to allow the various answers is the purpose of trusted computing.

---

[1] The author trusts the computer for book purchases but not for mortgages.

The Basic Problem of Trust

Why do rational individuals and companies trust a platform to perform one job, but they do not trust the platform to perform another task? Underlying the difference is an inability to trust or understand how the platform works. People assume that software does not work correctly or that viruses change how applications work. The difference in their level of comfort with a simple transaction, like a book purchase, and a complex transaction, like the mortgage signing, highlights the uneasiness that the lack of understanding creates. Platform users should feel more at ease with the following pieces of information:

■ The hardware nature of the platform provides protections.

■ The currently executing software is taking advantage of the protections.

■ When something does go wrong, the system has ways to provide protections from the "badness."

■ Mechanisms are in place to allow the verification of information reported from the platform.

The design of a trusted computer should attempt to provide the information that a user needs in order to trust a platform. While you have many technical ways to provide these types of protections and information, Intel's security initiative codenamed LaGrande Technology (LT) is the Intel hardware building block that allows for the creation of a trusted computer.

One important piece of information to remember is that trusted computing is not about creating a 100-percent secure platform. A completely secure platform is one that is turned off, has no connections to the outside world, is buried in concrete, and does no work. In other words, there is no such thing as a completely secure platform. Attackers, with sufficient time and money, are expected to succeed. What trusted computing provides is a way to understand the current state of a platform, have some entity evaluate the state, and then make a decision whether the platform is appropriate for the current job.

A trusted computer assumes that attackers will continue to attempt to subvert the protections on the platform. The trusted computer assumes that some of the attacks will succeed. The trusted computer assumes that successful attacks could have no effect on other uses of the platform. All of these assumptions point back to the need for an outside observer to understand the current state of the platform.

Future versions of a trusted platform might provide additional protections from attacks that current platforms do not. Being able to differentiate between old versions and new versions is a critical component of a trusted platform.

The Trusted Computer and LaGrande Technology

OK, we have a problem[2] and we need solutions. The previous paragraphs suggested that the trusted computer helps to solve these problems. What are the basic properties of the trusted computer? Subsequent chapters cover these points in detail[3], but for a quick teaser, here are the attributes of a trusted computer:

- *Isolation of programs.* It keeps program A from accessing information of program B.

- *Separation of user processes from supervisor processes.* As an example, the system provides a way to ensure that user applications do not interfere with the operating system.

- *Long-term protected storage.* It can store a value that has protections in some place that lasts across power cycles and other events.

- *Identification of current configuration.* It can provide the identity of the platform and the identity of the software executing on the platform.

- *A verifiable report of the platform identity and current configuration.* An outside observer has a mechanism that allows her to query the platform and obtain an answer that the observer can validate.

- *Provide a hardware basis for the protections.* Simply changing the software does not provide the protections necessary for a trusted computer.

---

[2] Everyone has some sort of problem, but please just limit yourself here to just computing problems.

[3] Otherwise this book turns into a 20-page white paper.

When reading over the list, you might not see that it contains many changes from today's platform. That perception is only partially correct. While some applications require no changes to take advantage of a trusted platform, other applications might need an entire rewrite. One area that must change is the operating system (OS). While the interfaces that the OS presents to an application might not change, the way that the OS handles the interface and provides the actual operations of the interface is sure to change.

If LaGrande Technology is an implementation of a trusted platform, then by inference LT implements the basic trusted computing attributes. The first, and arguably the most important LT feature is its ability to make hardware changes to the platform. The changes do not occur only in the Central Processing Unit (CPU) but throughout the platform on various hardware elements. Providing the changes in the hardware meets one of the trusted computing basic requirements. The other items of isolation, long-term storage, and verifiable reporting are all features that LT provides.

Before going any deeper on what LT is and is not, you should have a basic understanding of the terms used in the description. These terms mean different things to different people, depending on the context in which the words are used. Our first order of business is providing definitions for these terms so that you and I are thinking along the same lines. Ambiguity leads to incorrect decisions, and incorrect decisions in a security setting normally lead to bad things happening.

Basic Definitions

The computer security industry, like any other industry, produces a language that often trips up newcomers. To spare you these problems, the next couple of pages provide the basic definitions of very important terms.

Our Definition of Trust

When discussing trusted computing, you first need to agree on the definition of trust. In general usage, trust has many meanings. Many meanings for the same term could lead to confusion and disaster that provokes mistrust. To avoid the resulting mistrust, let's establish one and only one definition of trust in use for this entire book. The definition of trust is:

> An entity can be trusted if it always behaves in the expected manner for the intended purpose. (TCG 2004)

The entity in the definition is a computing process or a human or something else. It doesn't matter. The definition makes no reference to the "goodness" of what of what is being trusted, as you can see when we work through some examples of this definition of trust.

First example: a standard doorknob. Normal individuals trust that if one walks up and turns the doorknob, the doorknob will work properly and allow the door to open. This action should occur each and every time, unless someone breaks the doorknob. Individuals trust the doorknob to work the same way every time. In fact, dogs and cats who open doors are trusting the doorknob to work correctly, too.

Second example: a program on a personal computer. Many users trust the platform to work the same each and every day. If one makes no changes on the platform, that trust is not misplaced. However, making no changes is usually impossible, so each and every day the platform changes, perhaps with additional applications installed from the Internet, occasionally with inadvertent user changes to files. The user wants to trust the platform, but having the same entity each and every day is difficult.

Third example: a platform infected with a virus. The virus causes the platform to do bad things, like sending the virus to all members of the user's address book. Everyone who can determine that the virus is present on the platform comes to trust the platform to perform the bad operations. This last example exposes a critical point. Relying entities do trust the infected platform to perform bad operations. As a result, trust does not equal goodness. Just because the relying party is going to trust the platform does not mean that the relying party trusts the platform to do a good job. The opposite is true; the relying party may trust the platform to do a bad job.

The Trust Decision

Critical to trusted computing is the use of our definition of trust. If one can determine that the same entity is operating, and if one can know the properties of that entity, the relying party has the ability to make a trust decision regarding the platform.

The crux of the matter here is the ability to know exactly what entity is operating. The information cannot be merely close or an approximation, it must be exact. Approximations leave doubt as to the exact entity and do not allow the relying party the opportunity to differentiate between entities.

The relying party can make a trust decision once they know the identity of the entity on which they wish to rely. The trust decision is based on the premise that, with the knowledge of the entity's identity, the relying party determines whether the platform can be trusted to provide the services for the intended task.

The relying party can query a trusted platform and obtain the current status of that platform. The relying party then makes a decision to trust the platform or not. The relying party can trust the platform to perform operation A but not operation B. That is, just because a relying party trusts the platform to perform one operation does not obligate that relying party to trust the platform for all operations. In fact, the relying party can trust the platform to perform operation A at one instance of time and then decide at some other point in time not to rely on the platform. The role of the trusted platform hardware is to always work the same way and to report the current status of the platform accurately.

The Platform

With a complete definition of "trusted," the next word to define is platform. Intel normally focuses on the platform as an Intel architecture (IA) desktop or mobile personal computer, but in the trusted computing paradigm, a platform can be any computing device. It could be an IA-32 device, or it could be a cell phone, router, PDA or another such unit that uses IA components. LaGrande Technology (LT) is the Intel codename for the security mechanism on upcoming IA platforms; other platforms would require different mechanisms to provide a trusted platform.

The Client

Just so that the problem has a boundary, a client platform has two characteristics:

◼ A human user can put his or her hands on the keyboard to control it.

◼ The platform provides services for the individual.

This definition eliminates infrastructure platforms like routers and switches.

Please do not get too wrapped up in this definition at this point. Certainly, individual client platforms provide server functions and servers act like individual clients. Later chapters sort out the details of when and how LT provides protections for servers. The biggest item here is that LT does not apply to each and every platform that Intel produces. The LT focus is on the IA family of processors that power clients and servers.

Owner, User, and Operator

Those persons using the platform could have different roles and responsibilities. LT makes a distinction between three different roles: owner, user, and operator. The roles differ according to their interaction with the platform.

Owner. The owner controls the platform. The owner sets the policies that determine what features of the platform are in use and what features are unavailable. The owner may be remotely located; not required to be present in front of the platform.

User. The user is an entity using the capabilities of the platform. The user could be either a human or a computing process. The user can only use the capabilities of the platform granted by the owner. The user may be remotely located; not required to be present in front of the platform.

Operator. The operator is a human who has physical possession of the platform. The operator also can be an owner or user. The distinction is that, by definition, the operator must be physically present and manipulating the platform.

In a corporate setting, the owner would be the IT department, and the employee is both the user and the operator, normally. IT could perform maintenance or other operations, and thereby become the operator. In this setting, the IT department decides what capabilities of the platform are active. If the IT department decides that the platform needs to perform a special operation, the IT department can set up the platform to perform the operation. The user could disable the special operation but would experience some loss of services as a result.

In a home setting, the owner and user tend to merge into one combined role. In a home where only one individual uses the machine, that individual performs all of the roles; owner, user, and operator. In a house with multiple machines and multiple individuals, it's more than likely that one individual is the owner and the rest are users. In my house, for example, we have multiple machines and multiple children using those machines, so the author is the owner and the children are the users. Depending on who is actually operating the platform, either the author or one of the children would be the operator.

The Weakest Link

Attackers always look for the weakest link. Sun Tzu asks us, why would anyone attack the strong point when an easier path is available? In the early twenty-first century's computing environments, most of the protections are available on the servers. Server owners have made tremendous efforts to provide servers with protection from various attacks. Some of the protections extend to the client; most of those protections do not.

A comparison of the level of protection against the amount of attacks, as in Figure 1.1, shows that while attacks on servers and the infrastructure are mostly covered, client attacks are out of control. Remembering what Sun Tzu tells us, what device is an attacker going to focus on?

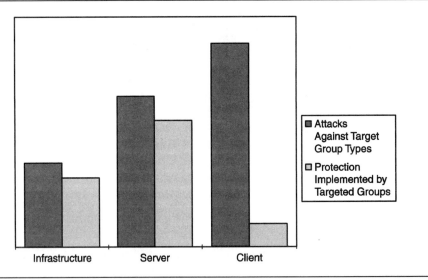

Figure 1.1   Protection Coverage versus Attack Incidents

The goal of LT is to increase the protections on all platforms such that the protections on a platform come close to mitigating the software attacks mounted against the platform.

Another way to look at the protection issues between the server, infrastructure, and client is to take a view of the enterprise as an enclave. As illustrated by Figure 1.2, the enclave model's architecture uses a common view of the world: things outside are bad; things inside are good.

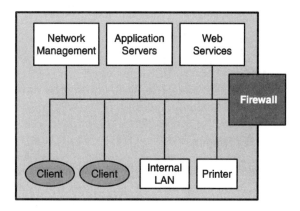

Figure 1.2   The Enclave Model of the Enterprise

The enclave combines platforms and services into a group and provides a wall around the group. The wall represents the protections provided to the group. The protections are both computational, like firewalls, and physical, like locked rooms. The wall treats entities very differently depending on whether the entity is inside or outside the wall. The wall does not imply that all of the entities reside in the same physical location. The connections are quite likely to be logical ones that extend across physical boundaries. The best example is a mobile PC that connects to the enclave from a hotel room. After setting up the appropriate channels, like a virtual private network (VPN), the mobile platform is a member of the enclave.

Outside entities are thought to be very bad, and a considerable expenditure of effort keeps those entities out. Firewalls, user authorization, special connections, and other mechanisms all provide the same underlying feature: keep the bad guys out of the enclave.

Inside entities should behave properly; hence they can use the services of the enclave at will. In some environments, the inside entities might have some restrictions placed on them, but once inside the enclave, the entity normally is trusted.

The attitude towards the inside and outside of an enterprise leads to a problem exemplified by a Far Side cartoon. In the cartoon two polar bears are standing next to an igloo. The igloo has a hole in the top. One of the bears is saying to the other bear "Just as I like them, hard on the outside, soft and chewy on the inside." The same is true for computing enclaves—if the attacker can get inside, the enclave is very soft and chewy, and attacks can succeed in all sorts of places.

Protection in the Enclave

By combining the concepts shown in Figure 1.1 and Figure 1.2, you can see why inside the interior of the enclave is soft and chewy; the protection levels do not match the attacks. The outside edge of the enclave is the firewall, the servers, and other infrastructure components. The inside is the client. If the attacker can bypass the enclave protections and directly attack the client, the attacker's chances of success are much greater. Therefore, the first entity to protect within the enclave is the client.

Effect of Providing More Protections

If Sun Tzu is right, and he is, then providing protections on one type of platform sends the attackers looking for some other avenue of attack. The other avenue could be on the client or it could be on the server.

Looking at the problem from an enclave point of view shows that focusing on one type of platform creates the "igloo effect" again. The would-be intruder bypasses one type of platform that has sufficient protections to attack the vulnerable platform.

The end result of the enclave view is the realization that all platforms in the enclave are going to need the protections of trusted computing. If LT focuses on clients in the first release, future versions may focus on other devices. Most likely future devices would need the protections of LT because the attackers would have found a new avenue of attack. The LT protections can help mitigate that threat. Check out Chapter 15 for some of the potential ideas for the future.

Basic Cryptography

When many people first hear about trusted computing, their first reaction is that it all revolves around cryptography. While cryptography provides many of the building blocks for trusted computing, cryptography is not the main focus. For a reader of this book, a simple understanding of cryptography is all you need to cope with the security properties of LT.

If you really want to dive deep into cryptography, try these two outstanding books, both listed in "References" for your convenience: *Applied Cryptography* by Bruce Schneier (Schneier 1995) and the *Handbook of Applied Cryptography* by Menzes, van Oorschot, and Vanstone (Menzes 1996).

Symmetric Encryption

Symmetric encryption protects information using the same key for encryption and decryption. That is, both the message sender and the message recipient need to have the same key. Symmetric algorithms are fast, and they normally add little or no extra information to the message. The issue is how both sides get the same key. Simply sending the key without any protections, or in the clear, does not work, and encrypting the key with a symmetric algorithm would still require the transmission of a key. One way to handle the transportation of these keys is to use a trusted courier. Embassies used to send keys in the briefcases of consular officials. The method works, but in the world of computing, sending briefcases with keys to all of the members of your address book is not practical. Another problem is that one needs a different key for each potential recipient. Having a key for each member of your address book and keeping track of the keys is an impossible task.

Some common symmetric algorithms are; DES, AES, RC4 and Blowfish. The mathematics behind these algorithms might differ, but they all have the same feature: that is, the same key that encrypts information decrypts the information.

Asymmetric Encryption

Asymmetric encryption uses a different key for encryption and decryption. The encryption portion is public and available to everyone; the decryption portion is private and available only to the key owner. The public and private nature of the key portions leads to their normal names: the public key and the private key.

Asymmetric encryption solves the problem of key distribution inherent in symmetric cryptography. The encryption key is public and the key owner can distribute the key to all who want to communicate with the key owner. No security is lost with multiple entities holding the public key.

The problems with asymmetric cryptography revolve around the circumstances of its use, in terms of both speed and size. Performing the mathematical operations necessary to perform asymmetric cryptography is orders of magnitude slower than the operations necessary for symmetric cryptography. The cipher text that results from an asymmetric encryption is larger than the plain text. The expansion can be quite large, depending on the actual algorithm.

Combination

A best known practice is to combine the two types of cryptography when creating systems. The result is known as *enveloping*; the bulk encryption of data uses a symmetric algorithm and the key for the symmetric algorithm is encrypted using an asymmetric algorithm. The bulk of the file uses symmetric encryption for speed and size considerations. The key for the symmetric algorithm uses asymmetric, where the speed is not a consideration and the expansion is not an issue because the key size is only 20 to 30 bytes.

Cryptographic Hash

A cryptographic hash takes some input and creates a fixed-size output. Cryptographic hashes have some important properties:

- Given the hash output, you have no way to determine the input to the hash.

- Changing one bit of the input causes at least 50 percent of the output bits to change.

- Input to the hash is order-dependent. Hashing A then B does not produce the same value as hashing B then A.

One way to think about cryptographic hashes is that the hash provides the "identity" of an entity. Normally, the entity is some piece of software, like a document or program code. Knowing the entity's identity is an important requirement for many of the trusted platform operations.

Trusted Channel and Trusted Path

Moving information from one location to another requires some sort of channel or path. In trusted computing, the terms have unique meanings and actually are not interchangeable.

Trusted Channel

A trusted channel moves information between two computing entities. A connection between two computers is a channel; a trusted channel adds the properties of integrity and confidentiality of the information.

The integrity of the trusted channel guarantees that the information arrives at the receiver exactly as it was transmitted by the sender. The confidentiality provides assurance that any entity who can observe the channel gains no knowledge of what the data on the channel looks like.

Trusted Path

The trusted path moves information between a computing entity and a human. The path requires some activity on the human's part to recognize that the path is present. Quite often, the trusted path indicates the presence of a trusted channel to the human.

Combination

Combining a trusted channel and trusted path gives the human using the trusted platform assurance that the platform is properly communicating with the human. On the Internet, for example, the SSL protocol provides a trusted channel between two computing entities, the server and the client. The SSL connection provides the integrity and confidentiality for the messages. The little lock icon on the bottom right of the browser window is the trusted path that indicates to the user the presence of the trusted channel. In a perfect world, before the user sends confidential information across the Web, the user would look to the bottom right to verify the presence of the trusted channel.

What is LaGrande Technology (LT)?

In a couple of paragraphs, I am not going to answer that question completely. This entire book is the answer. The quick, elevator-pitch answer is that LaGrande Technology (LT) provides a way to protect information from software attack. LT does not act stand-alone; rather it makes use of numerous platform components to create a protection boundary. Initially, LT is incorporated into client platforms, and subsequent versions are likely to appear in other platform types.

As you read through the rest of this book, you should obtain a clearer answer of what LT is, and more importantly, how you can make use of LT in the future. To be blunt, LT should provide solutions to the following trusted computing attributes:

- Isolation of programs

- Separation of user processes from supervisor processes

- Long-term protected storage

- Identification of current configuration

- A verifiable report of the platform identity and current configuration

- Provides a hardware basis for the protections

Each of these attributes does drive LT features, and by the end of the book, you should understand how LT satisfies these trusted computing attributes.

Chapter 2

History of Trusted Computing

Although this report contains no information not available in a well stocked technical library or not known to computer experts, and although there is little or nothing in it directly attributable to classified sources, the participation of representatives from government agencies it its preparation makes the information assume an official character. It will tend to be viewed as an authoritative Department of Defense product, and suggestive of the policies and guidelines that will eventually have to be established. As a prudent step to control dissemination, it is classified CONFIDENTIAL overall.

—Willis Ware, 1970 Task Force on Computer Security

The concept of trusted computing is not new. Very early on, security researchers were looking at trusted computing. The first computers did mostly government work of a sensitive nature. From the "bombes" that helped decrypt the German Enigma traffic to the mainframes that helped with Venona,[1] the computer was dealing with very sensitive information.

---

[1] The bombes were special purpose computers that automated the task of looking for the day key in use by the German military. The bombes were huge but they did a fantastic job of finding the day's key. Venona was the code name for a project that read messages from various Soviet embassies to Moscow. The task was to search through thousands of messages looking for patterns. Many of the messages were read. Doing Internet searches on these two terms could yield a wealth of information.

When a platform performs a single task, never changes from that task, and never shares information, dealing with sensitive information is a much simpler chore. Platforms that can share information and operate on multiple programs provide many opportunities to leak data to unauthorized entities. Multiple programs also provide an opportunity to disrupt concurrently running programs.

Early Papers

In the early 1970s, a series of papers funded by the U.S. government focused on computer security. These papers form the basic building blocks for trusted computing. The following discussion is by no means exhaustive; rather the list highlights some of the major findings of those early researchers.[2]

1970 Task Force

In 1970, long before personal computers, a computer task force made a seminal report on computer security (Ware 1970). The task force, led by the Rand Corporation, was attempting to define the security requirements for computer systems that had a mixture of users and systems. While the thoughts of the group were concentrated on time-shared mainframes, the actual results hold true for client and server platforms of today.

The task force had some specific recommendations for both hardware and software. The hardware recommendations were:

- *User isolation*. The isolation requirement stated that each user program must be isolated from every other user program.

- *Supervisor protection*. The supervisor, or the entity managing the user programs, must have protection from every user program. One distinct recommendation was to create a user mode and a supervisor mode. The user mode would be restricted and the supervisor mode would have complete control of the system.

- *Assurance against unanticipated conditions, including an interrupt system*. With programs not always operating correctly, something unexpected could always happen. The system must have the ability to handle the unexpected events in a set manner.

---

[2] The author is a great lover of history and reading historical documents and findings. You can provide the impetus for solutions to today's problems by rereading these papers and coming to the understanding that many of the issues we face today are not new, that they are variations on an old theme.

The software recommendations were:

- ■ *Language processors and utility routines*. For code in assembly language, the recommendation was to make the code particularly difficult to secure. High level languages—think FORTRAN[3] at the time this document was produced—should use libraries of evaluated utility routines.

- ■ *Supervisor program*. The key to the hardware's supervisor protection lay in these characteristics:

    - *Run as much of the supervisor as you can in user mode.* This recommendation seems to have fallen on deaf ears. Many operating systems of today require user applications to have access to supervisor mode, and the size of the operating system is growing exponentially. Much of LaGrande Technology (LT) is an attempt to separate user and supervisor modes and to allow the supervisor to place portions of the supervisor into user mode.

    - *Clean up after sensitive data is in use.* After a user program uses sensitive data, the supervisor must ensure that all sensitive data is not available to any other process. While user mode should perform the cleanup, the supervisor must enforce the protection of sensitive data.

    - *Orderly startup and shutdown.* This point is very important. The requirement is for a controlled startup that puts the machine in a known state. The shutdown must occur in a way that properly validates all sensitive information. Remember, this is a requirement in the design of LT.

    - *Certified ability to control access to files.* The recommendation was to ensure that all file accesses were validated, and that they went through a known control point.

One point to remember with this paper is the date, 1970. The requirements for a secure system are being defined before personal computers, before the Internet, before computers on every desk. The requirements come out of trying to share a computer that does more than one job at a time.

---

[3] While the author hates to admit it, he actually coded FORTRAN on punch cards.

Bell-LaPadula

By 1976, research was taking some of the task force recommendations and diving deeper. The Bell-LaPadula paper (Bell 1973) presents a mathematical model of a secure system. The paper contains descriptions of all of the "actors" in a secure system and of the operations that are necessary to enforce the security. The basic building blocks are:

- *Domain separation*. Separate processes make sure that the resources of one process are not available to any other process. This recommendation matches the user isolation and supervisor requirements of the 1970 task force.

- *Identification*. The identity of the user is very important. The identity allows the system to make decisions about use that are based on the user's identity. For example, a user might be granted access to a process only during regular business hours. Without properly identifying the user, the system owner would have no way to enforce the use restriction.

- *Authorization*. Using the user identity, the system owner gives the user permission to perform various operations. As in the previous example, the authorization might allow the identified user access to the process during regular business hours or during weekend hours, depending on the job function of that user.

The Rainbow Series

In 1985, the U.S. Department of Defense released the "Rainbow Series." The individual volume that people most often remember is the "Orange Book" (Department of Defense 1985), which describes a trusted computer system, the evaluation criteria for a trusted system, and how to use the trusted system. Other colored volumes in the rainbow of this series describe the nitty-gritty details of the trusted system and its use.

Security System Evaluation

The Rainbow Series begat the European ITSEC evaluations, and the combination of the Rainbow Series and the ITSEC begat Common Criteria, an international agreement on how to evaluate security systems. Evaluation is way beyond the scope of this book. If you are interested in looking at evaluations, the Common Criteria Web site is listed in "References."

The Rainbow Series is a wonderful source of the requirements for a trusted system in the 1980s. It defines how to build, distribute, and use the trusted system. What it does not contemplate is how to work with a personal computer. The whole thought process behind the Rainbow Series, and the Orange Book in particular, takes place in the context of a mainframe computer sitting in a computer room. The idea that the user would be able to load programs, or change the operating system, is just not possible with the Rainbow Series. It turns out that getting an Orange Book evaluation of a PC is very difficult and depends on the system being "locked down." The begins to solve many of those issues.

Industry Response

The U.S. Department of Defense was both a definer of trusted systems requirements and a purchaser of trusted systems. Industry provided to the government both the hardware and software to meet the Department of Defense requirements.

On the hardware side, industry leaders like IBM, Control Data, Digital, and others, defined and developed mainframe computers that provided the underlying features that enable trusted systems. From the ability to create user modes and supervisor modes, to the ability to separate applications, to the ability to handle unexpected operations, mainframe hardware supported trusted system development and deployment.

On the software side, mainframe operating systems used the hardware and provided the separation recommended by the various research papers. Some operating systems and applications implemented the mathematical models of Bell-LaPadula. A rich history of operating system research attempts to implement the necessary controls. A Google search of topics like "Trusted MACH," "Fluke," "Flask," and "SELinux" would show you the ongoing research to define and implement trusted operating systems.

The Future through the Past

Combining all of the original research leads to a list of requirements that contains the following main points:

- Domain separation
- Handling of events not anticipated
- Separation between user and supervisor modes
- Platform capabilities in the hardware to support the other requirements

The idea now is to combine the research requirements with the list of requirements from Chapter 1 to form the new requirements for a trusted computer. Table 2.1 provides that combination.

Table 2.1 Trusted Computer Research Requirements

Requirement	Research Requirement	Comments
Isolation of programs	Domain separation	Isolation is the same as domain separation.
	Handling unanticipated events	Isolation can provide a mechanism to handle unanticipated events.
Separation of user from supervisor	Separation of user from supervisor	The trusted platform requirement matches the research requirement.
Long-term protected storage		Original research does not call out need for long-term protected storage.
Identification of current configuration		Original research assumes that platform identity is not an issue.
Verifiable report of current configuration		With no identity issues and an assumption of secure software delivery, no reporting of platform configuration takes place.
Hardware basis for protections	Hardware basis for protections	The trusted platform requirement matches the research requirement.

A very interesting turn of events: the table has three requirements from the original research and three brand-new ones. To discover the reasons for the three new requirements, you need some more history, moving ahead in time to the personal computer era.

Personal Computers

One way to compare today's personal computers and the trusted computing research of the past is to consider the environment in which the research was focusing. The researchers were moving from dedicated machines performing a single task to generic machines capable of performing tasks simultaneously. One major concern was that when the machine switched from one task to the other, the possibility of leaking information was present. For those old enough to remember, these machines' one common architecture was the central mainframe and user's timesharing of the mainframe's resources. Compare that to a network today and you should see many of the same issues still remain. Also be aware that many differences exist and those differences drive our new requirements. To understand the security needs of a personal computer, one must understand the internal workings of the platform.

About Common Terminology...

A brief personal digression: As you can see in the biography on the back cover, I came with a background in software and learned hardware through working at Intel Corporation. In the very first few days, terms like front-side bus, North Bridge, and ICH just seemed like a foreign language.

As most engineers know, each discipline has a language all of their own. In the early days of LT, it was really fun to attempt to combine the languages of hardware engineers, software engineers, and the security architects. I would love to have back some of the time we spent trying to merge all of the terms and get the team reading from the same page. It reminded me of a comment made about the social dynamics during the filming of Grand Prix, the movie about auto racing. The real race car drivers started talking about camera angles and film speed, and the actors started talking about corner speeds and brake points.

To understand LaGrande Technology (LT), a basic understanding of the platform components is critical. In addition to understanding the terms, knowing the history of the changes to the Intel® architecture will help you to understand the security initiative's direction.

Figure 2.1 illustrates the basic components and includes some of the synonyms in use on the platform.

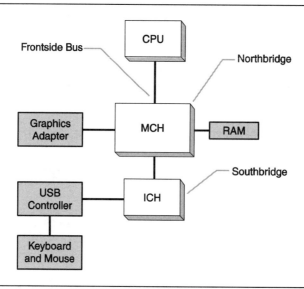

Figure 2.1   Basic Components

The definitions for each component are:

■ CPU. A central processing unit is the main processor for the system.

■ MCH. The memory controller hub is the component that connects the CPU to random access memory (RAM). Newer platforms contain a graphics MCH (GMCH). Common aliases for the MCH include the Northbridge.

■ ICH. The input/output controller hub is the component that connects system devices, such as network cards, disk drives, audio components, and others to the system. The ICH can assume aliases like the Southbridge.

■ Chipset. The specific combination of a processor, MCH, and ICH into a coordinated unit is called a chipset.

■ Front-side bus (FSB). As the connection between the CPU and MCH, the FSB allows for multiple CPUs to communicate with a single MCH.

CPU Internals

The CPU, or processor, has some internal state and packing issues that influence the LT architecture.

Protected Mode

Protected mode provides the "rings" in a processor. When you see a reference to ring 0 or ring 3, that's a reference to the protection mode in the processor. The protection modes actually provide four rings: 0, 1, 2, and 3. Figure 2.2 depicts the layers of protection mode rings.

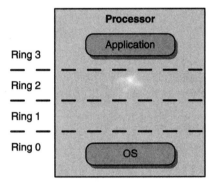

Figure 2.2   Protection Mode Rings

The intent of the ring architecture is to provide separation of the operating system (OS) and the applications that the OS manages. The ring structure also gives the OS a way to separate,[4] and layer functions in the OS to improve the ability of the OS to protect itself. Chapter 3 explains how a current OS uses the ring structures.

---

[4] Consider Table 2.1 and the requirement for user and supervisor separation.

Memory Management

The processor supports management of physical memory through segmentation and paging. In this simple introduction, I cannot possibly explain all of the options, permutations, and usages for managing memory. The canonical reference is the *IA-32 Intel® Architecture Software Developers Manual, Volume 3: System Programming Guide* (Intel 2003c). Chapter 3 of that document gives a much deeper overview of how to manage memory.

Figure 2.3 shows a simplified view of the memory management system.[5] Additional controls and tables provide the complete range of memory management.

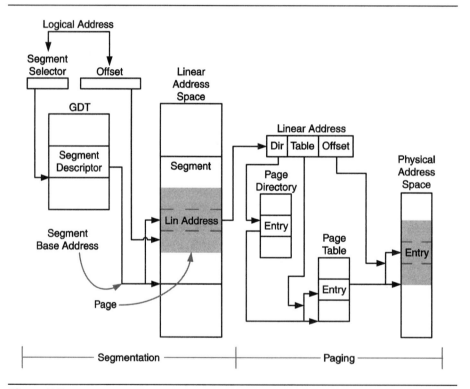

Figure 2.3   Memory Management

---

[5] The author knows that the definition of "simple" here does not seem to fit, but trust me, this explanation only scratches the surface of the mechanisms in use here. Do not miss the main point: to go from an address in a program to the real physical page, you pass through control points that system entities can manage.

When an application requests access to a memory location, the system follows this map to convert the address that the application needs to a physical memory page and location.

1. The logical address breaks down into two components, the segment and offset.

2. The segment indicates a selector that provides a base page address, and adding the offset produces a linear address.

    ■ If paging is not in use, the linear address would point to a physical address location.

    ■ Converting the logical address into the linear address is the segmentation task of memory management.

3. If the memory manager is using paging, the linear address maps to three components: directory, table, and offset.

4. The processor uses the directory to locate the table, and then it adds the offset to produce a physical address.

    The directory and table can indicate that the contents that should be in a physical address are currently not in memory, and the memory manager must load the correct physical page. This process is called *page swapping* and is the mechanism behind the swap file in use by operating systems.

Segmentation and Paging Control. An important property to understand from Figure 2.3 is the control issue. Notice that the entity controlling segmentation and paging controls the mapping of logical address to physical address. From an application standpoint, two successive accesses to the same logical address can result in two different physical addresses.

The memory manager is under no obligation to expose the complete physical address space. The physical address space in use can have holes and not allow access to specific physical address pages.

The controls that manage segmentation and paging start with Control Register 3 (CR3) and include the manipulation of the paging entries.

Front-side Bus

The connection between the CPU and MCH passes messages that allow control of the chipset and access to memory. The front-side bus (FSB) allows for the connection of multiple CPU packages onto a single MCH.

The LT design only works in topologies with a single MCH. Systems built with multiple MCH units cannot support the initial version of the security initiative. Chapter 16 discusses the issues of multiple MCH topologies.

Multiple CPU Systems

When the term CPU comes up, most people think of the CPU package that is put into a platform. A synonym for CPU is processor. An LT-enabled system provides support for multiple CPUs. The support ensures that all processors are operating in a consistent fashion.

MCH

The MCH connects the CPU to memory. The MCH also provides a connection between the graphics adapter and system memory. Some MCH units are actually a Graphic MCH, which has an integrated graphics adapter.

On a typical personal computer, the system has only one MCH. The MCH is not a field-replaceable part and is permanently mounted on the motherboard. Some server designs use multiple MCH units to handle multiple CPUs and complex memory topologies.

Memory

All CPU requests for system memory travel through the FSB, through the MCH, and to the actual memory DIMM. The MCH can "snoop" the memory request and either block it or re-route the request to some other entity. For information held by the ICH, the MCH snoops the address, recognizes the address as one held by the ICH, then routes the request to the ICH.

Display Adapter

The MCH can either contain an integrated display adapter or it can provide a connector for a discrete display adapter. Discrete display adapters connect to the MCH on a variety of busses, the newest being the PCI Express[†] bus.

ICH

The ICH, as the input/output controller hub, provides the connections to most of the platform peripherals. Platform peripherals include keyboards, USB connections, BIOS memory, and other busses like PCI Express.

Keyboard

The keyboard connector normally uses either a USB connection or the PS2 port. Most desktop systems use the USB port for keyboard connections and most laptops provide a PS2 port for connecting an external keyboard. In the context of a trusted platform, either connector can provide the ability to protect the keyboard input.

USB

The ICH provides at least one USB controller hub. Numerous peripherals use the USB connections to attach the device to the platform.

A critical requirement for the USB connection is the need for a driver to discover and route messages to the attached devices. The driver determines which devices are visible to applications, when the devices get service, and the routing of messages from the attached devices. Requiring a driver also inhibits the use of the bus and devices on the bus during startup operations. Without a driver, the peripherals are invisible; attempting to require the device during a startup process requires some sort of intermediate driver.

LPC Bus

The Low Pin Count (LPC) bus provides a simple bus that does not require any drivers to access the devices on the bus. Typical platform components that reside on the LPC bus include the BIOS boot block and the Trusted Platform Module (TPM).

The LPC bus is a slow bus running at a normal speed of 33 megahertz. Not only is the bus slow, but the data path is narrow. The reality is that sending information to a device on the LPC bus is like sending information through a cocktail straw.

The LPC bus does have a redeeming factor: it is so simple, the devices on the bus are available very early in the startup sequence. The availability of devices on the LPC bus provides an excellent location for devices that can support trusted platforms.

Current Intel® Architecture Security Support

Current processors based on the Intel architecture already support some security features. LT might add additional features, but the current support is essential to enable LT.

Rings

The privilege levels, or rings, are the first instance of security support in the Intel architecture. The Intel processor manual explicitly states that rings ". . . protect application or user programs from each other" (Intel 2003a). The implication is that the rings are a security device to provide domain separation. The reality is that the rings *are* a domain separation mechanism. LT makes use of the rings as one of the building blocks for the security solution.

Using the rings allows the user-supervisor separation as requested by the early security research. Remember the 1970 task force recommendation to isolate the user program from the supervisor? Executing the supervisor in ring 0 and a user program in ring 3 provides the separation necessary for security purposes. The rings have been part of Intel architecture since the Intel 286 processor.

Protected Mode

The Intel 286 processor included another security feature: protected mode. Protected mode uses the segment register contents as selectors, or pointers, into descriptor tables. Protected mode features include:

- Descriptors that provide 24-bit base addresses
- Maximum physical memory size of up to 16 megabytes
- Support for virtual memory management on a segment swapping basis

Protected mode mechanisms include:

- Segment limit checking
- Read-only and execute-only segment options
- Hardware task-switching and local descriptor tables that allow the operating system to protect application or user programs from each other

Protected Mode for Security

Protected mode provides security properties just as the rings do. Control of the segment descriptors allows the operating system to separate one user application from another user application.

Paging

With the introduction of the Intel 386 processor, a new security feature became available: paging. Paging provides an excellent mechanism for domain separation.

Looking at Figure 2.3, Memory Management, notice that the entity that controls the segmentation and the page tables controls which program can access a physical address. If the supervisor properly controls the page tables, then another factor in domain separation is present.

Security Properties

With the rings, segmentation, and paging, it would appear that all is in place to provide domain separation. Well, let us update Table 2.1, creating Table 2.2, and see how the current hardware matches the trusted computing requirements.

Table 2.2   Current Requirements Supported

Requirement	Hardware Support	Comments
Isolation of programs	Paging, segmentation and paging	Support for isolation but no real support for unanticipated events.
Separation of user from supervisor	Ring 0 and Ring 3 separation	Ring 0 manages the separation.
Long-term protected storage		No feature supports requirement.
Identification of current configuration		No feature supports requirement.
Verifiable report of current configuration		No feature supports requirement.
Hardware basis for protections	Yes	Whole point is that features are hardware.

The support is not too bad. The requirements from the basic research are present, but the new requirements are not met. That situation would be reasonable because the new trusted requirements did not influence the original designs. Before filling in the table, the next few chapters provide detailed coverage of the current environment and how designers and attackers make use of the current architecture.

What Is Happening Today?

The problems that exist in the world today, cannot be solved by the level of thinking that created them.

—Albert Einstein

Part II describes the situation today. From virus and Trojans to buggy programs, all cause loss of data. The current hardware on the PC platform does not provide sufficient building blocks that allow a programmer designer to mitigate the issues. Part II exposes some of the current warts in a PC platform.

Chapter 3: The Current Environment

Many users and program designers are unfamiliar with the width and breadth of attacks that are in the "wild." The wild is where attacks are not just in a lab, but are actual attacks that land on an individual's platform.

Understanding that changes to a platform, where change relates to manipulating software, can cause problems to applications. Manipulating software would include installing new software, applying patches or changing the configuration options of executing software.

One should understand what a "bad" platform is. How does one find a bad platform and what does one do with a bad platform?

Chapter 4: Anatomy of an Attack

The best way to understand what to protect is to attack it. Chapter 4 defines an application and then attacks the application. To understand an attack, you need a definition of who the attacker is and what resources the attacker has available. As LaGrande Technology provides protection from software attacks, the attacks in Chapter 4 use software mechanisms. Tying all of the attack mechanisms together reveals a common underlying vulnerability.

Chapter 3

The Current Environment

If you put tomfoolery into a computer, nothing comes out of it but tomfoolery. But this tomfoolery, having passed through a very expensive machine, is somehow ennobled and no-one dares criticize it.

—Pierre Gallois

Part of the inhumanity of the computer is that, once it is competently programmed and working smoothly, it is completely honest.

—Isaac Asimov (1920–1992)

In today's personal computer environment, a PC works perfectly if things are set up correctly, but if the PC is not set up correctly, you have the classic "garbage in, garbage out" scenario. Is that right? Or, can a well set up machine still give you garbage that is glorified because it came from a computer? A trusted platform believes that both are situations are possible and acceptable. The rationale behind the two chapter quotes is that from a trust standpoint, both quotes describe a trusted platform. Asimov really hits the nail on the head with the point that once you know what is happening it *always* happens in the exact same way. Gallois points out that if we do not understand what we are dealing with then the answers we get from the device are no better than tomfoolery.

To resolve these issues, the first task is to understand the computing environment of today, what works and what does not work, why we trust platforms to perform certain jobs but do not trust them for other jobs.

Platform

A platform[1] involves a combination of components. In this chapter, the discussion covers four areas:

- *Hardware.* The CPU, chipset, and other silicon components.

- *Operating System* (OS). The software that directly controls the hardware and provides services to applications. The OS includes drivers which extend the OS to control new hardware. The new hardware normally consists of plug-in devices.

- *Applications.* Software that provides services to the user.

- *Configuration.* The hardware and software have countless control options. The combination of the control choices is the current configuration.

Hardware

CPU, chipset, and other devices—the hardware provides the basic execution environment for the platform. While many think of the hardware as a monolithic entity, in reality the hardware devices are unique components, each providing important services.

The interesting issue in a security context is the fact that the hardware has configuration options. Some examples of hardware configuration are:

- *CPU frequency.* The Pentium® processor family provides for a range of operating frequencies and voltage levels. The choice between speed, heat, and power consumption leads to a wide variety of configuration options. Some combinations of frequency and voltage can cause the processor to operate incorrectly. Most BIOS and operating systems protect from these dangerous settings, but it is possible to set the values incorrectly. If the CPU no longer operates correctly, what happens to any security assurances? Checking for these types of hardware configurations is an important feature of LT.

---

[1] Do not focus too strongly on the word "platform." The platform could be a client and as such a desktop or mobile platform. The platform could be a server and servers come in many flavors: stand-alone, branch office, blades, etc. The point to recognize here is that all platforms have the four areas under discussion.

■ *DIMM settings*. The types of DIMM that are used and the way that the hardware controls the DIMM can also affect security. It is possible to configure the chipset improperly and cause the various FSB addresses actually to point to the same address. Validating the current settings is a large security concern.

These settings, and others, set up the hardware to perform certain operations. When some entity wishes to rely on the hardware, the current configuration is vital to any assessment of the platform.

Operating System

The operating system provides management of the hardware and a set of services for applications. The operating system also contains a wide variety of configuration options, many of them security-sensitive. Some of the issues with the operating system revolve around the basic architecture of the OS.

Ring Use

Chapter 2 described the rings that Intel® architecture provides. The idea behind the CPU architects was to provide the ability for domain separation in an Intel architecture processor. Figure 3.1 shows what the Intel architects had in mind on the right and what the OS vendors implemented on the left.

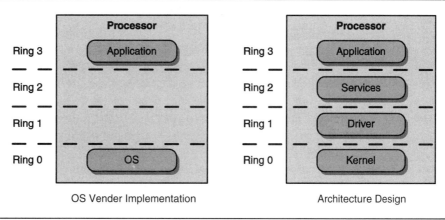

Figure 3.1 Ring Use Intended by Architects versus OS Vendors

For whatever reason, the OS vendors did not use all four of the rings, they only used two. The use of only two rings, and the non-use of the other two rings, has serious security implications. By combining all of the OS activities in a single ring, all of the activities share the same security level. With a constant change in drivers, the security of the OS is constantly changing. As described further in Chapter 5, many attacks occur due to the use of ring 0 for all system-related activities.

It is possible to redesign an OS and use all of the rings; the disadvantage is that the OS, most drivers, and some applications must be rewritten. Requiring software vendors to rewrite most of the platform software, thereby invalidating the old software, is not a viable strategy for the security initiative.

Drivers

The OS requires drivers to access hardware devices. The system has drivers for hard drives, LAN cards, graphics adapters, and other hardware devices. Most drivers require ring 0 access to properly function. Allowing multiple drivers access to ring 0 breaks any domain separation that the OS is attempting to provide. Chapter 5 shows how attackers make use of ring 0 access to perform their attacks.

Drivers also present another security problem: interactions with other drivers. Drivers may attempt to access resources that other drivers are already using and sometimes it proves almost impossible to remove the conflict. Not removing the conflict can cause the OS to work erratically and this problem is difficult to diagnose.

Some applications require specific versions of a driver. If the user loads two programs that require different versions of the driver, one of the applications could work incorrectly.

It is possible to install two or more drivers that attempt to manage the same device. While this occurrence is somewhat rare, the correct running of the platform is almost impossible when it occurs. A user can find it very difficult to determine that the two drivers are present.

The end result with drivers is that it is very important to understand the exact identity of each and every driver that is in use by the OS.

Configuration

In addition to the drivers, you have numerous configuration options in the OS. Some of the configuration options have security implications, like Internet connection options, driver load policies, and others. Installing an OS from scratch gives anyone a glimpse of the multitude of OS configuration options. These configuration options represent the executing environment of the platform, even more so than the OS code. While the code is what is executing, the configuration is the real identity.

Attempting to report the current OS configuration to outside observers is a difficult task. Many current operating systems do not have the basic design that allows for the reporting of the configuration information.

Applications

Applications mirror the issues with the OS drivers and configurations, with one additional issue: is the application even installed on the platform?

Installation

The first issue to consider—and this issue should be a simple one—is if the application is installed on the platform. Most applications leave quite visible indications that the application is present. Some applications do not.

A very interesting question regarding the installation is: what version of the application is present? The version is very important when attempting to find platforms that need to upgrade the application.

Drivers

Applications can require drivers to complete the applications' tasks. During installation, the application installer can install the required driver. The problem comes when the application installer does not properly check for a previous driver and installs a version of the driver that causes problems for other applications on the platform.

Configuration

In addition to installation and drivers, applications require configuration. The configuration choices made by the user who is installing the application can affect the security properties of the platform.

Malware

Simply put, malware is an application on the platform that performs actions that the platform owner does not like. The malware can attack the platform it resides on, or the malware can use the platform to attack other platforms. Either way, the malware performs actions against the wishes of the platform owner.

Malware has code, possibly drivers, and configuration options. The malware looks like any other application on the platform. Some types of malware even appear in the installed list of applications; other malware attempts to hide its existence on the platform.

Anti-virus (AV) programs attempt to find the malware regardless of the installation method. When the culprit is found, the AV program attempts to eradicate the malware. The eradication attempt might or might not be successful. Information regarding the existence of malware on a platform allows outside entities to make trust decisions regarding the platform.

Malware Components

Malware has three basic components:

■ *Distribution mechanism.* The distribution mechanism moves the malware from one platform to another. Using the human virus analogy, think of the distribution mechanism as the sneeze that distributes little droplets of the virus throughout the room. A very common distribution mechanism is to send e-mails using the infected platforms e-mail distribution list.

■ *Infection mechanism.* The infection mechanism provides the way for the malware to penetrate the platform. Just as the sneeze only distributes the droplets around the room and the virus needs to get inside and start multiplying, malware needs to arrive at a platform and then get beyond the protections. Programs with buffer overflow issues provide a wonderful source for malware to infect platforms.

■ *Payload.* The payload triggers after the new platform is infected. The payload can be benign, discomforting, or fatal. A human virus can cause a little nasal drainage, give you the two-week flu, or be Ebola and kill you. Malware can be a nasty message on your screen, a use of all of your resources, or a reformat of your hard drive.

A specific instance of malware would pick one or more distribution mechanisms, one or more infection mechanisms, and one or more payloads. The newer forms of malware use combinations of distribution and infection mechanisms to attempt to bypass platform protections.

Break Once, Run Everywhere

Some protection mechanisms have a very undesirable property, known as Break Once Run Everywhere (BORE). A system that enables BORE attacks is, most likely, improperly designed. BORE attacks occur when the attacker, or malware, finds a shared secret. Consider a system that uses a symmetric key to encrypt messages. Normal best practice is to use some sort of asymmetric encryption to protect a random symmetric key and distribute the public portion of the asymmetric key pair. What happens if the system designer thinks: "That asymmetric stuff is just too hard, I will put the same symmetric key on all the platforms and protect the key really well." The designer might be successful in protecting the key on all the platforms, but what happens if the protection fails? If the attacker can recover the key on just one platform, the attacker has the key that works on all platforms. In other words, the attacker breaks the protections once and can now run the attack everywhere.

Notice that the designer made the decision to share a secret. Any time you have a shared secret, you have a possibility of a BORE attack. Obviously systems must share secrets; otherwise no encryption would be possible. What is dangerous is to share the same secret on many platforms.

Configurations

The thread tying hardware, OS, and applications together is configuration information. To understand what makes up the current environment, an evaluation requires the type of hardware, the operating system, the applications, and the configuration options for each one.

Changing the configuration can cause the platform to misbehave. Detecting changed, or improperly configured platforms, is very difficult. What is necessary is some mechanism to report on the environment in a manner that reflects an accurate measurement of the configuration and is verifiable by the entity requesting the measurement. Chapter 7 explains mechanisms to perform those two operations.

Finding Bad Platforms

So with all of the potential issues, how does one define a "bad" platform? The answer is that those who wish to rely on the platform should be the ones to determine what is good or bad. A platform, and the platform's current configuration, could be acceptable for one use but not acceptable for some other task. What is necessary is a mechanism that allows those wishing to rely on the platform a good view into the platform's current configuration.

Current platforms have few or no mechanisms that provide the information to outside observers. Those platforms using the Trusted Platform Module (TPM) from the Trusted Computing Group (TCG) have the ability to report information; the question then becomes what information can the platform report? The Intel safer computing initiative makes heavy use of the TPM (see Chapter 11).

Subsequent chapters build on the themes of allowing outside entities to determine their trust in the platform and providing mechanisms that allow accurate measurement of the current platform configuration.

Chapter 4

Anatomy of an Attack

So in war, the way is to avoid what is strong and to strike at what is weak.

—Sun Tzu, *The Art of War*

Sun Tzu was talking about attacking with armies. However, the principles he wrote about centuries ago are the same when discussing attacks on computers. The malware writers use the easiest mechanism available to them. We are going to create a simple application and then show how attacks can defeat the protections in place for the program. We will not show the exact mechanism used to mount the attack nor will we go anywhere near how to distribute malware. After all, it is not the purpose of this book to be a hacker's how-to manual, but show you what malware can do.

We will follow the development of an application and the programmers' response to various attacks. Our application is very simple with only one task. The application displays a special number when requested and allows the updating of the special number. For reasons that we will not try to figure out, attackers want to see the special number and some attackers want to change the special number.[1]

---

[1] To be more specific, the special number can only be 42 and any attempt to change the ultimate answer should not be possible. To understand the reference to 42, the author advises the reader to read another book, *The Hitchhikers Guide to the Galaxy,* where the rationale for 42 becomes clear, or at least not so obscure.

From the discussion of malware in Chapter 4, the assumption for our attack is that the distribution and infection mechanisms for the attack, or the specific instance of the malware, are effective on our platform. Moreover, because the payload directly attacks our application we need to mitigate the effect of the malware's payload.

From the standpoint of our application, the malware payload provides fatal attacks. The application designer, from the standpoint of our example, is not able to defend against either the distribution mechanism nor the infection mechanism. Obviously, closing the distribution or infection vulnerabilities would be very desirable in real life, but for our example, those choices are not available.

From a strictly technical viewpoint, many malware instances blend the distribution, infection, and payload components. Our example does not try to deal with those blended threats; rather the focus of this example is on the effects of the payload. Real world applications and protections are unable to make the same simplification.

Being that the author of the book is both the author of the application and the malware, the author gets to place some restrictions on the malware.[2] The purpose of our malware is to highlight issues on current platforms and to illustrate platform vulnerabilities.

The malware has one restriction: it may only use software processes— that is, no hardware modifications. While hardware attacks are certainly possible, we are not going to focus on them here. We define *hardware attacks* as those using a physical modification to the platform or using probes on the platform busses or memory. The focus on software attacks over hardware attacks comes from the responses to the following questions:

1. Have you ever been a victim of a malware process (virus, Trojan, etc.)?

2. Have you ever been the victim of a hardware attack (where the attacker actually used a probe on your platform)? [3]

The vast majority of users answer yes to question one and no to question two. Therefore, while we could concern ourselves with hardware attacks, the majority of users only need protection from software attacks.

---

[2] Obviously, real malware has no restrictions. The author has no illusions that malware would not try to use any and all potential vulnerabilities. When looking at real attacks, the author assumes the best, and worst, from attackers.

[3] If you are a current, or former, member of an agency tasked with keeping your country's secrets safe, the author assumes that some other country is very interested in what you are trying to protect.

Programmer versus Attacker

Let us remember the purpose of our application: it keeps track of a number, displays that number upon request, and allows for the updating of the number. The goal of the attacker is to discover what digits make up the current special number or to find a way to update the special number whenever the attacker wishes. Remember that the attacker is limited to software-based processes for the attack.

The first attack is the simplest. The malware merely reads the special number from the hard drive. Since any process can read a file from the drive, the application really has no protection against this foray.

The defense against this first attack is equally simple: encrypt the special number on the hard drive. The question to answer now is, "Where does the encryption key come from?" The most common first response to the attack would make a crucial mistake. Your first thought might be to encrypt the file using a symmetric key embedded in the program. At first blush, the new design looks like a good response because malware can no longer simply read the file and the information has protections using encryption. All attacks have mitigation. Remember the break once and run everywhere (BORE) attack described in Chapter 3? The decision to create shared secrets on many platforms was the fatal mistake. If you put the same symmetric key in every instance of the program, the design enables the attacker to break once and run everywhere. The attacker merely needs to find the key once, and then redistribute the malware with the symmetric key embedded in the malware. A very simple way for the attacker to discover the key is to run a debugger on the application and watch for the decryption process.

Well, shoot! You have an encrypted special number, but the encryption is providing no protection whatsoever. You must have a way to protect the key in the application. The normal response to this situation is: make it harder to run the debugger. The security term for this defense is *obfuscation*. Obfuscation mechanisms can be very simple or very complex. The result is the same. If one attacker is able to see their way through the obfuscation, all attackers now have the encryption key. While the obfuscation mechanism can be quite creative and make the attackers' job much harder, in the end, the obfuscation mechanism is likely to fail and allow the exposure of the file encryption key.

Obfuscation is not the answer. What you need is a different key for each instance of the application. Where does the unique key come from? The system must have a process whereby the application gets some unique value and uses the unique value, or a derivative of the unique value, as the key. Think about where you provide uniqueness to applications on a daily basis. The answer is passwords.

So, we update the application to require use of a password to obtain the encryption key. The password, or unique value, eliminates the BORE attack. Knowing the value on one platform does not allow the attacker to redistribute the same encryption key in the malware. Each platform has a unique value. Having a unique value forces the malware author to find the key for each application instance.

Normally, keys are just a random sequence of bits with a specific size depending on the encryption algorithm. Well-formed passwords do not normally fit into that definition. One method of converting a password into a key is to apply a cryptographic hash to the password. The resulting hash value has a fixed size and a nice mix of bits.[4]

The application needs a new screen for the password entry. The user enters the password, and the program takes the password as input for a two-step operation. First, it applies the cryptographic hash to obtain the encryption key. Then, it uses the encryption key to decrypt the special number on the hard drive. If the user picks a good password—that topic has fodder for more than one book—the key protects the special number from malware and no BORE attack is possible.

Application Today

Our application now protects the special number from simple reading by encrypting the special number, and it protects the encryption key by requiring a password. The elements of our application are:

■ *Special number* that the application displays and updates

■ *Special number display*, the portion of the application that displays the special number to the user

---

[4] Be very careful about relying too much on the fact that the cryptographic hash has mangled the password. A cryptographic hash must work the same way every time, so if your password is "pass," the result is a well-known value and everyone in the world knows the value. The hash merely converts the password into a more convenient form; it does not add additional protections.

■ *Update display*, the portion of the application that accepts updates from the user and changes the special number

■ *Password entry*, the portion of the application that requests the users password and then applies the cryptographic hash to obtain the encryption key

■ *Special number protection*, the portion of the application that uses the encryption key to encrypt or decrypt the special number

Application Components

The question we need to ask now is, "Can malware view or disrupt our application?" To answer the question, let's see how each of the components works and take an attacker's view of them. The components are:

■ Display window to request the password

■ Reading keystrokes for the user-ID and password

■ Password processing that applies the cryptographic hash to the password and obtains the encryption key and decrypts the special number

■ Decision to display the special number or the decrypted special number

■ Display window to output the special number

■ Process to update the special number

The components combine to provide the application the ability to request from a user their password, read the password from the keyboard, and process the password to determine whether it is a correct one. The components pass information between themselves using normal internal programming mechanisms, such as shared memory, shared threads, and other such programming conventions.

Unfortunately, all of these components are susceptible to malware. Let us look at the potential malware attack points.

Display Windows

The application has three windows that it presents to the user:

■ User-ID and password screen

■ Special number display

■ Special number update

The program creates a window by using system calls to create a display frame buffer. The display adapter reads the frame buffer and mixes the information from other display buffers to create the analog[5] information that allows the monitor to display the window. The entire process uses system memory, from the creation of the display window to the frame buffer.

While each of the windows displays different pieces of information, the basic process is the same for each—process the frame buffer from system memory.

Reading Keystrokes

The user enters the user-ID and password one character at a time at a keyboard. The mechanics of this operation are:

1. The keyboard generates a scan code, a value that indicates which key was pressed.

2. Send the scan code to the keyboard driver, code that is normally part of the operating system.

3. Convert the scan code into an ASCII character.

4. Send the ASCII character to the program requesting the input.

The generation of the scan code occurs in a hardware device, but after its generation, all of the processing occurs as software processes that use system memory.

The keyboard driver, running at ring 0, provides the conversion from the scan code into the ASCII character and sends the ASCII character to the operating system. The operating system then sends the ASCII character to the application that should receive the keyboard input. The keyboard driver and the operating system reside in system memory.

---

[5] Yes, we have digital display adapters now, but the real issue is taking information from the display buffer and converting the information into a format that the monitor can properly display.

Password Processing

As the user enters the password at the keyboard, the keyboard sends each individual key code, through the keyboard driver, to the application. The application takes each keystroke and builds the entire password. When the user indicates that all characters of the password are present, the program processes the characters through the cryptographic hash. Other types of processing are possible and could include making all of the characters upper case or other such character manipulations. At this point in the process, the application has not determined whether the password is correct, just that a password is present. All of the processing occurs in system memory.

Program Decision

With a processed password, the program needs to use the processed value to continue processing. Since the processed password is the key to decrypt the special number, the program decision is easy, just attempt to decrypt the special number, and if the decryption is successful, the password was the right one. An easy way to determine whether the decryption was successful is to place some fixed values along with the special number to display in the file on the hard drive. After performing the decryption, if the fixed values are present the decryption was successful and hence the password was correct. If the fixed values are not present, the decryption was unsuccessful and the password was incorrect.

Our application uses a separate mechanism to make the decision to display the special number after decryption. While it is not necessarily the most robust mechanism, this approach highlights another type of possible attack. After the decryption, the program code contains a simple yes/no switch. The code checks for a specific value, and if it is present, the program displays the special number. If that value is not present, the code does not display the special number. All decisions and comparisons occur in system memory.

Malware Attack Points

Attacks need a vulnerability to exploit. Where are the vulnerabilities in our program? The vulnerabilities for software attacks all revolve around one main idea: manipulate memory. If the attacker can gain access to memory supposedly assigned to the program, the attacker can read or change the memory. Reading the memory would allow the attacker to disclose either the special number or the password. Changing memory would allow the attacker to change the instruction flow of the program.

The other vulnerabilities are within the input and output of information to the user. These two areas, while being susceptible to memory manipulation, get specific consideration for how to manipulate the information.

Manipulate Memory

The IA-32 ring structure provides a good protection to keep programs from accessing each other's memory. However, applications that run at ring 0 have access to all of memory, including all of ring 3. Having access to ring 0 allows an attacker to read the memory of all running programs.

Therefore, the goal of an attacker is to gain access to ring 0. Stated in the context of malware, if the infection mechanism gains access to ring 0 the attacker wins. It is possible that an infection mechanism working only in ring 3 can compromise an individual application, but for our purposes, we are considering only attacks in ring 0.

What runs in ring 0? The first, and major component, is the operating system itself. Certainly, it is possible to corrupt the operating system, but a simpler method is to install a driver. Drivers are the lifeblood of current operating systems. They allow the use of new hardware without a change to the entire operating system. The manufacturer of the hardware normally writes driver code. To perform properly, driver code normally runs in ring 0.

The attacker wants to corrupt the OS, corrupt an existing driver, or install a new driver. Any of these mechanisms allow the attacker access to ring 0. Once the attacker has access to ring 0, the attacker has access to memory. The attacker uses this memory access to read data allocated to the program.

For our sample application, the two items in memory to which the malware wants access are either the password or the special number. If the malware gains access to the password, or the processed password, the malware can display the special number or modify the special number whenever the malware wishes to do so. After decryption, if the application keeps the special number in memory, the malware can search the application's memory and discover the special number.

These two attacks succeed due to the ability of the attacker to gain ring 0 access. In current systems, no mechanisms mitigate ring 0 access. The only successful defense is to ensure that nothing happens to the code running in ring 0.

Changing the Program

A related attack is for the attacker to manipulate memory and change how the program actually works. The attacker changes the op codes of the program such that the program no longer works properly. A common change is to alter the program so that it no longer makes the proper jump after evaluating the password. In this attack, the attacker does not learn the password and cannot masquerade as the true user. Instead, the program no longer works properly and treats invalid passwords as correct passwords. This attack can be somewhat mitigated by using various digital signature mechanisms on the program to ensure that no changes are made to the distributed program. These mechanisms are only as strong as the code that enforces the digital signature check, which normally consists of sections of code that run in ring 0. The signature check code itself is then susceptible to ring 0 attacks. Alternatively, one can attack the signature check code and then attack the program in question. This strategy is harder, but doable.

DMA Access

While ring 0 is the most likely place for an attack to occur, a totally separate mechanism provides access to memory. Direct Memory Access (DMA) allows a peripheral, like a PCI card, to directly access memory without any CPU involvement. The design point around DMA was to allow fast memory access to devices. It works very well. It also avoids any protections managed by the CPU. In fact, a DMA device has access to all of memory, making a DMA access similar to a ring 0 access. The attacker can manipulate the device to perform a DMA to the program's memory. The result of this attack is the same as if the attacker had access from ring 0.

An attack through DMA requires the attacker to convince the device to perform the memory access and to have the ability to communicate with the device to get the results of the memory access. This attack is very plausible.

Manipulate Input

Malware can obtain the password directly from the keyboard. Either the attack can corrupt the current ring 0 keyboard driver or it can insert a malicious keyboard driver in front of the normal keyboard driver.

Changing the Keyboard Driver

The first technique for corrupting the ring 0 keyboard driver is just a special case of memory manipulation; manipulate the current keyboard driver. The attacker would manipulate the driver such that in addition to performing the normal keyboard driver duties of accepting the keystrokes, the driver would send a copy of the keystroke to some other entity.

Chaining Keyboard Drivers

The second technique is to insert or *chain* a new keyboard driver that intercepts scan codes before sending the keystrokes to the real keyboard driver. The interception would send the keystrokes to some other entity.

Chaining drivers is a common occurrence and was a design feature of many of the original drivers. The underlying ability to chain must be a feature of each driver. In many ways, chaining is the easiest attack to perform. It provides the same information as manipulating the normal driver, but it is much easier to distribute and install. Since the information obtained through this technique is the same as the previous technique, the attacker still has to wade through all of the data, but the attacker does get the password.

Receiving Keystroke Entity

Using either of the previous two techniques, the malware intercepts the keystrokes and sends them to some other entity. The "other" entity could be a program running on the infected platform, or it could be a program running on another platform, and the interception process sends the keystrokes across the Internet. The attacker might have to wade through lots of keystrokes to determine the password, but one easy mechanism to find the password is to parse the data looking for the user-ID. Once the user-ID is located, it is an easy matter to look at the keystrokes that occur directly after the user-ID. The password should be right there.

The result of the interception is the same; the attacker has access to the password. Once the attacker has knowledge of the password, the attacker can discover or change the special number at any time.

Reality of Keyboard Sniffers

An Internet search for "attack keyboard sniffer" yields over 45,000 hits. The term *keyboard sniffer* is description of the malware that intercepts keystrokes. Sniffer malware has come as greeting cards or programs to "watch your spouse." Some sniffer programs have stolen bank account numbers and bank passwords. The effectiveness of these sniffers has been outstanding, with users losing information and money.

Manipulate Output

Malware that manipulates the output is trying to trick the user into entering the password into a program other than our application, to display the wrong special value, or to disclose the special value during the display.

Phishing

A phishing attack is where the attacker attempts to convince the user to perform a normal operation at the wrong time or location. An example would be creating a Web site using zero '0' instead of letter 'o' in the .com. Does one really notice the difference between .com and .c0m? The current font makes it obvious, but for many fonts, the difference is very subtle.

From the standpoint of the malware attacking our application, the phishing attack would be to display a fake screen asking the user to type in the password. Having the user type in the password to a fake application allows the fake application to forward the password both to an outside entity and to the real program. The role of the outside entity is the same as in the keyboard sniffer attack, but here, the user kindly indicates what the password is by entering the password in the password field.

The malware must have knowledge of the application and of the display window that the application uses, but as the information is normally not a secret, it is an easy attack to mount.

A separate but related phishing attack is for the malware to display a false special value. In this attack, the malware has no knowledge of the real special value; the malware merely makes up a new special value and display the malware's guess of the special value. It's called a Denial Of Service (DOS) attack because the real user does not have use of the real special value.

Screen Scraping

Remembering how the display adapter takes information from the display buffer and mixes it to create the display information gives a hint on how the malware can obtain information. The malware locates the frame buffer, which is held in system memory, locates the special number display, and then "scrapes" the information from the display buffer. If the application displays the password on the display, the scraping could obtain the password also.

Changing the Display Driver

The malware could accomplish any of the previous techniques to obtain the information by changing the display driver. Just as the keyboard driver controls the input, the display driver controls the output. If the malware can corrupt the display driver, then the corrupted driver can perform phishing or screen scraping.

Reality of Output Manipulation

An Internet search for phishing yields almost 6 million hits. Some phishing schemes can fake Web sites, fake login screens, fake banks, and facilitate all sorts of attacks. While mixing metaphors, phishing is a growth industry.

The Internet search for screen scraping results in 300,000 hits, with many of the Web sites offering how-to documents.

Attack Overview

Figure 4.1 illustrates the attacks in this chapter. Each of the arrows illustrates generically one of the attack vectors.

■ Arrow 1 shows an attack on the display screen through either a scrapper or manipulated driver.

■ Arrow 2 shows an attack on the keyboard driver

■ Arrow 3 shows an attack where the malware directly reads the memory of the application

■ Arrow 4 shows an attack where the malware manipulates the application and bypasses a yes/no decision

These attack summaries are not an exhaustive list of all possible vulnerabilities. They are just examples to show the difficulties that the application has in attempting to protect itself.

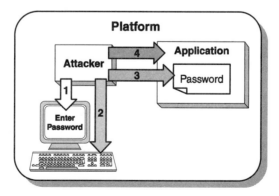

Figure 4.1   Attacks on an Application

Mitigating Attacks

Our application is under attack. We are losing control of both the special value and the application password. The attacks are coming through ring 0, with malware changing keyboard drivers, display adapters, the program itself, and through all sorts of other attack vectors. When the malware attacked our application previously, we were able to adjust the application and provide protections to the special value.

How does an application mitigate a problem with a keyboard driver? The application has no control of how the operating system installs and keeps track of drivers. If the driver is executing, it has access to ring 0 and has access to the sensitive data the application wants to protect.

No modifications are available that we can make to the application that provides ring 0 protection.

Hardware Mitigations

Without additional protections from the hardware and underlying software, our application is unable to protect itself. The purpose of LaGrande Technology is to provide the hardware and software necessary to provide these new levels of protections.

The mechanisms in LaGrande Technology are going to have to protect the memory of the application from other applications, from ring 0 access, and DMA devices. The next few chapters are going to lay the groundwork for the mechanisms and describe how the attacks to which our application is susceptible are mitigated with LaGrande Technology.

Part **III**

LaGrande
Technology Design

*When you travel, remember that a foreign country is not
designed to make you comfortable. It is designed to make
its own people comfortable.*

—Clifton Fadiman

Part III describes the design of LaGrande Technology. From objectives
and features to the basic design of the features, Part III covers the
"meat" of LaGrande Technology.

Chapter 5: LT Objectives

This chapter describes what LT does, and what LT does *not* do. LT
does not provide 100-percent security—nothing does. The trick is to
understand what has protection and where no protection is available.
There is no way to understand what has protection unless one
understands the attacker and the resources of the attacker.

Chapter 6: LT Design Principles

Chapter 6 describes the design principles that led the LT design team.
The principles have been around for many years and have guided many
security products.

Chapter 7: Protected Execution

Protected execution provides hardware domain separation. Chapter 7 describes how LaGrande Technology implements domain separation in an Intel CPU. The chapter provides an understanding of the CPU resources under control and protection of the execution environment. The chapter does go into some low level CPU details and the reader needs to have an understanding of IA architecture.

Chapter 8: Attestation

Chapter 8 provides a base primer on attestation. After the primer, the chapter shows how LaGrande Technology uses attestation. Chapter 8 introduces the Trusted Platform Module. Chapter 8 does not cover all of the details of a Trusted Platform Module, but it does include references to where to find the details.

A LaGrande Technology platform requires an attestation device. Without an attestation device, the LaGrande Technology platform cannot protect long-term secrets and is unable to report on the status of the platform.

The connection of the attestation device to the platform provides some additional functionality.

Chapter 9: Protected Input and Output

The user needs to communicate with a trusted platform. Many software attacks make use of this need and attack the user's input of information and the subsequent display of the information. Chapter 9 shows how to protect the user's input and an application's output.

There is a difference between a protected channel and a trusted path. Channel and path are very explicit terms and LaGrande Technology enables both and directly supports one.

Protected input allows the platform to protect user input from a keyboard and a mouse. There is a protected channel built between the platform and the input devices.

Protected output allows an application to display to the user information that the user can trust to be correct and not from any other source. The chapter covers how to create the appropriate channels and some information as to what the user needs to have the assurance that no spoofing of the display is occurring.

Chapter 5

LaGrande Technology Objectives

Good people do not need laws to tell them to act responsibly, while bad people will find a way around the laws.

—Plato (427–347 B.C.)

When trying to understand security, you must properly identify the objectives of the protection effort. You must understand what is and what is not protected. No security product provides 100-percent absolute security; all products have set objectives that define the security boundaries of the product. LaGrande Technology (LT) also protects some items and does not protect others. This chapter is all about the dividing line, defining what is inside the security boundary and what is not. The boundary definition comes from numerous sources and is not an exact bright straight line; rather the boundary line is a fuzzy curve with the final determination of the boundary being left to those entities wishing to rely on the LT platform.

The Basic Questions

A common tenet for security lies in the answers to the following questions:

■ What is being protected?

■ Who is the attacker?

■ What resources does the attacker have?

When one knows the answers to these questions, defining the security objectives becomes a boundable problem.

What is Being Protected?

LT needs to protect data. Not that all data on the platform is protected; rather LT protects only that data that is identified as being inside the LT security boundary. The data can be in use for various operations, including personal information like credit card numbers, Internet transactions, or keys to protect information.

Who is the Attacker?

The attackers are those who are attempting to obtain information protected by the platform. If LT is protecting a credit card number, the attacker is one who attempts to learn the credit card number. If LT is protecting an Internet transaction, the attacker is the one who attempts to read or disrupt the transaction.

Further identification of the attacker is not necessary. He or she could be a young hacker trying their first break-in or a member of a sophisticated crime organization. From the standpoint of LT, the identity of the attacker does not matter; LT must provide protections irregardless of the attacker's identity. Stated another way, LT must provide protections from the young hacker or the crime organization without knowing if the attack comes from the hacker or the crime organization. What will make a difference are the resources the attacker has access to[1].

---

[1] Do not make the mistake of ignoring the fact that data owners *do* care about the attacker, since the data owner needs to make the decision if the platform can properly protect the information.

What Resources Does the Attacker Have?

The attacker's resources break down into two categories: software and hardware. The rationale of breaking the resources down allows LT to focus on the software attacks and not consider the hardware attacks.

Software Resources

The first, and most important, resource an attacker can have is the ability to run software processes on the platform. The processes can be user applications (ring 3) or system level (ring 0). It does not matter how the attacker delivers the software to the platform. The attack software can perform all operations on the platform or the software can use resources of remote processes.

Ignoring the transport issue for software delivery allows LT to focus on the real problem: the events that happen after the software is present. If the LT security boundary tried to keep software from actually residing on the platform, an enormous effort would go into detecting when new software arrives on the platform and into attempts to control the delivery. The LT design point is not to be executing at all times, hence attempts to restrict software delivery would be very difficult.

Hardware Resources

When using a remote process, the attacker has a large amount of computing resources available. Thus, if the attacker obtains some information on the platform, she or he can use lots of computing resources remotely in an attempt to break any protections like encryption.

Stepping up from software attacks leads to hardware attacks. To mount a hardware attack, the attacker must have physical possession of the platform. While remote hardware attacks are possible, LT does not attempt to mitigate remote hardware attacks.

Remote Hardware Attacks

If you want to know more about remote types of hardware attacks, try a Google[‡] search on "TEMPEST hardware attack" and the resulting Web sites should give the information.

With physical access, you have no limit on the types of hardware mechanisms that are available to the attacker. The attacker can open the case. With the case open, the attacker can look around and use hardware tools like the ones that are available in a high school. The attacker usually does not have access to special probes or scanning electron microscopes. If the attacker does have access to these special resources, the attacker can defeat the LT protections.

LT is designed to provide protection from simple hardware attacks. What is the definition of a simple hardware attack? An exploit based on turning off the power and removing the battery is a simple hardware attack. Going to the local electronic store, purchasing twenty dollars worth of parts, putting the parts together and defeating the LT protections is a simple hardware attack. The LT objective is to mitigate simple hardware attacks.

Previous Platform Objectives

Platforms based on Intel® architecture have been a resounding success over the years. The addition of new features has expanded the use of the platform. The addition of security features must continue this tradition. Previous objectives of the Intel architecture platform, without regard to the security nature of these objectives, were:

■ Ease of use

■ Manageability

■ Privacy

■ Performance

■ Versatility

■ Backwards compatibility

The review of the previous objectives, and how LT affects them, leads to the set of objectives for LT.

Ease of Use

From a general viewpoint, the Intel architecture platform is easy to use. While it has some rough spots, overall many people are able to use the features and programs available on the platform. The operating system and the programs are a huge factor in this ease of use, but the underlying hardware allows the OS and programs to be written in a manner that enable easy use.

Adding LT to a platform must not make the platform that much harder to use. While some work to manage the LT parameters is necessary, their addition cannot change the users' burden fundamentally.

The best result would have a user able to purchase a new LT-enabled platform and merely plug it in to find that all elements work. The OS and programs that take advantage of LT would do so in a manner that is invisible to the user. While this goal might not be 100-percent achievable due to other factors, the design objective is to attempt this result.

Manageability

In a corporate environment, the ability to manage platforms is a critical total cost of ownership issue. It is difficult for a system administrator to know what software is available on a platform and how the software is currently executing.

If LT makes the management job even harder, then IT administrators will not allow the use of LT in their networks. One can successfully argue that with the ability to control what is executing on a platform, platform identity, and the ability to report the current platform configuration, the building blocks for reducing the management load in a corporate environment are present.

Privacy

If a platform contains unique values, the system design needs to ensure that the user has control of the uniqueness. The control of the uniqueness must be such that once a user makes their choice, the platform enforces that choice upon all future boots of the platform.

An LT platform will have uniqueness on the platform. The main source of uniqueness is the Trusted Platform Module (TPM). An LT platform must ensure that the mechanisms designed into the TPM to properly operate on the TPM uniqueness are available and in use.

It is important to be aware that various components using LT generate and store additional unique values on the platform. It is the responsibility of the creators of the additional platform uniqueness to adhere to privacy-sensitive implementations. LT provides assistance to properly expose and use platform uniqueness, but the final responsibility for proper management of the uniqueness lies with the creator of the uniqueness.

Performance

Intel has consistently provided platforms that increase in performance: not just speed, but the ability to get things done. This goal has been a driving force at Intel for many years.

You have two vectors to consider with LT and performance. The first vector is when a program is operating under LT protections; the performance of the program should be identical to a program not using LT protections. The second vector is that the overhead to manage LT should not be a major percentage of the computing resources.

The first vector implies that LT protections do not operate in the critical execution path. For example, LT should not have any effect on adding two numbers together. The objective to maintain performance while using the LT protections helps to ensure that software developers are not at a disadvantage when using the LT protections.

The second vector recognizes that all of the security provided by LT does not come for free. Security does incur a cost at some level. The LT design places the cost on the management of the security boundary and not during the execution of the protections. The time necessary to establish the protections becomes longer than the time spent if no protections were in place. Once established, the protections do not add any performance overhead, however.

Versatility

The beauty of the Intel architecture platform is the ability to allow others to innovate. The history of the platform shows that others have been able to innovate and expand what the platform can do. LT adds to this rich history.

The vision of the versatility provided by LT includes drastically different application architectures. The authors of LT do not have a crystal ball that informs them of all of the possible changes, but they hope that the basic building blocks of LT enable the new architectures.

By way of analogy, consider the history of display adapters. The author remembers the first display adapters and the beautiful green on green screens. To build "fancy" boxes, a programmer used the line characters └ ╫ amongst others. The idea of using these characters was to try to create boxes around certain areas. During programming, it was a painstaking task to count how many characters were necessary and where to put the T's to indicate sub-boxes[2].

How times change. The author is creating this book using a word processor that shows all of the diagrams in full color, with underlining, and beautiful lines and arrows. The original designers of the output systems did not foresee where output would go. The original designers *did* foresee that improvements would be necessary and provided hardware hooks that enabled and allowed others to innovate and create new architectures. LT is in the exact same situation. The basic building blocks are in place to provide software developers with lots of new architectures and ways to protect information.

Backwards Compatibility

Although listed last, backwards compatibility is a *huge* issue. In the early days of looking at what LT would be, the architects thought about an architecture that would do things in rather different ways. While the original idea had some nice security features, it did require the complete rewrite of the operating system. In addition to rewriting the OS, it also invalidated all currently written drivers. To the users of the platform, this complete change was unacceptable.

The goal of maintaining backwards compatibility cannot be absolute. As one adds security properties, some features do change. A good example is the restriction of no direct memory access (DMA) to pages protected by LT. Some applications that take advantage of DMA have to change. That change is the price to be paid for the additional security.

---

[2] Certainly, the author has counted more than his fair share of dashes, and he hopes never to count them again.

Protection and Attack Matrix

Can we answer the basic questions about LT security? I hope that the answer is yes. The graphic in Figure 5.1 should help you to visualize what is and is not protected.

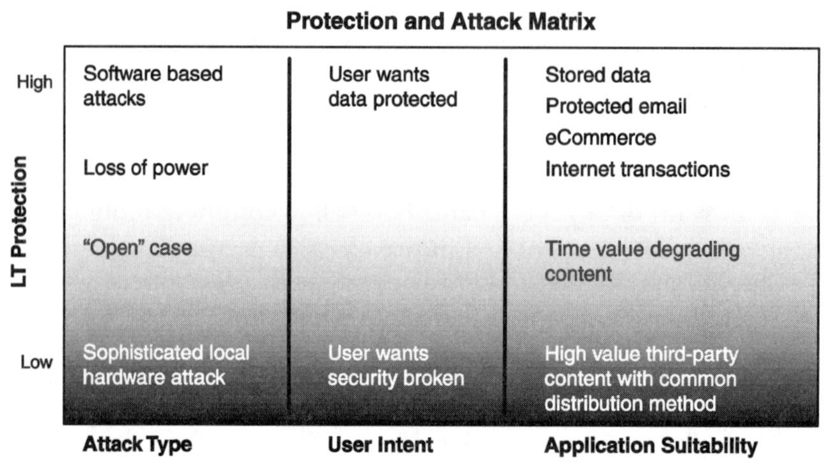

Protection and Attack Matrix

LT Protection	Attack Type	User Intent	Application Suitability
High	Software based attacks Loss of power "Open" case	User wants data protected	Stored data Protected email eCommerce Internet transactions Time value degrading content
Low	Sophisticated local hardware attack	User wants security broken	High value third-party content with common distribution method

Figure 5.1   Protection and Attack Matrix

The vertical axis indicates the amount of protection that LT can provide. A critical detail is that you have no definitive line between protected and not protected. This vagueness has a purpose. What constitutes protection for one user and application might not be protection for someone else. Security is not a bright line; it is a risk assessment. The idea of this matrix is to provide information that allows one to make a rational risk assessment of the protections that LT provides.

Attack Type

In Figure 5.1, the attack type progresses from software attack to hardware attack. We prevent software attacks and do not protect against sophisticated hardware attacks.

Software-based Attacks

Software attacks are the most prevalent attacks and mitigating these attacks will greatly increase the protections available on a platform. So, LT needs to protect against software-based attacks.

Where the software comes from should not matter to the protections provided by LT. The way a program loads, whether it comes from the hard drive or the Internet, does not affect the way that the program executes. An executable piece of code performs the same operation each time.

While data is under LT protections, LT must protect the data by preventing any process running in ring 0 or ring 3 from attempting to view or modify the data. Protecting data is not as simple as just ensuring that a software process is unable to access a physical memory page. Numerous other resources that are attached to the application relate to the data of the application. These resources include:

- *Registers*—the CPU has general-purpose registers, debug registers, and machine-specific registers. LT protection must ensure that only the application has access to the contents of the registers.

- *Threads*—the application can break execution into threads. Each thread has a register set and other resources attached. LT protection must ensure that only the application has access to the threads associated with the application.

- *Debug*—the CPU supports a rich set of debug operations. These operations include breakpoints and counters. Access to these resources by programs other than the application would leak information. Debugging is an operation that must occur at times. The design of systems using LT must be such that the application can determine whether it is accessed under a debugging environment and operate differently to avoid leaking information.

- *Counters*—the CPU in both normal and debug mode supports the creation of counters that provide information as to how many instructions have executed. These counters provide information that makes mounting timing attacks much easier.

Timing Attacks

A class of attacks that were discovered in 1996 has a direct bearing on the software protections provided by LT. Paul Kocher, a brilliant cryptographer, who discovered that small tidbits of performance information could lead to the exposure of the key for a crypto system. As Paul said:

> Crypto systems often take slightly different amounts of time to process different inputs. Reasons include performance optimizations to bypass unnecessary operations, branching and conditional statements, RAM cache hits, processor instructions (such as multiplication and division) that run in non-fixed time, and a wide variety of other causes. Performance characteristics typically depend on both the encryption key and the input data (e.g., plaintext or ciphertext). While it is known that timing channels can leak data or keys across a controlled perimeter, intuition might suggest that unintentional timing characteristics would only reveal a small amount of information from a cryptosystem (such as the Hamming weight of the key). However, attacks are presented which can exploit timing measurements from vulnerable systems to find the entire secret key (Kocher 1996).

The combination of debug registers, performance counters, and thread information can provide the resources necessary to mount a timing attack. As timing attacks can be a pure software attack, the LT protections must consider how to ensure the timing information is not available to attackers.

Loss of Power

While one might think of this event as a hardware attack, loss of power occurs in many different ways. Since many of the protections that LT provides come from internal mechanisms and a loss of power would remove those protections but not actually change what is in memory, LT needs to be robust and provide protections against this event.

If LT is protecting memory, and power is lost to the platform for any reason, when power is again applied and the platform reboots, the platform ensures that no information leakage occurred for data protected by LT.

Chapter 13 describes the complete actions that occur on a loss of power.

Open Case

The first step of physical attacks is where the attacker has physical access to the platform. By whatever means, the attacker has the platform where the attacker can manipulate the physical nature of the platform. Nevertheless, at this point, we do not assume that the attacker has unlimited resources. Instead, we posit that the attacker has very limited resources. The attacker has the ability to add in a new device on an open bus; for example, adding a new card in a PCI slot.

With the case open, the attacker has access to the busses of the platform. From a security standpoint, the busses break down into only two categories: fast and slow.

The fast busses are the front-side bus and the hub link. The front-side bus connects the CPU(s) to the MCH. This bus is very fast, 800 megahertz in early 2004, and it should continue to get much faster. The hub link connects the MCH to the ICH. This internal bus is also a very fast connection. We do not expect an attacker who just opened the case to be able to intercept and decipher information traveling on the fast busses.

Numerous other busses are on the platform, but from the LT perspective, the bus of interest is the Low Pin Count (LPC) bus. The LPC bus is slow and very simple. The design of the LPC bus does not contemplate lots of activity or high bandwidth use. The LPC bus provides the connection between the ICH and TPM. As a low-speed bus with a simple protocol, it is possible to watch the bus traffic with simple equipment. An oscilloscope and some publicly available documentation would give an attacker sufficient information to intercept bus traffic between the TPM and ICH. This "simple" attack requires a response from the LT design. Some mechanism needs to armor the traffic between the TPM and ICH. The TPM design provides for the creation of an encrypted channel between the TPM and devices using the TPM. This channel provides the armor that protects the traffic on the LPC bus.

It is difficult to launch a hardware attack without the right knowledge of the platform user. For instance, to watch the traffic on the LPC bus requires the use of probes and wires connecting the probes to some oscilloscope. I hope that the user would notice the addition of extra wires coming out of the platform. This watchfulness does not preclude the user from mounting the attack.

At the open-case level of attack, the platform should provide protections for the low-speed busses, like LPC, but it would not provide protections for the high-speed busses, like the front-side bus.

Sophisticated Local Hardware Attack

In this highest level of attack on the system, the attacker opens the case and has both the equipment and expertise to collect and interpret information from the high-speed busses. This attack represents a high level of system knowledge and monetary assets. The high-speed busses do not have protections in the first version of LT. Therefore, attackers with these resources would be able to pierce the LT protections.

Adding protections to the high-speed busses requires some very drastic changes to some basic platform components. Take, for instance, the example of encrypting information sent on the front-side bus. This solution works for the LPC bus, so why not use the same solution on the FSB? The LPC is a slow-speed bus, where data transiting from the TPM to ICH and elsewhere is a rare occurrence. In distinct contrast, for the information traveling on the front-side bus, speed is critical to the ability of the platform to execute quickly. Slow down a memory access and the system throughput degrades. Any attempt to encrypt a transaction would have throughput issues. Additionally, using more cycles to process the access can cause other devices to stall and further degrade throughput. With encryption on the high-speed bus, you also have the chance that the OS and drivers need to change. All of this leads to the fact that making a change on a high-speed bus can lead to changes in performance, backwards compatibility, and possibly versatility. For these reasons, the design of LT does not mitigate this type of attack. This decision does not imply that LT would never attempt to mitigate some of these hardware attacks.

User Intent

The user's intent is critical to the LT protection matrix. If the user wants protection, the only attacks to consider are software attacks. If the user wants to break the protection, then hardware attacks are possible.

One way to look at user intent is to use the following:

■ *Protect user's data from outsiders.* The information belongs to the user and the user wants the information protected. The user does not want to attack the platform.

■ *Protect outside data from the user.* The data owner wants to protect the data from the user. The user may want to break the protections. If the user does want to break the protections, the user may use all resources available to the user.

Protect User's Data from Outsiders

With the user wanting protection, the specter of a hardware attack is gone. The user has no reason to launch a hardware attack when the user wants the data protected. The only attacks that concern the user are software attacks launched by others. The main goal of LT is to provide protection against software attacks. The goals of the user and the platform match. The data under the protection of LT would have the protection that the user wishes.

Why are the hardware attacks off the table? Assume that the user wants LT to protect the user's credit card number. The user wants to protect the credit card number from software attacks. The user has no need to apply hardware attacks to the platform when it is an easy process to pull the card out of their wallet to obtain the number.

Protect Third-Party Data from the User

User intent is critical here. If the protection desires of the data owner and the user match, then both want protection from software attacks. The user has no desire to mount hardware attacks. LT provides good data protection here.

If the protection desires of the data owner and user do not match, then the user is motivated to mount hardware attacks. The user may mount hardware attacks as the user has physical possession of the platform. With the user mounting a hardware attack, the data owner has to consider the cost of the attack and the result of the attack. If the data under LT protection has a value that is less then the cost to mount the hardware attack, LT still might provide adequate protection. If the data under LT protection has a value greater then the cost of the attack, LT most likely does not provide adequate protection.

The valuation of the attack is not the only consideration. The third party could be distributing the data to a platform of today and accepting whatever software attacks were successfully exposing the data. When LT becomes available, even though the hardware attacks are present, the increased protection from software attacks makes the use of LT an improvement over the protections of today. The very fact that to break the LT protections requires a hardware attack could be a sufficient deterrent to keep the user from mounting the attack. The term in use for this deterrent is the "grandma" test. If grandma thinks the activity is bad, she will not do it. What the deterrent does is use the moral character of the user and moves an activity from where the user believes it is moral to immoral. Even though the user has the resources and opportunity to break the protections, the moral character of the user prevents them from mounting the attack.

Application Suitability

The final column in the matrix shown in Figure 5.1 combines the previous two vectors to show which types of applications are suitable for LT. Other applications can use LT, but the set of protections might not be sufficient to meet the application's need.

Stored Data

Stored data is data that is resident on the platform but not currently in use. This data is not in physical memory, but it uses some other storage medium. The typical media would be the disk drive, but other devices are possible. Stored data obtains protections from observation or use by the application encrypting the data. The encryption mechanism requires the protection of a key that can decrypt the stored data. LT provides the mechanism to protect the encryption key.

The attack points on the stored data are software attacks that try to recover the encryption key. LT provides the protections against software attack such that the stored data has protection from those software attacks.

Those entities wishing to rely on the stored data protection need to consider the potential of a user applying hardware attacks against the stored data encryption key. If the consideration is software attacks, LT provides mitigations against those software attacks.

Protected E-mail

Protected e-mail is a special case of stored data. The user wants to send and receive e-mail in a way that keeps other software processes from reading or modifying the e-mail. The information is specific to the user, and the user wants the information protected, so LT can mitigate software attacks. The protection mechanism would be a combination of LT memory protections and cryptography. The LT memory protection would provide coverage during the creation and viewing of the e-mail. The cryptography would provide protection of the e-mail during transit and storage of the e-mail.

Internet Transactions

Internet transactions represent an interesting type of data. The user might or might not want to protect the data. If the user is sending his credit card number, he wants protection. If the user is sending a confirmation of a bid price for an on-line auction, he might wish to cheat.

For information the user wishes to protect, an Internet transaction is another case of stored data, and LT can mitigate the software attacks.

For information that the user wishes to compromise, the grandma test works very well here. LT protects against software attacks, so the user is going to have to mount a sophisticated hardware attack. The attack mechanism would not sit well with grandma, and she would not compromise the information.

One additional type of protection that LT provides is the ability to know what application performed the operation. This is a very helpful item in a grid network. Grid networks are a combination of separate platforms that all combine to perform a single operation. In the late 90's there were some interesting uses of grid or distributed computers. One of the big projects was a project sponsored by RSA to find the cryptographic key for RC5. The key size was 64 bits and a huge amount of computing power was necessary to find the key. To obtain the necessary computing power, a large group of interested people[3] donated their spare computing cycles to search for the key. The interesting problem the designers of the system had to overcome was how to ensure that no one who reports results is lying. As the result would reward the winner with some money, there was additional motive for people to cheat. The designers used various techniques to isolate the application and detect cheating. The designers however were left with only performing obfuscation on the code, as they had no access to a secure area to execute a program. The designers of the software had this to say regarding their attempts to mitigate software attacks:

> **Why is distributed.net still not completely open-source with all parts of its source code?** Although we are providing all of the code linked on this page for public perusal, it is still necessary to keep select portions of the codebase unavailable for general distribution. Indeed, this is an aspect of our operations that we would very much like to be able to eliminate.

---

[3] The author was part of the group and all of the author's machines participated in the search

Quite truthfully, releasing binary-only clients still does not completely eliminate the possibility of sabotage, since it is relatively easy for any knowledgeable person to disassemble or patch binaries. This is actually quite a trivial task, so we urge you not to try. Indeed, security through obscurity is actually not secure at all, and we do not claim it to be such.

The source code available from this page is really all of the algorithmic code that would be of interest. The only code that is not present is the file-access and network socket code, which is not terribly interesting (nor pleasant to try to comprehend). The computational cores and platform-specific optimizations included in this package is what you would want to look at if you are interested in how the client works, or how you can increase the speed of the client for your processor.

A document that discusses many of these issues at much greater depth is available for reading, and discusses the more general problem of Operational Code Authentication. (Distributed 2003)

If the designers had LT available to them they could have solved their problem. Notice that the designers were not interested in protecting from hardware attacks—their concern was for those who were going to attempt to change the access or network code portions. To prevent cheating at the algorithm level, the system required duplicate attempts for the same key. The increase in computing power was offset by the assurance that work was actually being done.

Protecting the application from either manipulation or from performing unknown operations is an LT objective. Using the LT protections allows designers of these types of applications to mitigate these problems and have a higher assurance that their applications work properly in a distributed computing environment.

Time Value Degrading Content

What is time value degrading content? The best way to define this is to use an example. Consider a sporting event that is only available on pay-per-view. The providers want to protect the viewing of the event, but soon after the event occurs, the highlights of the event are available on the sports highlight shows. The value of the content degrades very quickly after the event is over. This is important in an LT context where the provider wants to use LT to protect the content. Most data loses value over time, the degradation time can be quite short or it could be hundreds of years. The value of the latest prizefight degrades quickly; the value of the Constitution does not degrade.

If the content provider wants to use LT for protection, the provider needs to evaluate a couple of issues. The first issue is how quickly the data degrades. In the sporting event example, the content degrades as soon as the event is over. With the degradation time so short, the protections need only be in place while the event is in progress. If the content provider believes that the LT platform can resist attacks, even hardware attacks, during the time of the event, LT provides sufficient protection for the content. If the content degrades slowly, then the attacks on LT may succeed before the value of the content reaches zero. Only the content provider can make this determination.

High Value Third-party Content with Common Distribution Method

High value third-party content is data that is difficult for LT to protect. If the data uses a common distribution mechanism, it is *very* difficult to protect. The reason is discernible by reviewing the matrix in Figure 5.1. This application is in the lower-right area, which means that the user wants to break the protection and that sophisticated hardware attacks are possible. Providing protection against sophisticated hardware attacks is not an LT objective, so this type of application may not gain appreciable levels of security by using LaGrande Technology. Based on the grandma test or other factors, LT may provide additional levels of security that the content provider wants to use, but implying that LT will solve all of the content provider's problems is incorrect.

A serious issue for the provider if they are using a common distribution mechanism is the Break Once Run Everywhere (BORE) attack. If the attacker can mount a sophisticated hardware attack on a single system and obtain the content, the attacker then has access to any other content using the same distribution mechanism. The attacker can also distribute the BORE information and allow other attackers access to the content.

The Features

Objectives are great, but to meet the objectives a product or technology needs features[4]. This section is a quick introduction to each main feature of LaGrande Technology. All of these features follow with a sub-section of their own:

- Protected execution
- Protected memory pages
- Sealed storage
- Protected input
- Protected graphics
- Attestation

Protected Execution

Protected execution provides domain separation on Intel architecture platforms. Protected execution provides isolation of all resources associated with an application. The resources under protection include memory and internal CPU state.

To implement protected execution, the majority of the changes occur in the CPU. Protected execution requires a change in the mechanisms that allow communication between the CPU packages and the chipsets that tie the packages together. One important piece of information the busses must communicate is the indication that all of the processors inside of a package are properly executing the domain separation feature.

---

[4] Well that is what marketing actually sells, so to keep marketing happy we need the features.

Protected Memory Pages

The CPU protects the application resources using protected execution. All memory access occurs when the CPU requests access to the page using the FSB to indicate to the MCH which page to access. The CPU protections do not change what the MCH does on DMA accesses.

To protect against DMA from outside devices, the MCH has the NoDMA table. The NoDMA table allows the MCH to have a view of which memory pages are under protection of the CPU. When any device other than the CPU operating in protected execution mode attempts to access a memory page, the MCH blocks access to the page.

Sealed Storage

While the CPU is executing data, it receives protection from the domain separation feature. From a platform perspective, data needs protection on a long-term basis. Storing data on a hard drive and then retrieving it needs to be a secure operation. The protected execution allows different configurations to use the LT protections. It is imperative that secrets held by one configuration are not made available to any other configuration.

The feature that provides this capability is called sealed storage. Sealed storage is a feature that the TPM provides. LT uses this feature to segregate data from one configuration to another.

Protected Input

When entering information, users need to have an assurance that only an application using protected execution can receive the key strokes for such things as pass phrases. The traditional mechanism for creating the assurance between a device and an application is a trusted channel. LT provides the mechanism to create a trusted channel between the protected execution environment and the keyboard and mouse. LT provides the necessary hooks that allow the execution environment to establish the channel.

Protected Graphics

Users need an assurance that what they see on a display window is truly coming from the application under protected execution control. As with input, the traditional mechanism for creating the assurance is to create a trusted channel between the application and the display adapter. LT provides the necessary hooks to allow the creation of the trusted channel between the protected execution environment and the display adapter.

LT allows for both integrated adapters and discrete adapters to participate in the trusted channels. The user sees no difference on their screen between an integrated or discrete device.

LT does not participate in the connection between the display adapter and the monitor. There are previously defined protocols that provide protection between a display adapter and the monitor and LT does not change how those protocols work.

Attestation

LT works in a heterogeneous environment; some platforms might have LT and others might not. When an entity wants to rely on the LT features, how does that entity determine whether LT is present on an individual platform? In addition, how does the entity determine how the protected execution environment is currently executing? To answer these questions requires a verifiable mechanism that reports on the current platform configuration. The Trusted Platform Module (TPM) provides this capability.

The entire process of measuring a configuration and reliably reporting the measurement is *attestation*. LT provides the appropriate mechanisms to measure the LT configuration and store the measurements on the TPM. The TPM provides the mechanism to report on the stored measurements.

Chapter 6

LaGrande Technology Design Principles

I am a man of fixed and unbending principles, the first of which is to be flexible at all times.

—Everett Dirksen

Saltzer and Schroeder (Saltzer 1975) in 1975 created a list of principles that security solutions should consider. The following is that list and a quick definition of each item:

- *Least privilege.* Limit access to resources to only those entities needing the resource.

- *Economy of mechanism.* Privileged code should be small and easy to verify.

- *Complete mediation.* Ensure all access to the secure area is authorized.

- *Open design.* The design should not be secret.

- *Separation of privilege.* Use two mechanisms to arbitrate the access.

- *Least common mechanism.* Limit the amount of mechanisms shared between the users.

- *Psychological acceptability.* The user should want to use the system properly.

The principles overlap and sometimes appear to conflict with each other, but in the end, the principles provide an excellent starting point for the architecture of LaGrande Technology (LT). By using the Saltzer security principles and the objectives from Chapter 6, one can create the LT design principles.

Security Principles

The security principles provide the framework for the overarching design. Understanding each principle individually illustrates how they combine into a coherent security design.

A critical building block for the LT design principles is the heavy use of virtualization, such as the enhancements provided by Intel® Virtualization Technology. The underlying capabilities of virtualization provide the perfect base for security operations.

Least Privilege

The definition of this concept is to restrict access to resources to a designated number of entities that should have access. For instance, instead of allowing all applications access to a memory page, restrict access to only the application that is using the page. The restriction comes from hardware providing services that a Virtual Machine Manager (VMM) can use to provide resource protection.

A virtual machine provides least privilege almost by default. The VMM ensures that resources allocated to one guest are not available to any other guest, the very definition of least privilege. LT extends the protections of Intel Virtualization Technology by protecting memory pages from DMA devices.

The concept of locality, and enforcement of locality by the hardware, restricts access to the TPM. Locality is a projection of least privilege.

LT does a very good job of providing and enforcing a least privilege design.

Economy of Mechanism

According to this concept, privileged mechanisms are to be as small as possible. When you are trying to evaluate a mechanism for security properties, which seems more possible to evaluate, 1,000 lines of code or 10,000,000 lines of code? The answer is obvious.

The LT mechanisms do not touch the entire CPU or chipset. The domain separation comes from Intel Virtualization Technology and does not require additional support. The launch process, while complex, uses one instruction. The chipset protection on the LaGrande Technology Control Space (LTCS) uses a small protection engine.

Is LT as small as possible? The answer is an arguable point. Einstein had it right when he said "Make everything as simple as possible, but not simpler."[1] The question to ask is, "remove *what* to make it simpler?" Removal of the NoDMA table allows DMA attacks, removing the VMM measurement allows the launching of attacks through VMM. Other evaluators of LT have made the same comment, "Oh, this is complex." The first question back to them has been, "what should we remove?" The answer has always been "I do not see anything you can remove."

Complete Mediation

This concept ensures that each time an entity accesses a resource, the protection mechanism authorizes the access. To authorize an access, the protection mechanism must be able to identity the source of the access request.

In LT, the physical page protections provide complete mediation of the access request. Any attempt by a guest to access a physical page results in the VMM gaining control. The VMM knows, from the VM exit information, the identity of the guest attempting to gain access to the page. The VMM then is able to allow or disallow the requested access.

The system also checks all DMA access to a physical page using the NoDMA table. Every DMA access uses the NoDMA table to ensure that the page is available for DMA access.

The LT system mediates all access to physical memory pages. When the LT system protects any other system resource, the same protections are in place.

---

[1] The author of this book also is the author of the LT security specification. So, simplifying and removing pages from the specification would be something the author would support.

Open Design

The open design security principle was not new to Saltzer and Schroeder. In fact, the principle is from the 1890s. The idea behind it is that the attacker knows your system, or put another way, you cannot keep your design a secret forever. If the system relies on a secret design, exposing the secret destroys the product.

The LT design is not a secret. Certainly, some information is not public, but the secrecy regarding the design is to protect Intel's intellectual property. Exposure of the design does not provide an advantage to an attacker attempting to defeat the LT protections.

The protection of secrets revolves around an encryption key and the ability of LT to keep the key safe. Exposure of the key only exposes the secrets on an individual platform; the exposure does not expand to every LT machine.

If the VMM properly protects pages, including the NoDMA table, an attacker knows how the system works. The attacker knows that each physical page reference causes the VMM to gain control and authorize the page access. No "magic sauce" is used in the LaGrande Technology recipe.

Separation of Privilege

The design idea here is that more than one mechanism provides the protections. In some security circles, the concept is "who is watching the watcher" and "defense in depth." LT separates protection into the hardware mechanisms and the software that manages the hardware. The management software is the VMM.

LT does separate the software and hardware necessary to access a physical page. The software performs the hardware setup, but the hardware enforces the policy. LT has a single software mechanism, the VMM, and a single hardware mechanism, the LT functions, to enforce the access to physical pages.

The separation of hardware and software provides a good balance between a policy-enforcing engine and a policy. The hardware is the engine and the software is the policy, with a distinct separation between these two roles. Additional protections to be sure that the hardware works correctly or that the software has the correct policy are not inherent in the LT design. The software can easily have additional checks for the correct policy, both through attestation and additional functions. At this time, no LT design adds an additional hardware mechanism.

Least Common Mechanism

The least common mechanism is, at first, a non-obvious direction. The idea is that the various mechanisms should *not* share common code or hardware. At first glance, you might think that this idea violates the economy of mechanism directive. In reality, you have no conflict. When a design shares a resource, the architecture must provide additional mechanisms to provide domain separation. If the architecture has two separate mechanisms, it becomes much easier to show the separation of the two functions.

LT has two basic mechanisms: Virtual Machine eXtensions (VMX) and the Safer Machine eXtensions (SMX). VMX provides the ability to create guests, and SMX provides the measurement and protections for the VMM.

Another requirement for the least common mechanism is that any common mechanism must be acceptable to all users. LT provides an excellent acceptance mechanism for the users. The measurement of the VMM and each guest allows a user of a guest to have a detailed knowledge of the VMM environment. The user has the opportunity to accept or reject the environment.

Psychological Acceptability

Psychological acceptance equates to the technology being easy to use and easy to understand. If the user is unable to manage the system and cannot understand the protections offered, the user cannot use or properly configure the system.

Some parts of LT are very easy to understand at the user level. Stating that one guest knows nothing about any other guest is a concept that normal users accept. Trying to explain the NoDMA table is not within the normal user's realm of expertise. Thankfully, the user need not know about the NoDMA table or understand how VMX provides domain separation. The user does need to control the VMM Environment. The VMM must provide adequate control surfaces, which allow the user to control the VMM without burying the user in superfluous detail.

Design Principles

The following requirements drive the LT design. The breakdown of these requirements is the purpose of the sections on assumptions, threats, and objectives. These high-level statements provide you with an overview of the LT design and help us to frame the questions about what LT does and does not do.

The LT hardware requires supporting software. A hard and fast statement that "LT provides a specific protection" is not correct. Only in combination with properly executing controlling software are the LT protection capabilities available. Since the combination is the key, understanding which controlling software is executing becomes a critical requirement.

High-level Requirements

The high-level requirements define the basic idea of LT: protecting data.

- An LT system must enable the protection of user data from software-based attacks while the data is being used, viewed, operated upon, or stored on the PC platform. The definition of data includes information and executable code.

- The LT protection must be available in environments designed to run many different general-purpose programs concurrently.

- LT protection architecture applies equally to desktop and mobile systems using single or multiple CPU, with a single chipset.

Environment Requirements

LT runs on Intel architecture platforms. The environment of the platform creates some requirements for LT:

- The LT architecture must enable backward compatibility. Backward compatibility allows the user to run legacy programs where the legacy program does not affect any protections provided by LT. LT may provide protections to the legacy program.

- Future hardware-based Intel architecture security technologies must provide comparable or better levels of protection going forward.

- LT Protection architecture should make no assumptions about the security of the pre-LT environment.

- The LT architecture should enable high-confidence measurement and reporting of the environment that is launched and protected by LT. The reporting of the measurement is not required to be always available.

User Assumptions

Both the designer of the platform and the user of the platform make some assumptions about how the user is going to interact with the platform. These assumptions drive some design principles:

- The user of an LT-enabled platform should *not* be considered an adversary.

- LT protection architecture must enable an opt-in mechanism that allows the system to be delivered to the user with the protections disabled as the default mode and the state of the protections to be clearly indicated to the user.

- Ease of use is a factor of the LT architecture and the environment that leverages the LT architecture.

- Third-party content protection is not a design goal of LT.

Attackers

Just as the designer makes some assumptions regarding the user of the platform, the designer makes some assumptions about those who wish to break the protections on the platform.

- The base of the hardware LT protections *must not* use a "global secret" such that the LT hardware protections are vulnerable to a Break Once and Run Everywhere (BORE) attack.

- Attackers with detailed knowledge of the PC platform, software architecture, and LT should not be able to launch a successful software-based attack.

- Attackers with physical access to an LT-enabled platform may be able to circumvent protections.

Protection Requirements

The LT system, at its very core, is going to protect some items. The items to protect include the following:

◼ LT must enable the ability to assign a physical memory page to a specific virtual machine and protect the page from other virtual machines and DMA device access.

◼ At a minimum, LT must enable a mechanism that protects keyboard, mouse, and display data from attack while the data is in transit to and from the LT-enabled protection environment.

◼ LT should enable a mechanism that indicates to the user that the keyboard, the mouse, and the display data-protection mechanism are operating.

◼ Any security secrets which provide a foundation of trust should be protected by a robust, long-term storage protection mechanism and a place for these secrets to handled, used, operated on that does not expose the secrets.

◼ Protections should apply across PC platform corner cases like Reset, Initialization, power management, BIOS configuration changes, etc.

Upgrade Requirements

LT architecture and implementations must enable a controlled, trustable mechanism for the user to upgrade the system as well as to migrate data under LT protection.

LT Non-requirements

It is critical to know what items are *not* under LT protection. These non-requirements provide the basis for drawing the protection boundary. While the boundary can be somewhat soft or fuzzy, it is important to know that the boundary does not include the following items:

◼ LT does not provide protection against hardware-based attacks.

◼ LT does not provide a "Trusted Path." LT does enable a trusted channel between the keyboard, mouse, and display, but it does not provide the indicator that the channel is present. The channel indicator is a trusted path; LT enables the path but does not display the indicator.

- LT does not provide protection from Denial of Service (DoS) attacks. Some items have increased protection in LT; other items are susceptible to DoS attacks. LT is not required to prevent all DoS attacks directly.

- LT does not directly indicate the current LT operating status. The software using the LT protections should provide visible indications to the user of the current LT operating state.

LT Protection Boundary

After knowing what the requirements are and what the potential use models are, the next question to ask is "What are the protection boundaries?" In other words, what does LT protect and what does LT not protect?

The easiest way to protect information in a PC is to limit access to the physical memory page. If an application cannot gain access to a page, all of the information on the page has protection from the application. Since the LT goal is to protect from software attacks, denying an application the ability to access a page provides the protection. While the physical memory is important, other resources require protection. These resources include hardware configuration settings, input/output devices and ports, and other system entities.

The previous discussions around requirements, design principles, and security principles point out the need to draw a boundary around what does and does not have protection. One way to describe the boundary is to use the mechanism of a Target of Evaluation (TOE) from the Common Criteria (Common 2002). A TOE produces a description of the protection boundary including the entities and mechanisms in and out of the boundary. This chapter does not create a complete TOE, but it does go into the building blocks necessary to create a TOE. The exercise of determining the components inside and outside of the boundary was helpful to the original LT architects.

From an LT standpoint, the domain separation breaks when a software process obtains access to a protected resource. If a ring 3 application accesses a protected ring 0 memory page, the access represents a break. If one guest accesses the memory of another guest without permission, the access also represents a break.

Page Protections

Four mechanisms for a software process to gain access to a physical page are:

■ The software, as a guest of the Measured Virtual Machine Monitor (MVMM), can request access to a physical page by referencing the virtual page address. The internal CPU process translates the virtual page access to the actual physical address and routes the physical page request to the memory controller. The software can be executing at any privilege level, ring 0 through ring 3.

■ The software can program a device to access a physical page. Devices access physical pages on a very frequent basis to move information from the main system memory to a storage or network device. These memory accesses do not require CPU control; hence, the paging mechanism is not in use. The term for such a direct access to memory, bypassing the CPU, is Direct Memory Access (DMA). Software configures the device by indicating which physical page the device should use for the DMA accesses.

■ Display adapters are a special case of DMA device access. Special tables are made available to the display adapter so it can create and display the output screens. The display adapter needs quick and efficient access to the display buffers so that reasonable display frame rates are possible.

■ System Management Interrupts (SMI) result in a mode switch in the CPU and the bypassing of the paging mechanism. The SMI handler code can currently run in modes that do not support paging.

The security boundary that LT requires must take into account all four of the physical page accesses in the previous list. Figure 6.1 shows the LT physical page protection from a layer point of view.

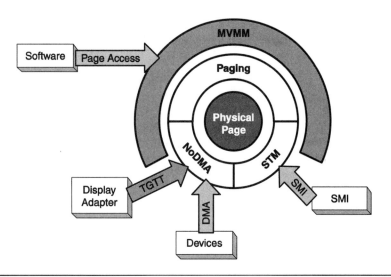

Figure 6.1   Physical Page Protections

The four boxes match the four areas listed in the previous paragraph and show the initiation of a software request for access to a physical page. The components that control the accesses are:

■ MVMM and the paging mechanism

■ NoDMA table

■ Trusted Graphics Translation Table (TGTT)

■ SMI Transfer Module (STM)

The MVMM provides a large portion of the protection as the MVMM manages the paging mechanism, the NoDMA table, and cooperates with the STM. The remaining sections describe the controlling mechanisms.

Paging Mechanism

The paging mechanism with a page table and ring structure has been in the CPU since the time of the Intel386™ processor. LT does not require a change to the paging mechanism. The paging mechanism provides separation of processes from ring to ring. The idea is that a higher-level process has no access to lower-level process information. A ring 3 process is unable to access ring 0 process information without the permission of the ring 0 process. The paging mechanism also can separate processes inside of rings other than 0; any ring 0 process has access to all of memory.

Ring 0 controls the paging mechanism by manipulating CR3, the register that contains the base address of the page directory. Any entity that can control CR3 has the ability to control access to physical memory. Operating systems control CR3 to provide process separation and to ensure that applications only gain access to real physical memory. VMX adds additional paging support. VMX allows the VMM to control CR3; the operating system in the guest only sees a virtual CR3. When the OS makes a change to CR3, the hardware causes the CR3 change request to invoke the VMM and the VMM ensures that the CR3 change is allowable. The paging mechanism also uses page tables and other controls; any manipulation of these controls by an OS requires validation and acceptance by the VMM.

The VMM control of the paging mechanism is what provides the protection from software manipulation of physical pages. All software accesses must use the mechanism built by CR3, with the VMM validating any change to CR3 and the page tables, the VMM ensures that the OS only has access to a proscribed set of physical pages. The VMM uses this control to segregate one guest from another. By assigning a physical page to one guest and never allowing the physical page to be in use by any other guest, the VMM provides the base level of domain separation. The control of the paging mechanism by the VMM is the crux of the domain separation protection. If the VMM is unable to control the paging mechanism, it cannot provide domain separation.

LT makes use of the exact VMX control of the paging mechanism. The VMM has complete control of CR3, and no additional controls are needed. You only need to understand which VMM is controlling CR3. The understanding requirement again points to the necessity of understanding which VMM is controlling the platform.

NoDMA

The paging mechanisms under control of the VMM provide sufficient protections from any CPU software process attempting to access a physical page. What the paging mechanisms do not control is the ability of a DMA-capable device of directly accessing a physical memory page. The original reason for DMA was to bypass the paging mechanism and allow for faster device access to physical memory. Devices that make extensive use of DMA are network cards and disk drives. Changing the system architecture to require a DMA device to use the paging tables would add an unacceptable amount of memory access latency to those devices needing direct memory access.

The issue with DMA devices is, while they are hardware, most of them allow software to configure the physical memory pages that those devices use for DMA purposes. Software configuration of the devices would allow software to break the domain separation setup by the VMM and the paging mechanism.

With no change available to the system architecture and the continued need to perform DMA access, LT needs to add a protection mechanism that limits DMA access. The NoDMA table is the mechanism that LT adds. Figure 6.1 shows that the MVMM overlaps the NoDMA table. The overlap indicates that the MVMM controls the NoDMA table. While the DMA access bypasses the MVMM and the paging mechanism, the MVMM does control the NoDMA table. The NoDMA table is a chipset component, and the MVMM has the responsibility of maintaining the synchronization between protected physical pages in the paging mechanism and the indicators in the NoDMA table. If the paging mechanism and the NoDMA go out of sync, it is a distinct possibility that the protection mechanism has a leak.

TGTT

To create and display the screens, the display adapter needs quick and efficient access to physical memory. The mechanism in use is a special DMA access with sophisticated access patterns defined and bounded by one or more address-remapping tables. The remapping allows the dynamic change of page addresses in response to the needs of the adapter. As with any DMA device, the need to continue DMA access is critical to system needs, and changing the basic access is not possible in the LT architecture.

One change would be to indicate that the physical pages in use by the display adapter would allow DMA access. The DMA protections are binary, either no DMA or all DMA. Allowing graphic DMA access would allow any device access. One advantage that LT provides is the ability to create trusted channels between devices and drivers. One obvious device to use a trusted channel is the display adapter, which requires the creation of a trusted display channel. Many security solutions depend on the ability to create a channel between the application and the display device. The basic attacks on the display occur because the display buffers are in physical memory and susceptible to access by either applications or DMA devices. The display adapter uses DMA to gain quick access to the physical memory and create a display frame rate that is pleasing to the user's eye. To create a trusted channel, the mechanism must provide both protection from software processes and other DMA devices. If the LT system does not provide these base-level protections, you have no assurance that the information on the display is what the protected application sent to the display. For all of these reasons, simply not protecting the display buffer's physical pages is an unacceptable solution.

The LT solution is to provide special frame buffers for the display and disallow any DMA access except for the display adapter. In addition, the display adapter can only communicate to the frame buffers using certain addresses. Any other attempt by the display adapter to touch other physical pages using a DMA access requires the NoDMA table to allow the physical page access. The Trusted Graphics Translation Table (TGTT) is the mechanism that provides the frame buffer protection.

Just as control of the NoDMA table comes from the MVMM, control of the TGTT resides in the MVMM. The MVMM establishes the TGTT, assigns the physical pages to the TGTT, and configures the chipset and display adapter to use the TGTT. The MVMM must synchronize the physical memory pages in use by the TGTT with the NoDMA table and the use of the frame buffers by graphics applications. Failure of the MVMM to perform this task can result in the leaking of graphically protected information.

STM

The SMI Transfer Monitor (STM) provides protection of a physical page from access by normal SMI handling code. The STM is a security peer to the VMM. The STM and VMM negotiate the correct policies for what the SMI handling code should and should not do, and then the MVMM allows the STM to handle all SMI events.

SMI handling code in a non-LT system has access to all of physical memory. The code operates without knowledge of the OS and can manipulate any physical address. Obviously, allowing a software process this type of access does not maintain the protection boundary that the MVMM is attempting to create.

The MVMM cannot directly control the STM. The difference between normal execution mode and SMI is too great to allow the MVMM direct SMI control. The STM is a peer to the MVMM. Together, the MVMM and STM establish policy that allows the STM to protect those pages from access by the SMI handling code.

VMM

The VMM is the keystone of LT security. The VMM protects physical pages by enforcing correct page tables. Without the VMM protecting the page tables and any changes to the page tables, software processes in the CPU could gain access to a protected physical page. With the VMM, software processes only gain access when the appropriate process is executing in the CPU.

The VMM provides additional physical page protection by enforcing the correlation between the page tables and the NoDMA table. The VMM is the primary enforcer of protections from DMA device access. If the VMM allows pages under protection from CPU software access to have DMA access, the security boundary is broken.

The VMM, in conjunction with the STM, provides the protection of a physical page from SMI access. By managing the negotiation of protections with the STM, the VMM ensures that an SMI does not have access to a page under protection. As with the NoDMA table, it is the responsibility of the VMM to ensure the proper synchronization of page under protection and SMI access.

The VMM may not directly manage the TGTT, as the TGTT could be under control of a guest partition. However, the VMM does ensure that only one guest has access to the TGTT and enforces control of the trusted configuration space.

VMM Measurement

In numerous places, the protection boundary requires knowledge of the currently executing VMM. Any entity wishing to rely on the VMM wants to know which VMM is currently controlling the system. One of the major differences between LaGrande Technology and Intel Virtualization Technology is the launch of the VMM. Intel Virtualization Technology launches the VMM and allows the system to run; LT goes through numerous steps to ensure that the identity of the VMM is available.

Description of Measurement and Identity

A short digression is important here to define the terms "measurement" and "identity." In the LT architecture, the identity of a module, VMM, or any other application, is a cryptographic hash of the module. LT currently uses the Secure Hash Algorithm version 1 (SHA-1). The calculation of the hash is the measurement. Therefore, the measurement of the VMM requires a SHA-1 calculation of the VMM code and the VMM identity is the resulting hash output.

Obtaining the VMM Identity

The difficulty with LT is ensuring that the measurement process obtains an accurate measurement of the VMM. The term in use for the LT VMM is a Measured VMM (MVMM). Measuring the VMM does not change the properties of the VMM; rather it allows entities to evaluate the VMM's ability to manage the paging mechanism, the NoDMA table, the interaction with the STM, and other protection operations properly. It is entirely possible that some VMMs might do a good job and some VMMs might not. The ability to determine which VMM is managing a platform allows the entities wishing to rely on the platform the ability to make a trust decision.

Figure 6.2 shows the components necessary to perform the measurement of the VMM.

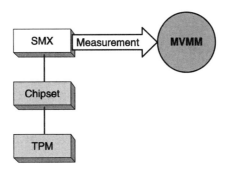

Figure 6.2   Measured Virtual Memory Management (MVMM) Measurement

The components of the VMM measurement are:

■ SMX instructions

■ Chipset hardware

■ TPM

SMX Measurement Instructions

The SMX instructions provide the ability to perform an accurate measurement of the VMM. To ensure the accuracy, the platform relies on the following components:

■ CPU synchronization

■ Authenticated code execution and measurement

■ Measurement of the VMM by the Authenticated Code (AC) module

■ Storing the AC module and VMM measurement in the TPM

With these mechanisms, the LT system provides an accurate measurement of the launching environment, the AC module, and the VMM operating environment. With those measurements, an outside entity can determine whether the system does provide the proper mechanisms to protect a physical page.

Chipset Hardware

The measurement process is not simply a CPU mechanism—the chipset must participate also. The chipset provides hardware mechanisms for the following features:

- *The ability to accept a VMM measurement.* The chipset provides a dedicated area that is only for storing the VMM measurement. The area allows for special addressing and special processing.

- *A way to ensure that only the SMX instructions can attempt to store the measurement.* When the chipset receives the measurement value there must be some assurances that only the CPU and an executing SMX instruction is storing the measurement

- *Passing of the measurement to the TPM.* After the chipset assures itself that the measurement value is coming from a valid SMX instruction, the chipset must pass the measurement value to the TPM

Storing VMM Measurement in TPM

The TPM stores the VMM measurement, and when requested, it can report the measurement value. The reporting of the VMM identity allows the entities wishing to rely on the platform the ability to evaluate the properties of the VMM.

LT does not change the TPM reporting capabilities. Storing measurement values in Platform Configuration Registers (PCR) and providing digital signatures of the PCR contents does not change in an LT platform.

LT does take advantage of the ability to report what platform entity is requesting access to the TPM. The TCG term for the access differentiation is *locality*. LT takes full advantage of the localities to ensure the proper handling, reporting, and recording of the VMM measurement.

Other CPU Resources

While physical pages represent the bulk of protections that an LT system provides, other CPU resources require protection. These resources include:

- *Input/Output ports.* Intel Virtualization Technology provides a mechanism to control every port. The VMM gets control whenever any guest attempts to access an I/O port. The VMM must allow or disallow the access. It is permissible for the VMM to allow one guest access to a port and disallow another guest access to the port. As the protections represent a policy, the identity of the VMM allows those wishing to rely on the VMM the knowledge of how the VMM enforces and sets I/O access policy.

- *Control registers.* In addition to CR3, numerous control registers affect the way that the CPU operates. Intel Virtualization Technology allows the VMM to control access and provide virtualization for these registers.

- *Machine Specific Register (MSR).* The control registers are the same on each CPU family. The MSRs are specific to a CPU family, and they might or might not be available on a previous or subsequent CPU family. The MSRs control many aspects of the platform, and some of the MSRs can affect the ability of the VMM to maintain the protection boundary. One example of the type of MSR that can affect the protection boundary is the MSR that controls the frequency and power to the CPU. Trying to run the CPU at a frequency and power level not properly tested could result in the CPU not operating correctly. Allowing software to access the MSR and change the settings could break the VMM protections. Intel Virtualization Technology allows the VMM to provide virtualization for the MSR.

Figure 6.3 shows that Intel Virtualization Technology provides virtualization of all of the CPU resources that affect the protection boundary. The VMM intercepts any attempt by software to access the CPU resources and the VMM evaluates the request and allows or disallows the request.

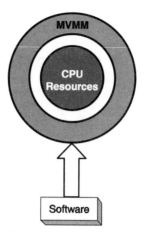

Figure 6.3   CPU Resource Protection

Keyboard and Mouse

The keyboard and mouse are special cases of input. The platform must provide the ability for the MVMM to create a trusted channel from the device driver to the input device connection. Providing a connection across all connection mechanisms—that is, wired, wireless, infrared, etc.—is not a design goal of LT. If an application wants to create the trusted channel all the way to the device across multiple connections, nothing in the LT architecture prevents the application from creating the connection.

Overt Channels

A working definition of a *covert channel* is "a mechanism that can be used to transfer information from one user of a system to another, using means not intended for this purpose by the system developers." The task of defining a system that is completely resistant to covert channel attacks is nearly impossible. For example, the internal clock that the system uses for time of day and process scheduling can also provide a covert channel. LT makes no claims to prevent covert channels.

However, the MVMM implementer must consider related threats. It is possible to transfer information between components of the platform using CPU and chipset control registers, status registers and I/O ports. Transfer of information can also occur using the persistent storage and state of attached devices. All of these data areas can allow the creation of direct communication channels between guest partitions. The term for this type of communication channel is an *overt channel*, which differs from the covert channel, as the covert channel does not directly leak information. An overt channel represents a security hole in the architecture. The hole allows direct guest communication outside of the physical page protections. The overt channel differs from normal guest communication because the data area's design did not anticipate inter-guest communication. Using the overt channel, an attacker might attempt to circumvent the inter-guest protections provided by virtualization and asset assignment. Overt channels are software attacks on the protection boundary of the system.

The MVMM should prevent the establishment of overt channel attacks. The MVMM must employ intelligent mechanisms that can monitor the complex behaviors of the previously mentioned data areas. The MVMM must be able to allow a guest to manage a device or control register properly, but it also must be aware of the possibility of an overt channel.

The possibility of an overt channel exists when devices allow the routing of information between the devices without any intervention by the CPU. An example of this type of exchange is a PCI peer-to-peer data exchange. The MVMM must provide the intelligence to monitor and control the data exchange, or the security policies must contemplate the potential vulnerability.

The MVMM must be aware of device settings not initialized when the system resets. Some devices do not reset to default values on system reset but retain their prior settings and respond to specific reset events. The data in the device represents another potential overt channel, albeit a channel that requires a platform reset. It is the responsibility of the MVMM to remove any information from these potential channels prior to MVMM shutdown and to scrub the areas during MVMM initialization.

The mitigation of overt channel attacks requires platform configuration and implementation-specific behavior. The definition of the specific behavior is outside the scope of the LT hardware but is within the scope of the MVMM. The level of protection that the MVMM provides is a design decision left to the MVMM designer.

Boundary Summary

The entities to protect on the LT system include physical memory pages, CPU resources, measurements of the VMM, trusted input, and trusted output. Table 6.1 provides an overview of each of the entities and the protections for the entity.

Table 6.1   Boundary Protections

Entity	Protection Mechanisms	Function or Activities
Physical Page	Rings and Paging	Provides protection from software processes running in the same VM.
	Virtualization	Provides protection between VM guests.
	NoDMA Table	Provides protection from DMA devices.
	STM	Provides protection during SMI events.
CPU Resources	MVMM	Protects internal CPU resources from access from VM guest or DMA access.
Measurements	SMX	Extensions to ensure the correct and proper measurement of the VMM turning the VMM into a MVMM.
	TPM	Provides a storage area for the measurements and a mechanism to report the measurements.
Trusted Input	USB host controller or Trusted Mobile Keyboard Controller (TMKBC)	The USB host controller provides protections for messages moving from the controller to the device driver.
Trusted Output	TGTT	The TGTT provides a special buffer for the display adapter to obtain display information that has protection from VM guest and DMA access.

The boundary of protected platform entities can continue to grow over time. Future versions of LT might add additional entities to protect and change the listed protection mechanisms. When the future boundary changes occur, they will add to the current boundary and not change the basic design principles. In fact, most of the design principles will never change throughout the lifetime of LT. As new threats appear, some principles may need modification, but the security principles will live on.

Requirements and Boundary Comparison

In Chapter 2, Table 2.2 lists the requirements for a trusted platform. When comparing the list to the features available on platforms today, some holes were obvious. With the LT protection boundary defined, table 6.2 revisits the earlier table and looks at the holes. You can see that they've been plugged.

Table 6.2   Current Requirements Supported

Requirement	Hardware Support	Comments
Isolation of programs	Paging, segmentation and paging	The VMM provides both paging support and the ability to handle events issuing from the guest.
Separation of user from supervisor	Ring 0 and Ring 3 separation	The VMM is completely separate from any guest. In addition, the guests are now separate from each other.
Long-term protected storage	SMX measurement and TPM	The TPM provides long-term storage
Identification of current configuration	SMX instructions	The SMX measurement process provides for the identity of the executing VMM.
Verifiable report of current configuration	TPM attestation	The TPM provides the ability to report
Hardware basis for protections	Yes	Mechanisms are in hardware.

Chapter 7

Protected Execution

No enterprise is more likely to succeed than one concealed from the enemy until it is ripe for execution.

—Niccolo Machiavelli

The success of LaGrande Technology (LT) depends on the creation of domain-separated processes. To provide that separation, the LT Security Architecture depends on the Virtual Machine Extensions (VMX) to create one or more virtual machines. The Virtual Machine Manager (VMM) provides the domain manager that establishes the virtual machines and manages the communication between virtual machines. For LT, it is the epitome of being Machiavellian, by concealing the execution processes from the enemy. A virtual machine can be general-purpose and run an existing operating system like Windows, or the virtual machine could be a specific application like a firewall. The LT system puts no requirements on the use model of a virtual machine.

The VMM has complete and full control of the processor. The VMM presents to each guest a processor abstraction and allows the guest to use the abstraction. The VMM controls processor resources, physical memory, interrupts, input and output, and communication between the guests.

VMX Operation

VMX provides the support for virtualization in the processor. VMX does not require any changes in the chipset. VMX is true virtualization and the virtualization state is not visible to a guest. It is possible for a guest to know the virtualization state. For instance, a guest design may require virtualization. If the guest is running, virtualization must be present.

When VMX is executing, the processor is in one of two states: VMX operation or VMX root operation. If a guest has control of the processor, the processor is in VMX operation; if the VMM has control, the processor is in VMX root operation.

When a guest is operating in VMX mode, the only mode a guest can operate in, the guest believes that the guest has total control of the processor. The reality is that VMX root mode restricts what the guest can do. The restrictions include: physical memory visible to the guest, operations the guest can perform, events that execute, and instructions that work without VMX root authorization. The VMM controls the guest VMX mode by setting various options only changeable in VMX root mode. Whenever the guest performs an operation under control of the VMM, the guest exits from VMX operation and transitions to VMX root operation. Exiting from the guest uses the VMEXIT event and the VMM receives control at a predefined entry point. After processing the event, and either allowing the event or blocking it, the VMM returns control to the guest by using the VMRESUME operation.

Figure 7.1 shows the layout of the guest and VMM, the various structures, and the directions of VMEXIT and VMRESUME. The guest in VMX mode has all of the normal CPU control mechanisms available in ring 0. Those control mechanisms include the Global Descriptor Table (GDT) and Interrupt Descriptor Table (IDT). When a system is operating without Intel® Virtualization Technology and a VMM, the ring 0 process has complete control of the GDT, IDT, and all other CPU control mechanisms. When Intel Virtualization Technology is executing and the guest is in VMX mode, the guest sees a virtualized copy of the GDT and IDT. The VMM, in VMX root mode, has control of the real GDT and IDT. The virtualization of these two structures is the basic mechanism that allows the VMM to control the guest and what the guest can do.

The net effect of running in VMX operation state is to restrict or "de-privilege" certain operations of the guest, while still allowing the guest the full use and utility of the normal privilege levels, rings 0 through 3. To illustrate the de-privilege nature of a VMX operation, Figure 7.1 uses 0D and 3D. Those rings and the 1D and 2D rings not shown are in the guest. The VMM has all four rings, 0 through 3, but the rings have full privilege. The designation of "D" indicates de-privilege and "P" indicates full privilege. The current implementation of a VMM does not use the other rings 1 through 3, but they are available, and a VMM implementation could use them.

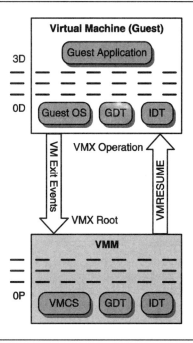

Figure 7.1   VMX Events

When the guest invokes one of the operations that cause a VMEXIT, like accessing CR3, the hardware fills in the Virtual Machine Control Structure (VMCS), passes control to the VMM, and transitions to VMX root operation.

VM Control Structure

The VMCS controls a number of functions relevant to VMX mode and transitions into and out of VMX root operation. The VMM is the only entity with access to the VMCS; no guest can access any VMCS structure. The VMM has VMX instructions that allow the VMM access to the VMCS. The VMCS includes:

- The *guest-state area* contains key components of processor state representing the guest's execution state and the cause of the most recent VM exit. This state is saved on a VM exit, as execution control reverts to the VMM, and this state is restored on a VMRESUME as control is passed to the guest. The VMM may modify this state to alter the behavior of the guest or to invoke a different guest.

- The *host-state area* contains key components of processor state representing the VMM. VMEXIT restores the area when transitioning from VMX operation to VMX root operation.

- The *VM-execution controls* regulate the processor's functions while in VMX mode. They determine, for example, which events, operations, and situations cause VM exits if they occur while the processor is in VMX mode.

- The *VM-exit controls* determine the components of processor state to save into the guest-state area on a VM exit and certain components of VMM state that load on a VM exit.

- The *VM-entry controls* determine which components of processor state load from the guest-state area on a VMLAUNCH or VMRESUME. In addition, they allow modification of the VMRESUME behavior, such as allowing the next VMRESUME to deliver an interrupt to guest software.

Notice that while only one VMCS is in the processor, and therefore only one guest can be "active" at any given moment, the VMM may selectively modify all guest states in the VMCS. Thus, a VMM can set up multiple guests and switch between them by explicitly saving and restoring guest VMCS state and associated controls from memory. The specific properties of such multiple-guest environments are determined solely by the VMM, which is also solely responsible for instantiating and managing each guest and its resources. It is possible to establish guests with fully private resources—that is, resources not accessible to any other guest—as well as to allocate resources to be shared between all guests or a subset of guests.

VMM Launch and VM Creation

Figure 7.2 illustrates the general process of launching a VMM, creating an initial virtual machine environment, and then adding a second virtual machine. This figure illustrates the general case, where launching the VMM occurs after an OS and its applications are already running. It is also possible to launch the VMM as part of an OS boot loader, or even during the BIOS. No architectural requirement says that the environment that initiates the VMM must be present as a guest during VMM execution. The VMM may establish a guest that contains the initiating environment or the VMM may never establish a guest that contains the initiating environment. The VMM could never establish a guest that contains the initiating environment, but when the VMM terminates, the environment to which the VMM passes control could be the initiating environment.

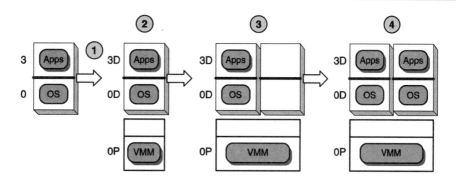

Figure 7.2   Creation of a Multi-partition Environment

The steps described here represent only an abstract view of the process. Detailed descriptions, including the specific instructions, VMCS settings, and VMM responsibilities are available in the appropriate platform manuals. Additionally, these steps identify only one process model, but multi-process variations are possible.

Step 1 in Figure 7.2 illustrates the initiating software loading a VMM into memory and then transferring control to the new VMM. Step 2 shows the VMM instantiating a guest partition with the initiating software in the guest partition. Steps 3 and 4 show the VMM instantiating another partition and loading an OS into the new partition.

On first launch, the VMM performs its own self-initialization and assumes control over critical resources formerly belonging to the initiating OS that could represent violations of the VM perimeter—for example, the interrupt table and the now-guest OS page tables, amongst others. The VMM also configures the desired VMEXIT conditions that cause the OS or applications in the VM to trap back to the VMM. Once properly configured, execution control may return to the now-guest OS using a VMLAUNCH instruction.

Once control returns to the guest OS in its VM, execution continues normally within that VM. As configured by the VMM, certain operations may result in traps back to the VMM. The VMM may perform the operation as specified, perform only a portion of the operation, substitute another operation entirely, or reject the operation with or without notice. As an example, an attempt by the guest OS to change an entry in the guest OS page table results in a trap to the VMM, which selectively performs or discards the requested change, depending on whether the result would violate the boundaries of the virtual machine.

At any time after the initial launch, the guest or the VMM may recognize the need to run additional, specific software in a second VM.[1] The three main ways for the VMM to establish an additional VM are:

- *Current guest loads new guest memory.* This mechanism has VM#1 load VM#2 into the memory pages in the VM#1 physical page allocation, then has VM#1 inform the VMM where the pages for VM#2 are, and finally passes control to the VMM which instantiates VM#2. When allocating pages to VM#2, VM#1 removes the pages from VM#1 control.

- *Current guest relinquishes pages.* VM#1 would release pages under control of VM#1 and have the VMM instantiate VM#2 in a separate step. VM#1 has the option to fill the new pages with information or leave the pages blank. If VM#1 places information into the pages, the VMM should validate the starting state; if VM#1 leaves the pages blank, then the VMM must provide the code to execute in VM#2.

- *VMM maintains pool.* In this mechanism, the VMM does not assign all free pages to VM#1. Instead, the VMM maintains a pool of free pages, and when a new VM is necessary, the VMM assigns the pages from the pool.

---

[1] In other models, this decision may be made by the VMM itself. In which case, the VMM requests that the guest OS in the initial VM surrender an appropriate number of memory pages, after which the VMM may install the new VM into those pages.

To manage the physical pages, the VMM can use one, all, or any of the above mechanisms that the VMM desires. Each mechanism has plusses and minuses. The use model determines what is appropriate for a VMM and the guests it supports.

The VMM, by virtue of having total control, can reject or modify the request for an additional VM. The VMM has the ability to add additional pages, start multiple VMs on a single request, or stop the instantiation of the new VM. The VMM might or might not report the reasons for denying or modifying a request for a new VM.

Once the memory pages, and optionally, other resources such as specific IO ports, have been removed from the VM#1 context and reallocated to VM#2, VM#1 no longer has any ability to touch those resources in any way. Neither can VM#2 access any resources allocated to VM#1, unless, of course, such sharing is explicitly supported by the VMM. This separation is the essence of domain separation and the underlying security assumption for LT.

Protected Virtual Machines

The LT Security Architecture Specification appears to define two classes of virtual machines, standard and protected. The reality is that protected is the only class of VM. Whenever LT is running, a virtual machine has protection. The protection can be strong, with every possible event and resource protected, or the protection can weak, with many resources unprotected. The VMM controls the amount of protection that a guest receives. In the typical case, a VMM provides different levels of protection according to the guest's requirements.

Why do guests have different protection requirements? The answer lies in the task or tasks that the guest is performing. A guest that creates digital signatures and needs protection for an asymmetric private key has very different properties from a guest that manages a printer. A generic guest that operates a complete operating system has very different requirements than a single-purpose guest. No one size fits all type of protection. The VMM and the guest must combine to provide the appropriate level of protection for the guest. The mechanism through which the guest informs the VMM of the protection requirements is a function of the services that the VMM supplies to the guests.

For the sake of simplicity and ease of reading, the SAS discusses two types of guests: standard and protected. The definition of standard is a guest that only uses virtualization and does not attempt either to protect physical pages with the NoDMA table or to restrict access to I/O ports. The definition of protected is a guest that protects all resources. Numerous other definitions are possible; the point of naming them is to provide labels in the document.

The LT design places no architectural limit on the number of guests the VMM can support. The design places no architectural limit on the mix of guest protections. A VMM could support one protected and one standard guest. The VMM could also support four protected and two standard guests. Implementation issues could limit the number of guests, and they could possibly limit the protections available to a guest.

When each guest gains control of the CPU, the normal protections for the ring (0, 1, 2, and 3) are active. A guest is not able to change or manipulate the ring protections and allow a guest to bypass ring protections for memory or process resources. A guest should have no access to VMM resources. The VMM can expose services that make use of VMM resources, but not provide a direct access to any VMM resources.

Varieties of implementation models are possible when considering the VMM and the guests. LT does not require or enforce any specific model. The VMM designer can cooperate with the guest designer; in fact they may even be the same entity. When the VMM and guest designers cooperate they can create symbiotic models of communication and control. If the VMM and guest designers do not cooperate, either through mutual distrust or ignorance of each other, the models of communication and control are set by the VMM and the guest has no control over the interfaces. Figure 7.3 illustrates some models that can occur.

The left model, labeled A, shows a VMM that provides no services for either the standard or protected guests. A guest that is unaware of the VMM does not attempt to use any VMM services. A legacy OS would be unaware of the VMM and would not require specific VMM services to execute applications.

The middle model, labeled B, is a picture of a special-purpose guest that requires kernel type services from the VMM. The kernel services could be specific for the guest or the services could be generic. A special-purpose guest can be either a standard or a protected guest.

The right model, labeled C, shows a VMM that provides kernel services to guests that have their own operating systems. The kernel services in this model could provide both special and specific guest services.

The real model for a VMM is going to be the combination of all of the previous models. The VMM does support those guests that are unaware of virtualization, those guests that require a VMM, and those guests that make use of the VMM when it is present. No model is right or wrong. The system designer needs to take protection, throughput, ease of use, and other such considerations into account when deciding how to create and use the VMM and guests.

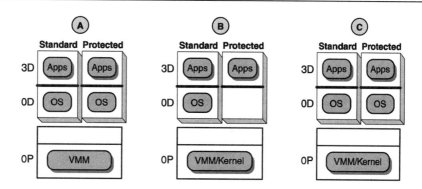

A: VMM provides no services to guest OS.

B: VMM provides complete kernel services. Normally represents a special-purpose guest.

C: VMM provides kernel services and guests provide OS type services. Represents a very common model.

Figure 7.3   VMM Environment Models

VMM with No Services

The VMM provides no additional services to any guest. The VMM is opaque to the guest and the guest must be self-sufficient. The VMM does provide:

■ Domain separation

■ Resource protection

■ VM life-cycle support

■ VM scheduling, though this may come from a guest

■ Limited inter-VM communication

The rationale for this type of VMM lies in the simple nature of the VMM. The VMM code base is smaller than a VMM with services, and with the smaller amount of code, one might think that a security evaluation would be easier to perform. The lack of services limits the security and functionality claims of the VMM. Fewer claims and services provide developers of the VMM with an opportunity to make fewer mistakes in design and implementation.

VMM with Kernel Features

The guest must have knowledge of the VMM when the VMM provides kernel features. The VMM determines the mechanism that exposes the service to the guest. Of the many types of communication mechanisms available, the VMM may use one or more to expose VMM services.

With the VMM providing services, the ability to create special-purpose guests is possible. Using the services of the VMM, the guest can concentrate on a single purpose. The LT architecture does not require a single-purpose guest; it merely allows one. The VMM service of providing communication between guests now becomes a much more important service. Since a single-purpose guest only does one job, other guests are going to require the service that the single-purpose guest provides. While some services might have a low bandwidth, the assumption is that many guests have high bandwidth requirements. Hence, the communication between the guests and the VMM are critical.

The VMM is free to provide any service that the VMM developer wishes to expose. The VMM may provide services to only one guest and no other guest; the mix, content, and availability of services is a design decision for the VMM designer and implementer.

Measured VMM

System designers can write an infinite number of VMM implementations that support LT. The variations occur due to the fact that the VMM is a piece of software and you have an infinite number of ways to write a program. Even after writing one VMM, you can update and modify the original code. Whether it is a human or a process, any entity that wishes to rely on the VMM to provide a specific set of services and assurances wants to know the identity of the VMM executing. In fact, the entity wishes to know if *any* VMM is executing. The simple answer is to ask the VMM who it is and let the VMM respond. Allowing the VMM to answer works fine when the relying party believes the VMM will not lie, but what happens when the VMM can lie? As the VMM has total control of the CPU, it is very easy for the VMM to report any identity for itself. Why would a VMM lie? Two obvious reasons are:

- The VMM wishes to masquerade as some other entity.
- Some attack corrupted the VMM and the attacker wants to hide.

In a world with VMMs that do and do not lie how does one tell them apart? The answer is the identity of the VMM. The VMM is just normal software with a special job to do. Creating an identity of the VMM is as simple as computing a cryptographic hash of the code. Cryptographic hashes—and from now on hash means cryptographic hash—have very interesting properties.

The interesting property that is most important to the VMM identity is: a change in a single bit of the VMM code causes a major change in the resulting hash value. One cannot change a single instruction without changing the hash value, which is an excellent property for identifying a VMM. The bottom line is that any change to the code means that the VMM has a new identity.

Hashes are very accurate in reporting the identity of the information presented to the hash. The issue is what entity sends the information to the hash algorithm. Asking an entity to measure itself does not work since that entity can present false information to the hash algorithm if it wants to lie. Some other mechanism, one not under control of the entity to identify, must present the information to the hash algorithm.

In the LT case, the entity to identify is the VMM, but the VMM has complete control of the CPU. Some hardware that is not under control of the VMM must measure the VMM. Measurement of the VMM occurs prior to giving the VMM control of the CPU. LT provides a hardware mechanism, in use during the invocation of the VMM, which properly runs the VMM image, or binary, through a hash algorithm.

With the measurement made, and the VMM identity in storage, the VMM is now a Measured VMM (MVMM).

Measuring the VMM

To have an assurance of the proper calculation of the VMM identity, or the measurement process, the measurement and launch of the VMM must meet the following requirements:

- All measurement and storage of the measurement must occur prior to passing control to the VMM.

- The measurement process must occur in a manner that defends against spoofing of the measurement.

- The launch process must ensure that all processors run the same VMM.

- The launch process must ensure that all processors start at a known entry point.

- The VMM must complete VMM initialization prior to allowing any other entity to execute.

- No other bus masters, processors, devices, or cache snooping can subvert the VMM measurement and/or VMM launch.

- No misconfiguration or misrepresentation of processor, chipset, or platform state must be able to subvert the launch.

Launching the VMM

When booting the platform, the BIOS performs the job of configuring the platform. The BIOS runs once and then allows the OS to manage the platform. With a MVMM, a user might want to run one MVMM for one task and then another MVMM for another task. If the process of measuring and launching the MVMM only occurs at once per boot, then to change MVMM, the user would have to reboot the platform, an undesirable user experience. To avoid this situation LT provides for a "late launch" of the MVMM. Late launch means that the measurement and launch of the MVMM can occur at any time after platform reboot. In addition, LT contains a provision to exit from the MVMM and allow another MVMM to launch. A launch of a MVMM can occur at any time, during BIOS processing, or during OS execution. The number of MVMMs that can launch and exit is unlimited. The time between invocations of an MVMM is unlimited, too. The interesting fact is that events occurring prior to the MVMM launch do not affect the launch. For instance, the launch could be the first time since boot that a MVMM launches or it could be the hundredth launch of a MVMM; it does not matter.

Prior to the launch, the launching entity locates and loads into memory two code modules. One module is the VMM that the launch process measures. The other module verifies certain system configurations to ensure that the hardware operates in a manner that allows the VMM to protect system resources. The chipset's specific Authenticated Code (AC) module has a digital signature from the chipset manufacturer, and it executes only if the launch process can verify the digital signature.

The GETSEC [SENTER] instruction starts the measurement-and-launch sequence. The instruction broadcasts a message to the chipset and all processors. In response to this message, the other processors perform basic clean-up, signal their readiness to proceed, then they wait for a signal to join the VMM.

Once all other processors have signaled ready, the initiating processor continues the process by loading, authenticating and executing the chipset-specific authenticated code module. This module is tests for an acceptable system configuration, enables chipset protections, and builds the initial NoDMA table that covers the MVMM. This module then measures, registers, and launches the MVMM, starting at an initialization entry point.

The MVMM initialization routine completes the system configuration changes, including redirecting INITs, SMIs, interrupts, and others, and then issues GETSEC [WAKEUP] messages to the other processors to bring them under control of the MVMM. At this point, all processors and the chipset are correctly configured.

Protecting Secrets

One of the promises of an MVMM is that if an entity knows how the MVMM acts, the MVMM should be able to keep a secret. The original term for the LT VMM was "Secure VMM" or SVMM. However, the reality is that the LT hardware has no way to know whether the VMM is secure or insecure. The hardware can provide an accurate measurement of the VMM, but it cannot make the trust decision. A VMM can protect secrets, but an outside entity must make the decision to trust the VMM to do so.

A VMM's ability to protect that secret is a major feature, and one that attackers will try to exploit. Since a VMM is software, the VMM's ability to keep secrets is not always perfect. To differentiate between VMM's, and contrast one VMM's ability to protect a secret over another VMM, is a major reason for the Measured VMM. Knowing the identity of the MVMM allows the outside entity to understand what the behavior of the MVMM will be.

The LT system needs to keep the following categories of secrets:

∎ *Application secrets.* In this category, each application keeps secrets from any other application. The mechanism that allows this secret-keeping is in the ring and paging mechanisms. If the application is running in ring 3, all ring 0 processes in the same VM have access to the application secret.

∎ *VM secrets.* In this category, each of the VM guests keeps secrets from all other guests running under control of the VMM. The mechanism that provides the secret protection is in the paging mechanism and the VM segregation under control of the VMM.

∎ *VMM secrets.* The VMM needs to keep secrets from all guests running under the VMM's control. Keeping this secret is a matter of keeping the VMM physical pages separate from all of the guests. In addition to keeping secrets from all of the guests, the VMM needs to keep secrets from all other possible VMMs. Keeping secrets from the other VMMs allows VMM segregation. The mechanism keeps secrets across VMM invocations. In other words, if a secret is held by MVMM #1 and MVMM #2 executes; #2 will not have access to the secrets of #1, but #1 can recover its secrets upon invocation of #1.

The VMM can provide a variety of services to protect application and VM secrets. The ability for a VMM to provide the appropriate services is another reason to know the identity of the VMM that is executing. Other than the normal hardware mechanisms, LT provides no special support for keeping these secrets.

The VMM secrets require special hardware support to implement. The crux of the matter is the identity of the VMM. By using the VMM identity in the Trusted Platform Module (TPM), LT provides a way to use sealing capabilities of the TPM.

An obvious way for a VMM to keep VMM secrets is to create a root key, protect all VMM information using the root key, and seal the root key to the VMM identity in the TPM. This mechanism relies on the sealing properties of the TPM; sealing information requires the exact same measurements to be present in the TPM to release the information. This property is exactly what LT provides for an MVMM: accurate measurement of the VMM, and proper reporting of the measurement to the TPM. Chapter 9 contains the details on the TPM.

Establishing Secrets

With the seal property, it is easy to prove that the exact same identity is running each time. But, what informs the relying entity the first time that the environment will properly protect secrets? Here the whole stack comes into question. An application should only establish a secret if the application believes that the VM will provide the protections necessary for the application to keep a secret. A VM should only establish a secret if the VM believes that the VMM will provide the protections for the VM to keep a secret. The VMM should only establish a secret if the VMM believes that the hardware can provide the protections necessary to protect the secret. This chain is a direct reflection of the previous section's comments regarding protecting secrets, with the difference that the entity wants to know the identity prior to establishing the secret.

Two mechanisms are in play during secret establishment. First, VMM measurement and launch provides the identity of the VMM in a way that software cannot manipulate. The second mechanism is the reporting capability of the TPM. The measurement process stores the VMM identity in the TPM. Using the native TPM capabilities of reporting on measurements, the TPM provides to entities wanting to rely on the platform the information necessary to make the decision to trust the platform and VMM and to allow the VMM to establish secrets.

The most important point of this process is that the LT hardware does not tell the entity that is about to use the platform to "trust me"— rather the platform says "here is who I am." Then, the entity makes its own trust decision. This flipping of who makes the trust decision is critical to how LT works. By providing the identity of the VMM, the relying party can make different decisions, depending on the type of operation about to occur. The first time, the entity might trust the MVMM, and the next time, the same entity might not trust the exact same MVMM. Security and trust are not "pushed" from the platform; instead, the relying party "pulls" the identity and then evaluates the identity.

The actual protocols are far more complex, in part because they include mechanisms to protect the user's privacy. See Chapter 9 for a detailed description of the attestation requirements, supporting hardware and protocols.

Boundary Conditions

The MVMM must maintain control of all resources, errors, or exceptions. Once measured and established, no event should be able to call into question the identity and integrity of the MVMM.

Examples of such events include system reset, INIT, SMI, S3 or S4 sleep states. In any of these cases, the event may remove or bypass the protections established by the MVMM launch, leaving the code and data in the formerly protected memory exposed.

As a rule, the LT Security Architecture addresses these events by:

■ Preventing the system event while the MVMM Environment is launched

■ Redirecting the event-handling code into the MVMM

■ Confining the event-handling code to a guest VM

■ Scrubbing the system memory following the event before allowing any unknown code to execute

See Chapter 10 for detailed descriptions on the handling of each system event.

Chapter 8

Attestation

All human history attests
That happiness for man,—the hungry sinner!—
Since Eve ate apples, much depends on dinner.

Don Juan. Canto xiii. Stanza 99.
—Lord Byron (1788-1824)

With all of the features that LT provides, how does an entity determine whether or not any specific platform has LT? Since LT platforms coexist with platforms that do not have LT, what provides the information that a specific platform has LT, and if it does, indicates which MVMM is executing? Finally, why should the entity requesting the information believe the response from the platform? Attestation provides the answers to all these questions.

Attestation requires roots of trust. A hardware or software mechanism that one implicitly trusts is called a *root of trust*. A platform needs the following roots of trust to be able to answer the questions posed:

- *Root of Trust for Measurement (RTM)*. The RTM provides an entity that is implicitly trusted to provide an accurate measurement. The RTM can be a static entity like the PC BIOS boot block, or the RTM can be a dynamic mechanism that is provided by LT.

- *Root of Trust for Reporting (RTR)*. The RTR provides an entity implicitly trusted to report information accurately and verifiably to outside entities.

■ *Root of Trust for Storage (RTS)*. The RTS provides an entity that can be trusted implicitly to store information without any interference or leakage of the information.

The various roots normally come as a package. The roots of trust for reporting and storage, RTR and RTS, are difficult to put into different entities on the platform. The Root of Trust for Measurement, RTM, depending on the platform, may or may not be combined with the RTR and RTS. On an LT platform, the RTR and RTS are part of the Trusted Platform Module (TPM) and the RTM is not part of the TPM.

TPM Design

The TPM definition comes in two parts, the main specification and a platform-specific definition. The main specification,[1] *TPM Main Spec* (TCG 2005b), defines the properties that must be present on every TPM no matter what type of platform. The platform-specific definition provides the information that is necessary for implementing a TPM on a platform. The platform-specific spec on which LT depends is the *TCG PC Client Specific Implementation Specification for Conventional BIOS* (TCG 2005a).[2] The reader needs to have both specifications available to answer any question regarding the TPM.

One important piece of information is necessary to understand the *TPM Main Specification;* the specification does not mandate internal TPM design. A TPM vendor is free to implement most of the internal functions in ways that allow the vendor to differentiate the part from other TPM vendors. A good example is the speed of the device; there are no requirements in the specifications as to how fast the TPM should perform an RSA operation. One vendor could create a part that made the RSA operation a priority and another vendor could have a part that made the SHA-1 operation a priority. Both implementations would be correct.

[1] For the remainder of this chapter, the term main spec or specification refers to the *TPM Main Spec*.

[2] Herein after cited as *PC Client Spec*.

Figure 8.1 shows the basic TPM functions in a block diagram form.

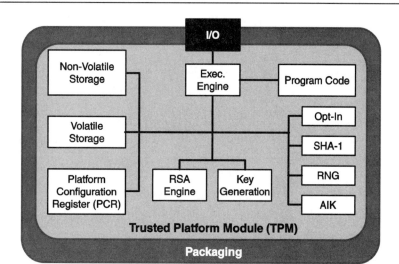

Figure 8.1   Basic Trusted Platform Module (TPM) Design

TPM Basic Components

The subsequent sections describe each of the TPM basic components.

Input and Output

All commands must enter and exit the TPM through the I/O port. The *TPM Main Spec* does not indicate what the I/O port shall be. The *PC Client Spec* identifies the I/O port as the LPC bus with a specific address on the bus.

The choice of the LPC bus is an important design decision. The bus on which the TPM resides must provide the CPU with access to the device without having to rely on interrupts or buses that require software stacks to operate. This access is very important when performing operations with an AC module that runs in a very restricted environment. The LPC bus definition includes the address for the I/O port and the registers that control the TPM communication.

The command that the TPM receives must arrive in a predefined format that includes a unique ordinal number to identify each command. For each ordinal, a predefined set of parameters provides the information that is necessary to execute the command and that must be present with the ordinal. With each ordinal, the TPM specification defines the exact bit pattern necessary to pass the command to the TPM. All TPMs, regardless of platform type, must accept the bit streams for all command ordinals. The TPM is not required to actually perform the function specified by the ordinal; the TPM only has to accept the bit stream. The TPM can return the unsupported ordinal error for all optional ordinals in the *TPM Main Spec*.

For input and output, the TPM is a slave device. The TPM never initiates any operation, but always responds to a request. Having the TPM reside on the LPC bus is a natural fit; the TPM is a slave device that always responds to commands and all devices on the LPC bus must be slave devices. The master of the LPC bus is the ICH, which controls all communication on the LPC bus. Should any device other than the ICH attempt to initiate an LPC command, an internal ICH fault occurs.

Addressing Other Platform Resources

The PC TPM, by being a device on the LPC bus, is severely restricted on what platform resources it has access to. The TPM does not have access to main system memory; the ICH blocks such accesses. In fact, the TPM has no access to any resource using a memory address; the ICH blocks the memory request.

Changing Execution Flow

With the TPM as a slave device on the LPC bus there are major restrictions on what the TPM is capable of doing. Combine the memory restrictions and the response nature of the TPM and there is no way for the TPM to alter the execution flow of the platform. Stated another way, there is no way for the TPM to change how the platform boots, or how an application executes. There is a way for some portion of the BIOS, or application, to take information from the TPM, make a decision based on the information, and change the execution path. The subtle difference is that the entity using the TPM is making the determination about what to do; the TPM itself is not initiating the change.

The distinction between the TPM forcing the change and the calling entity is very important. The TPM receives a command to perform one of the defined TPM commands; the TPM executes the command and returns the result. The TPM has no knowledge of which entity is making the request.[3] The TPM performs the operations the same way each time the request is made. If the caller wishes to make a decision based on the TPM supplied information (which is fine) the TPM itself did not make the decision, nor did the TPM make the entity do something different.

Execution Engine

Upon receipt of a command in the input buffer, the TPM needs to determine the proper formation of the command. The execution engine parses the bit stream to ensure a well-formed command. After validating the structure of the command, the engine locates the appropriate code according to the command ordinal. Depending on the internal structure of the TPM,[4] the execution engine locates the program associated with the command ordinal. After locating the program code, the execution engine passes control to the specified ordinal program code.

The execution engine ensures that the distribution of commands occurs only for valid TPM commands. This assurance of proper distribution provides a level of security that guarantees only TPM-defined commands execute on the TPM.

Program Code

The program code for a specific ordinal, located by the execution engine, provides the logic for the ordinal. The code performs the following tasks:

■ *Validate the entire command bit stream.* While the I/O and execution engines perform some bit stream validation, the program code needs to complete the command validation. This activity includes determining the size of the command, which is ordinal-specific, and checking for optional parameters.

---

[3] Well almost no knowledge, see "*Locality*" later in this chapter.

[4] Remember that TPM vendors have the ability to create TPMs with different internal control mechanisms.

■ *Validate each parameter.* The program code knows about the form and type of each parameter. The program code validates those parameters capable of validation. Since some parameters pass in user data where the structure of the data is unknown to the TPM, not all parameters are capable of an internal validation. When passing this type of information, the caller is responsible for validating the parameter before sending the information to the TPM.

■ *Validate the command authorization* if the command needs authorization. See "Authorization Values" in this chapter for complete details.

■ *Perform the ordinal logic flow specified in the TPM specification.* Each command has a defined set of actions to accomplish. These actions describe the exact details of what the command does and does not do.[5]

■ *Create the response packet.* After performing all of the actions, the program code creates the response packet. If the command was successful, the content and format of the response comes from the actions. If the command was unsuccessful, the program code creates an error response according the rules for errors.

While the program code must perform all of the previous operations, the TPM manufacturer may implement the operations in any logically consistent fashion. This flexibility allows the manufacturer to build a TPM that meets different criteria. A manufacturer can create a TPM that is faster but costs more, or a manufacturer can build the cheapest TPM.

Non-Volatile (NV) Storage

As the Root of Trust for Storage, the TPM must provide some long-term values. The requirement in the TPM is that the information must be available when the TPM boots and that the information not be affected by power cycles. Non-volatile (NV) storage is the most typically used mechanism. When creating a TPM based on silicon, the TPM manufacturer will typically use a manufacturing process that allows for information to be stable when no power is available on the TPM.

Two uses of the non-volatile storage on the TPM are internal TPM values and defined ordinals.

---

[5] Well, actually it is close. As one TPM vendor told me, "David, we treat the order of operations as advisory." The point was that the exact order of operations in an ordinal is not mandatory and that there is more than one way to get the job done. Again, the flexibility for the TPM vendors is present and the vendors make use of the flexibility.

Internal TPM Values

The TPM maintains two 2048-bit RSA keys internally: the endorsement key (EK) and the storage root key (SRK). These keys provide the essence of the Root of Trust for Reporting, the EK, and the Root of Trust for Storage, the SRK. The EK is set once, and under normal circumstances,[6] never changes for the life of the TPM. The SRK would change when, and if, the platform changes owners.

In addition to the RSA keys, the TPM holds additional values necessary to manage the TPM state. Some of these values are permanent and some update on a limited basis. An example is the settings that the user selects for opt-in.

Defined Ordinals

Along with the internal use of the NV storage, the TPM provides a set of ordinals that allows outsider entities to use NV storage. NV storage in the TPM is not cheap. Other mechanisms provide NV storage at a much lower cost so the NV storage in the TPM needs to provide some extra value. The value that TPM NV storage provides is that the TPM authorization mechanisms validate each and every access to the TPM NV storage area. The TPM provides a small NV area. The assumption is that between the platform manufacturer, CPU manufacturer, and the OS vendor, little or no NV storage area would be available for general applications.

Burn Issues

NV storage has an interesting property; the NV area has a lifetime number of write operations.[7] Most NV storage manufacturers specify the maximum number of writes as some value around 100,000. While no counter stops the TPM from working at 100,000, the result is that the writes start to take longer and longer times. At some point, the attempt to write a new value takes longer than the timeout value for the command and the write fails. The number of reads to NV storage areas is not restricted.

---

[6] Like many of the TPM absolutes there are mechanisms to actually change the EK. The results of changing the EK are very large and many TPM vendors and platform users of the TPM may not expose the ability to change the EK.

[7] To be 100-percent technically accurate, the operation that causes a problem is changing a bit from 1 to 0. Some implementations take advantage of this fact and optimize how and when the device performs the erasure. While TPMs might use this type of optimization, in the context of this book, a write operation equates to an erase cycle.

With this limit, the TPM needs some mechanism to control when and how the NV storage is in use. The TPM provides that all writes to the NV area have an authorization that limits any entity's use of the NV area.

Volatile Storage

With the limit on writes to the NV storage area, the TPM needs storage that has no limit on the number of writes, and the volatile storage area fills that need. The volatile storage is used internally by the TPM for the following things:

- Keeping track of current internal TPM state
- Providing an area for cryptographic keys (not the EK or SRK)
- Authentication sessions
- Transport session
- Other sessions

The volatile storage could also provide program code space for very large commands. The TPM manufacturer decides how to use the volatile storage. Outside entities have no direct connection to the volatile storage, other than access to the results of various operations.

The volatile storage area does not persist across power cycles, so any information that needs to be persistent must have an external storage location, like a hard drive, or the information must reside in the NV storage area. It is possible to move information from one area to another, but the restriction on use of the NV storage area would require use authorization.

Secure Hash Algorithm 1 (SHA-1)

Secure Hash Algorithm 1, or SHA-1, is a cryptographic hash algorithm. Hash algorithms take a string of arbitrary length and produce a fixed-length output. Given the resulting output value, it is computationally infeasible to calculate the input. Also, hash algorithms are order-dependent; that is, hashing A then B results in a different value than if one hashes B then A. The SHA-1 output is a 20-byte value.

The TPM makes extensive use of the SHA-1. Some of the functions that use SHA-1 are:

■ Authorization values

■ Binding together of structures

■ Hashed Message Authentication Code (HMAC) validation

■ Creation of XOR strings

Authorization Values

The TPM requires authorization of many commands and uses knowledge of a value to prove authorization. The authorization value held in the TPM is a 20-byte value, its size chosen intentionally to match the SHA-1 output size, based on the assumption that the authorization value would be some pass phrase passed through a previous SHA-1 operation.

Binding Structures Together

The structures in use by the TPM contain both sensitive information and information that needs integrity protection. Many times the combination of sensitive and integrity information becomes too large a structure to encrypt in a single operation. The solution is to take a hash of the information needing integrity protection and include the hash value in the sensitive information. When checking the integrity later, the hash of the TPM calculates the hash of the integrity area, and then compares the resulting hash value with the hash value stored in the sensitive area. A single bit change results in a new hash value and represents a failure to validate.

This use model represents a basic construct that many applications use. An area that needs integrity protection has a hash value stored and protected by the TPM. When validation is necessary, TPM recalculates the hash value and compares it to the stored hash value.

Hashed Message Authentication Code (HMAC) Validation

When performing authentication checks, the internal mechanism that the TPM uses is the HMAC calculation. The HMAC definition is *RFC 2104-HMAC:Keyed-hashing for Message Authentication* (Krawczyk 1997). The HMAC calculation is

```
H(K XOR opad, H(K XOR ipad, text))
```

where

H	is the SHA-1 hash operation
K	is the key or the authorization data
XOR	is the xor operation
opad	is the byte 0x5C repeated B times
B	is the block length and the block length is determined by the algorithm in use
ipad	is the byte 0x36 repeated B times
text	is the message information and any parameters from the command

RFC 2104 requires the selection of two parameters to define the HMAC in use. These values are the key length and the block size. The TCG choose to set the values such that the HMAC calculations for SHA-1 are very easy. The resulting sizes are: key length (K) of 20 bytes and a block size (B) of 64 bytes.

Creation of XOR Strings

The TPM provides encryption using an XOR mechanism. The XOR mechanism needs an encryption string the exact same length as the plain text data. The TPM uses the *PKCS #1: RSA Encryption Standard, Version 2.1* (RSA 2002) and the Mask Generation Function (MGF) to create the encryption string. MGF generates a string using SHA-1, a shared secret, and a counter. While not particularly fast, MGF does provide a reasonably secure encryption algorithm.

Continued Use of SHA-1

The spring of 2005 saw the publication of some SHA-1 vulnerabilities. The TCG is aware of the SHA-1 vulnerabilities and future versions of the TPM are likely to add additional hash algorithms to the TPM.

Platform Configuration Register (PCR)

The PCRs are storage areas that keep track of measurements reported to the TPM. The *TPM Main Spec* (TCG 2005b) does not specify the number of PCRs, while the *PC Client Spec* (TCG 2005a) specification mandates that the TPM must have a minimum of 24 PCRs. Reading and writing to any PCR requires special TPM ordinals and the PCR are never directly written to.

Extending the PCR

When an entity wishes to store a measurement in the TPM, the entity wants an assurance that no other entity can change the measured value. The TPM provides this assurance by not allowing any entity to write directly to the TPM; the entity "extends" the specified PCR. The extend operation concatenates the current PCR value with the new value and performs a SHA-1 on the concatenated value. The resulting hash value is the new PCR value. Graphically, the extend operation looks like this:

PCR = SHA-1(PCR old value, new value)

Using the extend operation has some interesting properties. First, a single PCR can keep track of an unlimited number of measurements. Since each extend operation results in a 20-byte hash value, it makes no difference to the PCR storage requirements whether that value is for one measurement or one hundred measurements.

Second, the extend process uses the ordering property of SHA-1. To recap, ordering provides for a different hash value when hashing A then B, against B then A. This is the property you want when keeping track of measurements on a platform. With the extend process order dependency, an entity cannot pretend to occur after a certain event. The ordering is automatic.

Finally, the extend process also prevents an entity from attempting to create a log that essentially removes the entity's own measurement from the log. Assume that entity A measures entity B and stores the measurement in a PCR. Entity B wants to hide, so B makes it appear that entity C is currently executing. Entity B has to find a value that, when extended, results in the same value for entity C. This operation is computationally infeasible.

PCR Event Log

The PCR only contains the results of all of the measurements. The list of measured events is not available inside of the TPM. If the event log were internal to it, the TPM would need to reserve enough internal resources to hold the entire log. This problem becomes unbounded because the PCR can contain an unlimited number of measurements. The solution is to hold the log externally to the TPM. The log provides all of the measured values that extend into the PCR. Any verifier can validate the contents of the log by performing the extend operation in software. The resulting hash value matches the PCR value if the log is correct. When the log is incorrect, the verifier knows only that the log and PCR do not match, with insufficient information to determine why the log and PCR are out of sync.

Reporting the Current PCR Value

With the measurements held in a PCR, entities outside of the TPM require a way to validate the TPM report of PCR value. The TPM provides a digital signature of the PCR value that a requesting entity can verify is correct and fresh. The correctness comes from the format of the digital signature and the ability to validate the key that creates the digital signature. The freshness comes from the inclusion of information from the verifier. Typically, this information would be a random number, but it could be other types of data. The freshness prevents an attacker from replaying a previously good measurement report.

Resetting of PCR

A PCR can be static or dynamic. The difference between static and dynamic is when and how the PCR can be reset to its default value. A static PCR can reset only when the TPM itself resets. As long as the TPM is active, the PCR value continues to extend. The PCR cannot be reset independently without resetting the TPM. This property provides an excellent way to measure and keep track of events that occur during the boot of the PC and do not change after the PC is executing. The best example is information relative to the boot of the platform like the BIOS and OS loader.

A dynamic PCR can be reset independently of the TPM, so long as the process that resets the PCR operates under sufficient controls that an attacker cannot reset the PCR and supply incorrect measurement information to the PCR.

Random Number Generator (RNG)

Randomness is critical in a cryptographic system. The randomness provides a way to generate keys, both symmetric and asymmetric, and is a source of nonces that provide freshness. A nonce is a random number used once. While it seems like a simple thing to find randomness, it is in fact a very difficult problem. John von Neumann said it best:

> Anyone who considers arithmetical methods of producing random digits is, of course, in a state of sin.

The RNG requirement for the TPM is to avoid any sin and use mechanisms that can produce random numbers. The actual implementation of the RNG is a manufacturer-specific option. Sources of entropy allow a device to harvest the entropy, run the entropy through some processes, and output a random number.

Note

> A considerable body of literature is available to tell you how to create a valid RNG. Various software implementations are available for downloading. In addition, you can find reports on how to harvest entropy from various sources. Several of these resources are listed in "References" for your convenience.

RSA Engine

Asymmetric algorithms break key usage into public and private components. The TPM uses RSA for encryption and digital signatures. The standard key size for most keys is 2,048 bits. When used for internal encryption the TPM must use 2,048-bit keys.

When performing RSA encryption the TPM enforces the rules established by PKCS #1 V2.1. These rules require randomness (provided by the RNG) and masking (provided by SHA-1). The rules set forth by PKCS #1 provide mitigation against all sorts of esoteric attacks. By following these rules, the TMP uses a well-known algorithm and protocol and avoids the necessity of performing additional cryptographic evaluations.

When performing RSA digital signatures, the TPM provides for a couple of standard digital signature schemes. These schemes allow for the digital signature on a wide variety of internal TPM and external data. The schemes also provide for mitigation against attacks.

Key Generation

Applications using the TPM are not going to all want to use the same key. In fact, good security practice demands that the applications use different keys. Some key will provide data protection and other keys will provide digital signatures. It would be nice to predetermine how many keys the TPM requires but one is now in the child's game of "pick a number, 21; OK I pick 22, I win" where whatever number is picked will be wrong for someone. The end result is the requirement that the TPM have the ability to generate RSA keys on demand. All information necessary to generate the key must come from internal TPM resources.[8] The process for generating the key is:

- Obtain two random numbers. While the TPM could go looking for a source of randomness, one of the major reasons that the TPM has a requirement for an internal RNG is to provide the randomness for key generation.

- Determine whether both the numbers are prime numbers. This is the fun part of creating an RSA key. For the typical key sizes, the numbers are around 1000-bits. While knowledge of prime numbers has been around for thousands of years, and tests for determining if a number is prime are available, to perform an exhaustive test on the two numbers could take days. Obviously then the TPM does not do an exhaustive test but performs some sort of statistical test to gain an assurance that the number was prime.

  - The normal method is to first make the number to test odd, as the only even prime number is 2, and 2 has only 2 bits, not the 1,000 bits we are looking for. The TPM then uses the statistical tests to determine whether the number is prime. If the number is not prime, the TPM could add 2 to get to the next odd number, and try the tests again. If, after a certain number of tries, the TPM does not find a prime number, the TPM could discard the original try and get some more randomness from the RNG.

---

[8] The entity requesting the new key certainly provides the key type, protection or signing, key size, and other pieces of information, but the randomness must come from the internal TPM RNG.

- The testing for a prime number is not deterministic. That is, no one can tell you how long the TPM will take to find a prime number. While it would be great if we had some way to put a bound on the process, with today's processors and mathematical knowledge, prime number testing is going to take some indeterminate amount of time. Because of the indeterminate time necessary some TPM vendors "cheat"[9]— whenever the TPM is idle, the TPM is creating a list of prime numbers. Now, when the TPM gets a request to create a new RSA key, the TPM merely picks the next two prime numbers from the list and performs the rest of the math. If too many requests for new keys arrive in a short amount of time, the prime number list could be exhausted and the TPM would need to find a prime number in real time.

■ With two prime numbers, the TPM would perform the other mathematical operations necessary to create a RSA key pair.

Opt-in

The TPM contains a unique value, called the *endorsement key*. The platform owner must have an assurance that the EK is only in use for those operations that the platform owner authorizes. The authorization provides protection against the improper use of the uniqueness. Improper use of the uniqueness could create the ability for outside entities to correlate two different uses of the uniqueness, resulting in a loss of privacy.

The TPM is an *opt-in* device. Opt-in means that the platform owner must take specific steps to turn the TPM on. When shipped, the TPM is not operational. The TPM must have a mechanism that stores and keeps secure the platform owner's selection of the state of the TPM.

The opt-in mechanism must include some physical mechanism that an operator at the platform must manipulate to indicate that a human is operating the platform. This physical presence mechanism, when asserted, allows the TPM to validate that requests to manipulate the permanent state of the TPM have authorization from a human.

---

[9] Actually, I don't think of this proactive number generation as cheating. It is rather an excellent way to use the limited TPM resources.

Attestation Identity Key

The Attestation Identity Key (AIK) provides a mechanism for establishing that an entity is communicating with *a* TPM but not for determining *which* TPM. This distinction is very important when discussing privacy issues. If the requesting entity can determine from the key in use which TPM is in use, the entity could correlate uses and cause a loss of privacy. The EK is the Root of Trust for Reporting, but if every single report used the EK, then the correlation would be very easy.

The AIK provides a mechanism to report on TPM internal information like the status/content of a PCR, but not to use the EK directly.

Authorization

The advantage that the TPM provides to entities wishing to rely on the TPM is that many operations require authorization to execute. From the standpoint of the TPM mechanisms, there needs to be a mechanism that can prove to the TPM that the entity requesting the operation has the authority to do so. While it would be nice for the TPM to put up a dialog box or use a voice request, those options really are not possible. The HMAC mechanism provides a way to authenticate TPM requests.

The authorization of the command wants to perform the following actions:

■ Use a shared secret or a value kept confidential by both sides of the communication

■ One wants to prove to the other side knowledge of the shared secret

■ Neither side wants to transmit the shared secret over the communication medium

When an entity creates a new key, or other resource requiring subsequent authorization, the creation process includes the authorization value. When the entity wishes to use the resource, the request to use the resource includes the HMAC of the request and the authorization value, or shared secret. The TPM must associate with the resource, and permanently keep track of the authorization value.

A security concern, not just a theoretical one but a practical concern, is that some attacker could capture a request to use the resource and replay the HMAC calculation. With the request being the same and the authorization being the same, the HMAC calculation would result in the exact same value. To mitigate this vulnerability, the calling entity places into the request some randomness and includes the randomness into the HMAC calculation. Now the caller knows that the command sent to the TPM and the response from the TPM, which also uses the randomness, is fresh and not a replay.

TPM Functionality

The value of a TPM comes not from the basic building block features of the PCR or the RNG, but the combining of the building blocks into a new functionality.

Transitive Trust

The idea of transitive trust is to provide a way for relying parties to trust a larger circle of entities from a single root of trust. The process for establishing transitive trust is:

1. *Measure the next entity.* Measurement is the process of taking some data and performing a hash on the data. For transitive trust, the program code is the value under measurement. A quick example is the BIOS could measure the OS loader.

2. *Store the measurement.* The storage location is a TPM PCR and the measuring agent uses the `TPM_Extend` command to extend the PCR with the new value.

3. *Pass control to the measured entity.*

Figure 8.2 shows the process by which trust is extended.

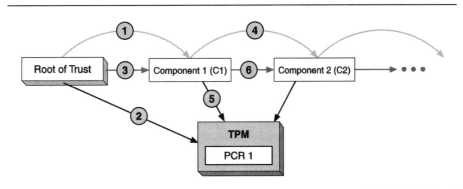

Figure 8.2   Transitive Trust

Combining the Root of Trust for Measurement (RTM), the PCR, and the Root of Trust for Reporting (RTR) allows a challenger to gain a verifiable picture of the current platform state. When the RTM measures the next component to gain execution control, any challenger can be assured that the measured component was in fact the component next in the execution path. This assurance comes from the challenger's dependence on the RTM. If the challenger trusts the RTM, the measured component really did get control.

Sealed Storage

Sealed storage provides a way to combine measurements and protection of external data. To help keep track of which thing is which, the following terms are in use for this section.

Data refers to the external information that the TPM is going to protect. *Value* refers to the current value inside of a PCR register. While it is possible, and normally desirable, to use more than one PCR register in the SEAL process, for this section all references to PCR refer to only a single PCR.

The idea now is for the TPM to provide protected storage of *data* combing the Root of Trust for Storage (RTS) and the *value* in a PCR. The protection uses encryption, the RTS, and measurement values, the PCR. Protecting the data is *Sealing* and recovering the protected data is *Unseal.*

Sealing

The seal process takes the external data, a requested PCR value, encrypts the data, and creates a sealed data package. The TPM returns the sealed data package to the caller and the caller is responsible for keeping track of the package and presenting the package back to the TPM when the caller wants to recover the data.

The seal process, internal to the TPM, ensures that only the TPM which creates the sealed package can unseal the package. The TPM ensures this type of behavior by including in the sealed package a nonce known only to the individual TPM. During the unseal proces, the TPM validates that the correct nonce is present in the sealed package. Figure 8.3 illustrates the seal process showing the external data, the measurement values, and the sealed data package.

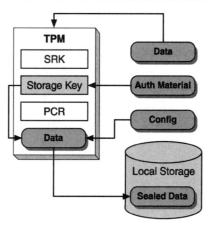

Figure 8.3   Sealing Data to the TPM

Of note is the actual key in use to encrypt the data. The key is a storage key that forms part of the Storage Root Key (SRK) tree. The key could use the SRK directly or a storage key many layers away from the SRK. For the seal process internal to the TPM, the key that performs the seal does not really differ from the other keys. From an application standpoint, you could have an operational difference, but the end result is a sealed data package that the application must keep track of.

The TPM does not perform any validation or checking of the PCR value during the seal process. The caller can specify any PCR value that the caller wishes. The platform may or may not be in the configuration that the caller is specifying for the unseal configuration, and that is intentional; the TPM only enforces the requested configuration during the unseal process.

Unsealing

While the obvious description of unseal is that it is the reverse of the seal operation, the obvious is not correct. While any entity can perform the seal operation, the purpose of the seal process is to *restrict* the unseal operation. It is necessary to define what the restrictions are and when does the TPM enforce the restrictions.

Before enforcing the restrictions, the basic unseal operations must occur. The basic operations are to decrypt the sealed package using the indicated storage key and validate that the decryption was successful. The decryption reveals all of the internal information and the external data. The validation ensures that the package information was not modified.

The first restriction is that the sealed package is only useable on the TPM that created the sealed package. The TPM enforces this restriction by ensuring that the TPM nonce included in the sealed package matches the internally held nonce.

The next restriction is the PCR value. The TPM compares the current value in the TPM PCR to the requested value in the sealed data package. If the two values do not match, the unseal operation aborts.

The combination of the restrictions is that the external data is only available to a caller when the correct measurement value is in the specified PCR. Any entity wishing to rely on the use of the data to a specific platform configuration can use the seal property and have a high degree of assurance that only in the right configuration does the data become available.

Transport Session

Well, assume that you have just executed an unseal command and the TPM is returning the sealed data back to the caller. The TPM_Unseal does not provide any protection to the returning data; any entity with access to the communication channel can see the unsealed data. If the data was an encryption key, having outside entities view the key might be a very bad thing. As callers to the TPM could be sending information across the Internet, there is a potential of numerous entities with access to the data.

The transport session is a response to the issue and a way to protect information traveling to and from the TPM. The transport session provides for the confidentiality and sequencing of information traveling from a requestor to the TPM. The basic features of the transport session are:

- *Confidentiality.* The transport session can encrypt data sent to and from the TPM. The mandatory encryption algorithm is XOR using MGF; however, individual TPM manufacturers can support a wide variety of additional algorithms such as AES or 3DES.

- *Sequence of commands.* The transport session groups a set of commands and provides a digital signature on all of the commands in the group. This grouping allows an entity to prove that a sequence of commands actually occurred. The sequencing can also include timing information that can show the exact time that the commands executed.

- *Total control.* The transport session can be exclusive, such that any command outside of the transport session causes the session to terminate.

Locality

One Root of Trust for Measurement (RTM) on a platform performs measurements from the boot of the platform. The normal designation of this RTM is the static RTM, or the RTM that keeps track of the information that statically defines the boot of the platform.[10] Other mechanisms could provide an RTM on the platform. LT has another RTM, called the dynamic RTM.

The dynamic RTM is a critical component of LT. Later chapters describe the actual dynamic RTM mechanism. What the TPM needs to understand is when the dynamic RTM is communicating with the TPM. An unspoofable hardware mechanism that the TPM can interpret must provide communications from the dynamic RTM. The TPM uses locality to provide this mechanism. The *TPM PC Client Specific TPM Interface Specification* (TCG 2005c) defines locality as:

> A concept that allows various trusted processes on the platform to communicate with the TPM such that the TPM is aware of which trusted process is sending commands. This is implemented using dedicated ranges LPC addresses and a new LPC "start" field. Six localities are defined: numbers 0 – 4 and Legacy.

The TPM definition provides for localities or indications of specific platform processes. The *TPM Main Spec* (TCG 2005b) makes no reference to what the localities are; the actual locality definition for the PC is in the *PC Specific Specification* (TCG 2005a). The TPM has five localities: 0 through 4. Each locality has a specific meaning.

■ Locality 4—Trusted hardware. The platform hardware ensures that only trusted processes have access to locality 4. Locality 4 assertions should be made by the hardware dynamic RTM. The locality 4 assertion allows the TPM to respond appropriately to dynamic RTM requests for measurement and resetting of PCR.

■ Locality 3—Auxiliary components. These components are optional and represent processes that gain control after the trusted hardware at locality 4 but before the normal trusted process runtime has control. The auxiliary component may or may not be part of the dynamic RTM.

---

[10] Review the TCG documentation for complete details on the static RTM.

■ Locality 2—The normal trusted operating system, as the trusted OS, gains control after the locality 3 and 4 processes have properly initialized the platform.

■ Locality 1—An environment set up by the trusted OS. The trusted OS does not have to use locality 1, but if the trusted OS desires, it may provide access to locality 1.

■ Locality 0 provides access to the TPM for the static RTM and any other processes operating after the static RTM.

■ Locality legacy. The 1.2 TPM provides for backwards compatibility with version 1.1. Since 1.1 did not have locality and did not have a standard communication mechanism, the ability to communicate with the TPM using old drivers is available. The legacy locality is the same as locality 0.

The chipset provides the locality mechanism. A reserved set of addresses correlates with the localities, as shown in Table 8.1, and it is the responsibility of the chipset to protect those addresses from any process that does not match the locality.

Table 8.1   Locality Addresses

Locality	System Address	LPC Address
0	0XFED4_0xxx	0x0xxx
1	0XFED4_1xxx	0x1xxx
2	0XFED4_2xxx	0x2xxx
3	0XFED4_3xxx	0x3xxx
4	0XFED4_4xxx	0x4xxx

Note: System address is permanent address on PC

Attesting To Information

The PCR contains the results of measurements provided by the RTM and other entities on the platform. The seal property makes use of the PCR and ensures that data is only available when the specified set of measurements is present. The unseal operation proves to the entity using the unseal operation that the correct configuration is present. But if the outside entity has not performed a seal operation, how does one prove to the outside entity that a current configuration is present? The answer is attestation.

Attestation is the process of providing a digital signature of a PCR or set of PCRs and having the requestor validate the signature and the PCR contents. The process is very simple; the entity wishing to validate the current platform configuration requests the `TPM_Quote` command specifying an Attestation Identity Key (AIK) to perform the digital signature, the set of PCRs to quote, and a nonce to ensure freshness of the digital signature.

The TPM processing is also very simple; validate the authorization to use the AIK, fill in a structure that shows the set of PCRs to be quoted, and perform a digital signature on the filled-in structure. The TPM then returns the digital signature as the output to the `TPM_Quote` command.

The entity requesting the attestation validates the digital signature by using the public portion of the AIK, validates the AIK by interpreting the AIK credential, and now evaluates the current configuration. If the configuration represents an acceptable configuration, the requestor can rely on the platform configuration.[11]

---

[11] Well, that paragraph certainly compresses lots of information. The validation of attestation values is a subject for an entire book, and is the current focus of the Trusted Computing Group Infrastructure Work Group. The ability to determine what an acceptable configuration is can be simple or complex and, as just stated, outside the scope of this book.

Measurement Agent

When attempting to rely on the attestation from a system, the evaluation of the "accuracy" of the measurement is vital. The RTM is supposed to provide a high degree of assurance that the start of the measurement chain is valid. The degree of difficulty here is that the RTM is a component outside of the TPM; the RTM is a *platform* component. How the platform is put together directly affects the ability of the RTM to start the chain of measurements. The purpose of LT is to provide a dynamic RTM that outside entities can rely on to accurately measure the VMM and truly move the VMM to a MVMM.

Use of the TPM

The TPM is a key building block of an LT platform. The TPM provides two roots of trust on the platform: the Root of Trust for Storage (RTS) and the Root of Trust for Reporting (RTR). The TPM is bound to the Root of Trust for Measurement (RTM) and the RTM uses the PCR to store measurements.

The PCR and the RTS combine to provide the seal capability, a key component in the ability of the LT platform to provide long-term protected storage.

The PCR and RTR combine to provide the attestation capability, which allows outside observers the ability to determine the current platform configuration.

The RTM, static or dynamic, provides the measurement values that drive the PCR contents.

The bottom line is that the TPM truly is a key building block for the LT platform and the TPM provides key services that allow LT to properly initialize and accurately report the current platform state.

Chapter 9

Protected Input and Output

I have only one eye, I have a right to be blind sometimes...
I really do not see the signal!

—Lord Nelson[1]

Trusted platforms protect the execution of programs, but execution of a program is not the only element of a personal computer. As important, or maybe even more important, is the communication between the platform and the human user. Input from devices like keyboards and mice; output from devices like monitors and printers. The interesting point for a discussion of trusted computing is, "Does the input really come from the user and is the user actually seeing the correct output?" Lord Nelson, with his single eye, could claim he did not see the information.[2] What is necessary with trusted computing is to find mechanisms that ensure the input and output mechanisms. To trust a platform, the user must trust the information flowing from the user to the platform and then back from the platform to the user. The trust also flows in the reverse direction—the program, and the entities distributing the program, want assurances that the user is providing the input and seeing the output.

---

[1] I was in England on 21 October 2005 and saw some of the festivities celebrating the 200th anniversary of the Battle of Trafalgar, in which the entire English fleet saw and obeyed Nelson's commands and defeated a combined French and Spanish fleet.

[2] This comment has been a classic comment from military commanders since the dawn of military activities. The essence of the comment is that if the commander does not receive additional instructions, the commander could make his own decision and do something different from the wishes of the chain of command.

Trusted Channel and Trusted Path

In the security literature, you see a distinction between a trusted channel and trusted path. A trusted channel involves communication between two computing entities, like two computers. A trusted path involves communication between a computing device and a human. Here's an example to explain the difference; most Internet users know that some Web sites make a security mechanism available. The security mechanism is commonly in use during Internet shopping. The security mechanism is the Secure Socket Layer (SSL). The connection between the client and the server, the actual SSL connection, is a trusted channel. The "lock" icon at the bottom of the browser indicates a trusted path between the server and the user. For a trusted path to work, the human must "do" something. In the SSL example, the human must look at the browser window and "see" the icon. Figure 9.1 illustrates the channel and path for SSL.

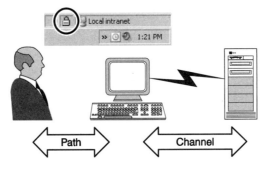

Figure 9.1   Path and Channel

LT hardware differs in that it provides the mechanism to create trusted channels, but does not mandate trusted paths. Stated another way, LT provides the ability to create trusted channels between the platform components, but does not require any display to indicate that the channel is present. The assumption is that MVMM designers create trusted paths, but no hardware requirement compels them to do so.

Why a Trusted Channel?

With the execution and storage of data protected by LT through the MVMM, why does input and output present any issues? The answer lies in how an application works. The application can only work with good information—the garbage in, garbage out (GIGO) principle works here. If an application that provides protection to a digital signature key allows the key to sign anything, attackers do not have to break the cryptography. Instead, the attacker merely presents bogus information and the application signs the information.

The following list is not complete, but shows the types of problems that the MVMM must consider when handling human input and output:

■ Data supplied from a secure input device, such as a keyboard, should not be readable by unauthorized applications. Obviously, this restriction is crucial for passwords or input from scanners.

■ Data supplied from a secure input device, such as a keyboard, should not be modifiable by unauthorized applications. For example, when entering financial data, the attacker should not be able to convert a user-specified amount of $100 to $234 by changing digits or to $1 by removing digits or to $1,000 by adding digits.

■ Data supplied from a secure input device, such as a keyboard, should not be *spoofable* by any application. That is, attacking software should not be able to fool an application into believing that user-generated keystrokes have occurred.

■ Data sent from a secured application to a secured output device, such as a monitor or printer, must not be readable by unauthorized applications. Such output often contains sensitive, confidential data, such as account numbers, tax records, or checks.

■ Data sent from a secured application to a secured output device, such as a monitor or printer, must not be modifiable by unauthorized applications. This restriction prevents the attacker from modifying what the user sees. As an example, in a check-signing application, the attacker could change the payee or reduce the amount of the check displayed to the user, to entice an approval for an amount other than the display.

■ Data sent from a secured application to a secured output device, such as a monitor, must not be spoofable by any application. That is, attacking software must not be able to fool the human into believing that the secured application generated the output. For example, attacking software should be unable to generate a password-entry dialog box that mimics a real dialog box. This example is a direct application of the trusted path issue; if the fake dialog box looks "close" to the real dialog box, and the user does not look closely, it is possible to fool the user.

■ The peripheral devices themselves could be a source for exposing information. Keyboards, for instance, accept the keystrokes that represent a password, so the keyboard design must not allow multiple entities access to the actual keystrokes. Saving the keystrokes in a buffer, and allowing the buffer to be read multiple times, allows an attack where the user types in their password, the attacker moves the keyboard to a new machine, and the new machine reads the keyboard buffer. Another example is a printer that buffers the last few pages of a document and allows the next printer user to reprint the pages stored in the buffer.

Trusted Channel Basics

At a minimum, a trusted channel represents a way to ensure that data travels from one computing entity to another without any interference. Most trusted channels also include the requirement of confidentiality, which means that not just any viewer of the channel can determine the contents of the channel. One mechanism that provides both properties is encrypting the data that is using the channel. Trusted channels come in two basic mechanisms: hardware or cryptography. Both have some advantages and disadvantages.

Hardware Trusted Channels

A hardware trusted channel relies on the physical nature of the platform to provide protections. A typical hardware trusted channel involves such fun things as buried traces, no visible pins, and no exposed vias. If you didn't understand those terms you are not alone; these terms are the province of the platform hardware engineers. The underlying idea of hardware trusted channels to is deny an entity with physical access to the platform the ability to watch or disrupt the electrical signals traveling between devices.

Two major issues with hardware trusted channels are: first, the channel must be designed and built during platform manufacturing, and second, the channel is only possible with devices that are in physical contact.

The first issue of designing for the channel during platform manufacturing is not serious; if the manufacturer wants to apply the time and effort to the protections, the hardware trusted channel is possible.[3] Few commercial platforms take the time and go to the expense to create hardware trusted channels.

The second issue is much more serious. The hardware nature of the protections applies to all links in the chain between the two devices. Some devices are very difficult to physically connect and even when physically connected, the attempts to provide hardware protection is impossible, or nearly so. What is necessary is some other mechanism to provide the trusted channel.

One interesting side feature of a hardware trusted channel is that the normal designs require no operational setup. With the physical nature of the channel, turning the platform on enables the protection.

Cryptographic Trusted Channels

The cryptographic trusted channel solves some of the hardware trusted channel issues while adding some new issues. The cryptographic channel solves the physical connection issue by encrypting all data traveling between the two devices. No more worries about the physical nature of the connection—in fact the trusted channel can be huge distances as the SSL connection between a Web site and a Web browser shows.

---

[3] For many platforms built to military specifications, the hardware trusted channel is a requirement.

The issue with cryptographic trusted channels is key exchange. To provide sufficient speed and bandwidth most, if not all, cryptographic channels use symmetric encryption. Symmetric encryption requires the same key at both sides of the channel. A truly ugly question now comes up, how to accomplish the key exchange.

Key exchange is not easy. The protocols are difficult, exacting, and sometimes use lots of bandwidth. To create a channel, though, the problem must have a solution. The steps to establish and use a trusted channel look something like this:

1. *Find both end-points.* It does not matter how the end-points are found; one side can look for the other. The search can be across the Internet or through buses on a platform.

2. *Say hello.* Essentially, one side sends a message that says, "I would like to start a channel."

3. *Verify the end-points.* One side verifies the identity and authorization of the other side, or both sides verify each other. The checking can be very simple or very complex. The checking can involve cryptography to validate and protect the answers.

4. *Create a session key.* The session key encrypts all data using the channel. The session key should be ephemeral, so that when the channel terminates, the session key is lost forever. Many protocols combine the end-point validation with session key creation.

5. *Establish channel.* With the session key at both end-points, all future traffic on the channel uses an encryption algorithm to encrypt all traffic. The "distance" between the two end-points does not matter to the integrity or confidentiality of the channel. As long as both sides properly protect the session key, no intervening entity can read the data. The cryptographic strength of the algorithm and key can affect the strength property. If a reasonable algorithm, such as AES, and a decent key size, such as 128 bits, is in use, then intervening entities have a very low probability of success.

6. *Terminate channel.* Either side can terminate the channel, at any time. One efficient and effective way to terminate the channel is to destroy the session key.

Trusted Channel Device Focus

Devices that support the trusted channel may also support usages without the trusted channel. Some devices must make provisions for continued use of the device when the focus changes from the trusted application to an untrusted application. One example of changing focus is the trusted channel to the keyboard—when the trusted keyboard driver has the focus, all of the keystrokes travel through the trusted keyboard driver. When an untrusted driver has the focus, the keystrokes may or may not travel through the trusted driver. Determining which entity has the focus is a critical ability of the trusted driver in order to properly handle the channel.

Device Support

With many types of human input and output devices in existence, LT does not attempt to provide a trusted channel to every one. The LT architecture does identify a few mandatory devices and provides the internal hardware support to create the trusted channels to those devices. No requirement says that all functions of the device must support the trusted channel. It is possible and permissible to create a hybrid device where some data uses the trusted channel and some data has no protection. The following is the list of hardware devices supported by trusted channels:

- *Display adapter*. The trusted channel may display information in one or more regions of the display monitor. The application establishing the trusted channel must create the trusted path to indicate the presence of the trusted channel. The display adapter may be either integrated or discrete. The design and security solutions for integrated and discrete adapters are different, as you can see in the following sections of this chapter.

- *USB peripheral*. The channel establishment requires the assistance of the chipset and the USB host controller.

- *Keyboard and mouse on a mobile platform*. The mobile platform for the built-in keyboard and pointing devices do not normally use USB for the connections. Attached peripherals do normally use the USB connectors. Establishing the trusted channel to the built-in devices requires assistance of the chipset and mobile keyboard controller.

Secured Discrete Graphics

Discrete graphics adapters plug into the platform. To create a trusted channel to the device, both sides need to understand the protocol and have the computing capabilities to perform the cryptography. Once the channel between the adapter and the device driver is set up, the channel needs no hardware assistance. LT only needs to support establishment of the trusted channel. As long as the discrete graphics adapter uses standard connections, like PCI or AGP, no additional hardware support is needed.

An issue arises from the need of the channel driver to validate the display adapter. The standard method of providing the identity and validation of the entity is to use a unique cryptographic key pair. Allowing the driver to validate the key pair, usually through a digitally signed statement of authenticity, solves the problem of establishing the trusted channel. However, this unique cryptographic key pair creates a potential privacy issue, as unique cryptographic values provide an excellent way to track platforms and possibly users.

As discussed in Chapter 8, the LT platform already has various mechanisms to properly handle the Trusted Platform Module (TPM) uniqueness. The designers of discrete graphics adapters would like to gain the same assurances that the uniqueness on the adapter is not available for misuse. To solve these problems, a change to the PCI Express definition is pending which adds a Trusted Configuration Space (TCS). The TCS requires changes at both the display adapter and the chipset. Using the TCS, the graphics driver can obtain the public key for the display adapter and use the public key while creating the trusted channel session key. Using this mechanism avoids exposure of the unique cryptographic public key.

Secured Integrated Graphics

Some chipsets provide, as a feature, an integrated graphics adapter. The requirement to create a trusted channel between the driver and the adapter remains the same. The protection mechanisms do change. No cryptographic protection is needed because the hardware itself can provide confidentiality and integrity. The creation of the channel uses the hardware identity inside of the chipset and a direct connection to system memory.

One way to implement such an integrated graphics engine would the *trusted sprite model*. This section only provides an overview of the trusted sprite model. Chipset manufactures are free to provide trusted graphics support in any manner that they wish.

Trusted Sprite Model

The characteristics of the trusted sprite model are as follows:

■ The adapter allows the creation of a *trusted surface* that is the size of the main display. The creation of the trusted surface comes from configuring an available hardware sprite as a "trusted" sprite.

■ The memory used to support the trusted surface is protected memory, accessible only to the MVMM or its designated secured driver, and the trusted sprite.

■ The trusted surface overlays the entire main display surface, such that any portion of the main display is visible only if the equivalent portion of the trusted surface has been set to be "transparent."

■ Any graphics mode changes, such as changes to display resolution or color depth, require that the trusted surface be torn down, the changes made, and the trusted surface reconstituted.

■ A special form of the "blue screen of death" is used if the trusted surface is enabled, preventing software from spoofing this display.

Figure 9.2 shows an abstraction of the trusted sprite model.

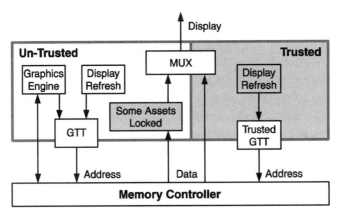

Figure 9.2   Trusted Sprite

The trusted sprite implementation supports a limited subset of display adapter capabilities. While modern display adapters allow a dizzying array of choices, the trusted sprite fixes most of the choices. The number of bits per display pixel, the available colors for each pixel, and transparency of the pixel are all choices limited in the trusted sprite.

One "choice" forced on the display adapter for the trusted sprite is the Z-order. In the typical X Y graph, adding the Z order adds depth.[4] The trusted sprite is forced, at all times, to reside at the top of the stack.[5]

Resource Management

Referring back to Figure 9.2, the right side of the diagram is the trusted sprite handling. The left side has the standard Graphics Translation Table (GTT) which provides the mapping between the memory controller and the graphics engine. Normal display operations occur when the graphics engine writes the display information through the GTT into the display buffers and the MUX engine reads the display information and sends the resulting display to the monitor.

---

[4] Think of the X and Y as defining a page and the Z axis defining the page number.

[5] Top of the stack is a Z value of 0.

The trusted sprite works just like the standard display but uses a separate GTT, the Trusted Graphics Translation Table (TGTT). The TGTT performs the same operations as the GTT but works with pages identified as holding the trusted sprite display information. Pages assigned to the TGTT are under control of the MVMM and the MVMM must ensure that each physical page in the TGTT is included in the NoDMA table.

The inclusion of the TGTT mapped pages into the NoDMA table is a critical feature of the trusted sprite display. The display adapter is going to read the memory display pages using DMA access and normally a page containing sensitive information blocks DMA access through the NoDMA table. The TGTT allows DMA access to the protected page if the request comes from the display adapter. The chipset enforces the display adapter DMA access to pages only in the TGTT. If the display adapter attempts to access a protected page, not listed in the TGTT, the chipset will block the read request.

The multiplexer (MUX) combines the video streams into a single sequence of display information that the monitor physically displays. The MUX has the important job of enforcing the Z order requirement and ensuring that the trusted sprite is always on top.

The sprite's buffer contains a composite of the virtual frame buffers across all secured applications currently using the display. Only the secured driver has access to the display buffer itself. This driver builds the composite image from the secured application's frame buffers.

Most of the integrated graphics controls, including the main GTT, remain fully accessible to the OS or applications running in a guest VM. However, selected modes that affect the overall display, such as resolution and color depth, are locked once the trusted sprite is enabled; any subsequent change to these modes requires first alerting the secured driver, which tears down the trusted display, and releases the lock over these controls. After changing the controls, the entity making the change alerts the secure driver. The secure driver then tests and locks the mode configuration and reestablishes the trusted display.

Panic Blue Screen

In normal use, the trusted surface always supersedes the main surface, ensuring that the secured driver has the final say in what data is displayed anywhere on the screen. A panic situation occurs when the CPU is unable to continue executing the normal flow of operations, but the CPU can make forward progress on some code paths. Think of this situation as one where the normal application and OS are unable to execute but the CPU has access to some special code that can at least display a message that something really bad is happening. In the event of a panic situation, the special code must display the characteristic "blue[6] screen of death" (BSOD) without any dependence on sophisticated protections and modes created by the MVMM. Typically, in a panic situation the system grants immediate and total control of the display to the main operating system's BSOD routine.

However, giving immediate control to some entity other than the MVMM or secure driver opens a hole for an attacker. Specifically, this would permit an attacker to mimic or induce a panic, by redirecting or hooking the routine that would normally display the BSOD. The attacker then displays a screen that purports to be the trusted display. Potentially, a clever attacker can detect when a specific trusted display, such as a password-entry dialog, is visible. The attacker would then force the panic and display the attacker's own copy of the password dialog, thereby capturing the user's password.

To prevent this attack, the following rules must go along with a panic mode implementation:

■ Panic mode is only enabled by setting the panic bit.

■ Panic mode immediately disables the trusted sprite.

■ Panic mode can only display white text on a blue background.

■ Panic mode cannot change any resolution settings, such as size, depth, etc.

■ Panic mode remains until after a system reset.

The first implementation of trusted graphics does not support a panic screen. Subsequent implementations might provide the panic screen support.

---

[6] The original panic screens were blue, OS/2 used black, and other colors are possible. No matter what the color, the panic screens get called a BSOD.

Human Interface Design

Discrete graphics adapters and integrated graphics adapters can provide the mechanisms to create trusted channels. These mechanisms do not address the issue of the creation of the trusted path. The entities using the trusted channels must create the trusted paths. Just as SSL creates the channel and then the browser puts the "lock" icon in the window, those entities using the trusted channels must create the "icon" that indicates the presence of the trusted channel. The human must then recognize the "icon" as the trusted channel indication.

Hardware solutions to the trusted path icon are possible, but the solutions have some very severe consequences. It is possible to include an additional LED that lights upon establishment of a trusted channel. However, you would need an LED for each trusted channel and a wire from the display adapter to the LED. Nevertheless, even the LED does not address the problem of indicating to the user which window in a multiple window environment is the trusted window. An additional problem is that putting a wire, an LED, and a hole in the case to display the LED is very expensive and does not solve all of the issues.

Better solutions exist when the entities using the trusted channel include the "icon" in the trusted display. Examples would include special borders, sequences of icons, and other types of information. The issue with special borders or sequences is that some secure storage of the path indicator has to be included. LT provides the secure storage through sealed storage. In fact, sealed storage is perfect for the protection of the path indicator, as sealing protects the value for the specific MVMM. A change in the MVMM results in the inability to recover the path indicator.

Trusted Input

What goes out must come back again, to paraphrase a famous quote. Just as there are multiple ways of creating the trusted output channel, there are multiple ways of creating the trusted input channels.

One reason that there are multiple input channels is that there are multiple input devices. Keyboards, mice, and other devices can be a Human Input Device (HID). HID can connect to the platform through a variety of busses. The most common of the busses are the USB and PS/2 busses and connectors. For a typical desktop system, LT will enable trusted input channels on the USB bus. Laptop systems will use a combination of USB and PS/2.

LT in the first version supports keyboard and mouse input. There is no special support for other HID devices. If the platform, peripheral, and application developer desire, they can create trusted channels to other HID devices. However, LT does not provide any direct support for these channels.

Peripheral or Bus

When adding support for a trusted input channel, the designers must make a decision regarding the endpoints of the trusted channel. One endpoint is internal to the platform and is in a trusted driver or application. The other endpoint is at the peripheral or at the bus connector. The decision regarding the peripheral is a very interesting one. Placing the protections directly in the peripheral protects the communication from the peripheral across all of the busses and software to the driver or application. If the trusted channel is a cryptographic trusted channel, the channel requires the peripheral to have the necessary cryptographic strength to protect the channel. Requesting the computing power necessary to perform encryption on a mouse might not be the best design. In addition, you have the key distribution problem—how the peripheral receives the keys necessary to protect the channel. Again fairly strong cryptographic mechanisms might need to be in place on the peripheral. Strong cryptographic processing power does not equal inexpensive devices.

From a USB bus standpoint, the USB controller is another location to apply the protections. On a PC system, USB connectors are built directly into the ICH. The USB connections use a built-in USB controller. Considering protections from software attack, the trusted input channel only needs to protect the HID input from the USB controller to the application. Protecting the HID input from the peripheral to the USB connector is an attempt to thwart hardware attacks, as there is no software executing between the peripheral and the connector.[7]

---

[7] Certainly if the USB connection is a wireless connector there is some software executing, but the software is not directly accessible to outside entities. USB wireless connectors currently do not normally have downloadable software.

Trusted Input Driver Endpoint

One side of the trusted channel remains the same in the face of the wide variety of peripherals and protection options; the CPU side of the channel. The CPU side of the channel always ends in a driver that controls the channel. Just as the trusted sprite always requires the TGTT and MUX, the trusted input channel always requires a CPU side driver. The driver understands the current application focus, if the current application requires trusted input, and how to properly distribute the HID information to the applications. If the trusted input channel is performing cryptographic protections, the driver knows how to set up the channel and how to decrypt the HID information. While each trusted input channel requires a specific driver, all of the drivers provide the same basic level of services.

Trusted USB Peripheral

For this type of protection the HID device creates the trusted input channel between the peripheral itself and the driver. The HID information has protection using a cryptographic trusted channel. The plus side to this design is that there is protection from hardware attacks; the minus side is that the peripheral requires cryptographic processing and appropriate key setup.

Another advantage of the secure peripheral method is that it places no hardware requirements on the platform to support the peripheral. Consider a protected keyboard and the support necessary to establish the trusted input channel. The two endpoints of the trusted input channel are the peripheral itself and the driver. The driver requires no special hardware support, just an execution environment that allows the driver to run without interference, the exact environment that LT provides. No requirements are on the USB controller or other USB devices, so the trusted input channel is independent of platform hardware support. The design allows the user to add a trusted input device at any time.

The main features of the *Trusted USB Peripheral* are:

■ Data to or from a trusted USB peripheral is encrypted when its "trusted" mode is enabled. Encryption/decryption logic is added to the USB peripheral. To hinder replay attacks, where an attacker captures a series of keystrokes or commands, then inserts them at a later time, and to hinder attacks based on deletion of keystrokes, the encrypted data stream contains sequence numbers.

■ You need not trust the primary USB stack. As the HID information is encrypted, and the driver knows how to decrypt the information, the USB stack is a pass-through device. The stack receives the encrypted packet and dispatches the packet to the trusted input driver without any need to decrypt the packet. Using the primary stack allows the system to process a wide variety of USB packets without the need to move the stack code into the MVMM or trusted input channel driver.

■ A trusted driver—part of the MVMM or a service in a trusted VM—handles the encryption/decryption of the trusted USB data on behalf of the trusted applications making use of the device.

■ The securable USB device is, by default, in an un-trusted state. Specific initialization of the device is required, including the generation and installation of the encryption key. New keys are generated each time the USB peripheral is reset, and they also could be generated at more frequent intervals.

The crucial aspect of this model is the requirement that the trusted driver have an *a priori* method of sending commands and data, including the encryption key, to the securable USB device without snooping, spoofing, or tampering. These configuration sequences cannot be done using the standard USB software stack, which is not trusted.

If the peripheral contains a unique public/private key and the appropriate cryptographic engines, the problem is solved—an authenticated key exchange can be performed. Both sides, driver and device, prove their identity and establish a common session key, all done safely even in the presence of hostile software or hardware snoopers between them. However, this solution adds significant cost to these devices, both in silicon and in manufacturing overhead.

Expecting a USB mouse to have sufficient processing power to create the cryptographic trusted channel is not really viable. In addition, setting up the trusted input channel key on the mouse is going to be very difficult.

Keyboards make excellent choices for devices that are trusted USB peripherals; a mouse is not a good choice for a trusted USB peripheral.

Verification of Session Key Creation

When initializing a trusted USB peripheral, it is important to verify that the peripheral is in receipt of the correct session key. The trusted input channel driver is responsible for exchanging the session key and validating the peripheral receipt of the key. The mechanism to pass the key can use cryptography, randomness, or user input. The choice is a peripheral manufacturer option. The details of any peripheral initialization mechanisms would be part of the specifications for the actual device.

The main attack to worry about here is a man-in-the-middle attack where the attacker takes the session key and creates two session keys: one for the communication between the peripheral and the attacker and one key for the communication between the driver and the attacker. Ensuring that the peripheral has the key is possible on a keyboard and extremely tricky with a mouse.

Trusted USB Controller

To combat the cost and key distribution and verification issues, the trusted input channel can occur between the USB controller and the driver. The USB controller is an integral component of the ICH and controls the USB connectors on the platform. The USB controller has the ability to designate any of the connectors as a trusted input channel port, the ability to create a cryptographic trusted channel, and the ability to properly turn on and off the trusted channel.

Making the USB controller as the trusted input channel peripheral endpoint has a couple of advantages:

- ■ *Cost.* With the endpoint in the USB controller, the peripheral will work without any modification. No modification implies that all USB peripherals could participate in a trusted input session as long as the USB controller had sufficient trusted input ports.

- ■ *Control.* The USB controller represents a single entity that the trusted input channel must control. The code to initiate and terminate the trusted input channel becomes much simpler.

- *Key distribution.* The key distribution problem now becomes one of moving the key between internal platform components, ICH and CPU, rather than an issue of sending the key across the wire to the actual device.

- *Software attack mitigation.* The USB software stack represents the first software component that attackers could manipulate to disrupt the HID input information. Placing the protections in the USB controller protects the HID information prior to the information being made available to the USB software stack. The USB controller then mitigates potential software attacks in the USB software stack or in any other software component prior to the HID information use by the driver.

The trusted USB controller is not a panacea. It has its faults, and the faults include:

- *Hardware attacks.* The connection between the USB controller and the actual peripheral is subject to hardware attack. As the trusted input channel terminates in the USB controller, the defense mechanisms against the hardware attacks are peripheral specific.

- *Hardware changes.* The trusted USB controller represents a change to the hardware. The support necessary to establish the trusted input channels requires changes to the ICH. Without those changes, the creation of a trusted input channel to the USB controller is impossible.

The USB controller represents a compromise between the protection provided by trusted peripherals and the support necessary to set up and operate the trusted peripheral.

Trusted USB Operation

From an operational standpoint, the choice between a trusted peripheral or the trusted USB controller represent no real difference. Both channels require setup and a driver that understands the channel. In actual use, a trusted peripheral could connect using a trusted USB controller.

After initialization, subsequent data transfers from the USB peripheral use the standard USB stack, with HID information encrypted using the session key.[8] The encryption only occurs when a trusted application has the focus and is requesting input from the user. All other HID information travels from the peripheral to the application without any protections.

The standard USB management controls work without modification. The USB stack still polls the devices, the USB stack still requests packet information, and the plug and play nature of USB devices is still active. For example, the USB stack polls the USB device periodically to check for its status, character count, running checksums, running hashes, or other parameters. The trusted driver may at any time, as a driver prerogative, decide to reset the trusted input channel session key.

Trusted USB Teardown

Prior to a safe termination of the MVMM environment and returning to non-VMM operation, the trusted input channel must be shutdown. The shutdown must follow a specific sequence to ensure that no HID information, supposedly under protection, does not appear to other applications without protection.

Shutting down either the trusted USB controller or a trusted USB peripheral requires that the channel endpoint "drain," or clean up, any potential HID information and invalidate the channel session key. With the potential HID information drained and the invalidation of the session key, no further communication on the previous trusted channel is possible. The MVMM should not release control of the platform until the MVMM terminates any and all trusted input channels.

Trusted Mobile Keyboard Controller

Using a trusted USB input channel to secure a keyboard or mouse is not sufficient for mobile systems. While some mobile systems do provide support for external USB keyboards and mice, the system normally integrates the primary keyboard and mouse. This integrated keyboard and mouse typically does not support a USB interface. Instead, it has an embedded scanning logic, a microcontroller, and state machines, collectively known as the Keyboard Controller (KBC). The KBC typically attaches to the platform via the LPC bus.

---

[8] Notice that the encryption occurs at either the peripheral itself or the USB controller.

In addition to reporting keystrokes and mouse inputs, the KBC often performs other mobile system management functions, including power management, battery management, thermal management, general-purpose IO, SMBus access, smart card access, and other services.

Applying the LT security architecture principles to the existing KBC represents some difficult challenges:

■ The KBC microcontroller runs firmware supplied by the OEM. While this firmware is not necessarily attempting to void trust, it contains no security analysis, evaluation, or certification to ensure that no exploitable holes exist.

■ Attempting to evaluate and certify this firmware would be difficult for a couple of reasons. First, the code often performs many platform-specific functions completely unrelated to keystrokes. Additionally, each OEM customizes this non-keystroke code, resulting in a wide variety of firmware that requires evaluation.

■ In many systems, the KBC firmware can be field upgraded. Typically, an upgrade supports fixes or extensions to power management or docking control. While the OEM may provide some degree of authentication before accepting such updates, this authentication does not operate at the same level that is used for the rest of the LT architecture.

■ The KBC interface is inherently not trustworthy because untrusted software can generate the I/O cycles that would result in access to the component, allowing it to snoop, delete, insert, or modify keystrokes that were intended for use by a trusted application. Similarly, most KBCs support debug commands that act as "back doors," providing similar capabilities to attackers.

Rather than attempting to fix all of these problems, and likely requiring significant changes in the industry standard KBC specification, the LT architecture calls out a parallel engine in the KBC specifically dedicated for trusted keyboard and mouse input.

TMKBC Overview

The Trusted Mobile Keyboard Controller (TMKBC) has two modes of operation: trusted and untrusted (legacy). The legacy mode operates exactly as defined today, using the existing KBC hardware, including firmware. The trusted mode operation uses a new dedicated hardware-only scan engine and new dedicated ports.

The new dedicated ports that provide trusted mode access to the TMKBC are accessible only using a new special cycle format on the LPC bus; other LPC devices do not decode this format. Software can only generate these new LPC bus cycles to the TMKBC through the chipset's memory-mapped Trusted Keyboard Port, which the chipset makes available to protected software.

The TMKBC operates in legacy mode using the legacy scanner and ports, until explicitly instructed to shift to trusted mode operation, which is enabled using a command sent through the restricted chipset port to the TMKBC trusted register space. A similar trusted register space command switches the TMKBC back to untrusted (legacy) operation.

While in trusted mode operation, only the new dedicated hardware scans the integrated keyboard and pointing device engine. The new dedicated trusted ports report all scanned data. The TMKBC may support other external devices, like PS/2 keyboards.

TMKBC Initialization

The TMKBC is already in use, in legacy mode, before the launch of the MVMM Environment. The MVMM must support the ability of a guest to initiate the conversation with the TMKBC in order to turn on trusted scanning.

TMKBC Operation

After the initialization phase, the TMKBC reports keyboard or mouse data scanned by the TMKBC to the protected driver. The TMKBC ensures that the scanned data is only available to the protected driver and is not available to any legacy port. The TMKBC also ensures against any loss of scanned data. The TMKBC must continue to accept some commands via the legacy port, especially those that are unrelated to keyboard input or mouse movement. For example, the legacy port may be in use to report commands associated with reading General Purpose Input/Output (GPIO) signals or inputs from un-trusted PS/2 devices.

The operation of the TMKBC places few requirements on the MVMM or its designated protected driver. The TMKBC remains in its trusted mode operation until it is reset or until the TMKBC receives a command to terminate trusted operation. Periodic polling of the TMKBC is not needed.

The protected driver should read keystrokes or mouse data from the TMKBC upon the signaling of an interrupt. Otherwise, subsequent keystroke or mouse data may be lost. Since this loss is always possible due to long interrupt latencies, the status information indicates whether an overrun has occurred. The run-time software is responsible for handling overruns.

TMKBC Teardown

Prior to a safe termination of the MVMM environment and returning to non-VMM operation, it is necessary to reconfigure the TMKBC to normal operation. The reconfiguration must make sure that any data in the TMKBC buffers is available only to the protected driver and to no other drivers.

Trusted I/O and LT

With the inclusion of the trusted display adapter and a trusted input channel, the LT platform provides the support necessary to secure communication between the user and a protected application. While the hardware mechanisms are in place to create the channels, the applications still have lots of work to do in creating the trusted paths. The mechanisms provided by LT enable applications to successfully create trusted paths and protect the trusted path components.

Part IV

LaGrande Technology Architecture

> *The secret temple of the Piranha women. Their architecture is surprisingly advanced.*
>
> —Dr. Margo Hunt. Cannibal Women in the Avocado Jungle of Death (1989)

The quote is not that good but the movie title is just great. It really is amazing what one can search for on the Internet. The previous chapters discussed the building blocks of LaGrande Technology, not how the blocks tie together. Part IV starts to provide the mortar for the blocks.

Chapter 10: LaGrande Technology Architecture

Chapter 10 is a real "rubber hitting the road" chapter. How software uses LaGrande Technology dominates the explanations. Chapter 10 introduces the standard partition, the protected partition and the domain manager. The three components together provide the framework for applications that use LaGrande Technology features.

How the components communicate provides some insight into the mechanisms that each component must provide to make the architecture work. An interesting discussion concerns what entities can provide the components. Who provides what gives some interesting results.

Chapter 11: Late Launch

Chapter 11 covers one of the author's favorite LaGrande Technology features. Late launch is one of the cruxes of the entire LaGrande Technology architecture. If one does not understand late launch, one does not understand what LaGrande Technology does.

The idea is that a platform user will want to start and stop the LaGrande Technology protections. Starting and stopping LaGrande Technology is very exciting as the protections are deep in the CPU and other motherboard components. Ensuring that only the authorized operations enable these protections drives many of the hardware changes required by a LaGrande Technology platform.

Chapter 12: Configuration Concerns

Chapter 12 describes how certain hardware configurations can allow software to breach the LaGrande Technology protections. The configurations that cause the problems are detectable so the architecture must provide the detection and mitigation mechanisms.

The major issue is how the platform handles system memory. Ensuring an evaluation of the memory configuration during the LaGrande Technology launch mitigates the configuration concern.

Our issues revolve around the loss of the memory configuration when the actual memory location could still contain some LaGrande Technology protected information.

Chapter 13: Hardware Attacks

The LaGrande Technology design principle is to protect from software attack. Most of the features provide protection solely from software and do not contemplate hardware attacks. Hardware attacks will occur and the LaGrande Technology system can defend against some of them. Chapter 13 describes the hardware attacks where the current system provides protection. The chapter also describes hardware attacks (not in detail) where LaGrande Technology does not provide protection.

Chapter 10

LaGrande Technology Architecture

Architecture starts when you carefully put two bricks together. There it begins.

— Ludwig Mies van der Rohe

The architecture of LaGrande Technology (LT) starts putting together the bricks available on the platform. The requirement is to protect software and use domain separation to provide the protection. Figure 10.1 shows the basic picture of LT.

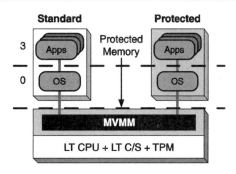

Figure 10.1   The Basic LaGrande Technology Architecture

The architecture has three main features:

■ The *standard partition* or the left-hand side (LHS), of the diagram is an operating environment such as one sees in non-LT platforms. This part is the execution area of today.

■ The *protected partition* or the right-hand side (RHS), of the diagram is the protected environment. This area is under the protection of LT. All applications running in the protected partition have protection from software attack.

■ The *Measured Virtual Machine Manager (MVMM)* provides the controlling entity that manages all partitions.

The protected partition and the MVMM reside in protected memory.

The Naming of the Sides

In the early days of LaGrande Technology project, a small task force of security architects was working on the design of LT. The group's output was going to be a specification that defined LT. The name of the specification was going to be something like "LT Security Architect Specification." As that moniker was much too large, the acronym of LT SAS appeared which was finally shortened to SAS. The series of meetings to work through the various sections of the document are known as the SAS meetings. The SAS continues to meet,[1] albeit with a larger group now, defining the security properties of LT.

When the SAS started on the task of defining what worked with what with whom and when, it became very apparent that some sort of naming convention was necessary. As the conversation went back and forth, covering items like protected or unprotected, known and unknown, secure and insecure—they all got mixed up. Someone would ask, "Where is the item at any point in time?" The diagram in Figure 10.1 was up on the white board constantly, and one of us would point to the left or right side and say "there." Figure 10.1 soon became "standardized" in that the standard partition was on the left side and the protected partition was on the right. The shorthand soon became to say simply left or right, and everyone in the room knew whether or not the information was under protection.

---

[1] I was the chair of the LT SAS, a role I both loved and hated. The meetings are known to have lots of discussions with many twists and turns. The normal SAS time slot is two hours and many a new person has come to the SAS with a 15-minute topic—when they leave two hours later they are a better and wiser person.

This shorthand worked very well for the security architects in the SAS. In fact, as the architects talked with others working on trusted computing projects, the terms left-hand side and right-hand side became the standard. For those working on these projects for any length of time, left-hand side always conjures up the image of something not under the protection of the platform, while conversely right-hand side always implies something receiving protection. The terms were so prevalent that the definition of the acronym of Left Hand Side (LHS) and Right Hand Side (RHS) are in the specifications.

Not surprisingly, marketing people feel that the terms LHS and RHS are not appropriate to use for a major new technology. Without the background of Figure 10.1, LHS and RHS do not really impart any information to a listener. When I gave the first presentation of LT at the Intel® Developer Forum (IDF), marketing asked me not to use LHS and RHS as the terms were just too esoteric. The LHS became the standard partition and the RHS became the protected partition. While the terms are much more descriptive of the type of partition, they do not have the ease of use the LHS and RHS do. Having briefed many people on LT, I still use LHS and RHS. When I communicate with other security architects who work for OS vendors or other hardware manufacturers, we continue to use LHS and RHS. I am going to attempt to keep the marketing folks happy in this book and use the approved names, "standard" and "protected." The reader must know though that when they hear or see someone talking about the LHS or RHS, the speaker is referring to Figure 10.1.

Actual Use

A funny thing happened with the architecture diagram: everyone realized that the diagram was really incomplete. One must come to grips with two realities when looking at Figure 10.1.

First, the diagram does not actually represent what most MVMM vendors are likely to implement. Intel® Virtualization Technology allows for an almost unlimited number of partitions. Why should LT limit the possibilities to only two? The answer is that LT does *not* limit the number of partitions; the MVMM can have one, two, or twenty partitions.

The second is that the difference between protected partition and unprotected partition is arbitrary. All partitions automatically have protection between each other that is a function of Intel Virtualization Technology. The real protection attribute comes from individual page protection that prohibits DMA access. Certainly, the MVMM would normally provide protection for itself from DMA, but individual partitions could easily have a mixture of protected and unprotected pages.

With these two issues, it becomes very difficult to differentiate between the partitions again. So, for the sake of sanity, the terms protected partition and unprotected partition continue to be used throughout this book. However, the reader is admonished to remember that the designation is only one of convenience and real partitions have a mixture of protected and unprotected physical pages.

Measured Virtual Machine Monitor

The MVMM is the controlling software in an LT system. The MVMM provides:

■ Memory arbitration

■ Resource assignment

■ Communication channel

■ Partition lifecycle

You must remember as we discuss the MVMM that the MVMM is just a *Measured* VMM. The basic capabilities and responsibilities of a VMM do not change when the VMM becomes a MVMM.

Memory Arbitration

The MVMM provides control of all memory and resources in the system. If an application needs access to a physical memory page, the application uses a memory address. Using the page table entries, the CPU evaluates the address and converts the virtual address into a physical address. The setup of the page table entries is under complete control of the MVMM.

Memory arbitration is the basic building block for guest partition isolation. Ensuring that each and every memory access complies with the policy set by the MVMM, and that the CPU enforces the memory access policy, is the crux of MVMM protection capabilities.

Memory arbitration is an inherent feature of any VMM. The MVMM adds no real additional properties to the memory arbitration feature of the VMM.

Resource Assignment

The MVMM controls, in addition to physical memory, all resources of the platform. Disk drives, display adapters, USB devices, and any other device one uses on the platform are all under control of the MVMM.

All memory-mapped resources are very easy for the MVMM to control; they appear as memory addresses, so the MVMM treats the address as a protected page. The entire MVMM page controls map onto the controls for the resource.

Resources that are not memory-mapped require specific support from the MVMM. The MVMM must be aware of how entities communicate with the resource and then the MVMM must be able to intercept, or virtualize,[2] the access.

Communication Channel

Guests are going to want to talk with each other. While it is certainly possible to simply require guests to have an Internet connection and use the Internet for inter-guest communication, the reality is that direct guest-to-guest communication is mandatory. The MVMM has complete control of how each guest communicates with any other guest.

Partition Lifecycle

A major feature of the MVMM is the ability to launch and terminate a guest partition. The MVMM contains, either explicitly as a standalone entity or implicitly as part of the code, the policy on when and how to launch and terminate guest partitions. Entities wishing to rely on the MVMM, and its guest partition lifecycle management policy, must have the ability to obtain validation of the currently enforced policy. For MVMMs that have the policy implicitly embedded in the code, attesting to the MVMM identity also confirms the guest partition lifecycle management policy. For MVMMs that have explicit policy statements, the MVMM must be able to show which policy the MVMM is enforcing and how the MVMM loaded the policy.

---

[2] Chapter 15 talks about possible future enhancements, such as the handling of resources.

Standard Partition

Defining the LHS as a standard partition implies that the LHS is the normal situation that a user expects. This is correct. The standard partition does run standard operating systems and applications. The OS and applications need no modification to run in the standard partition.

The standard partition provides protection from software attack. Information held in the standard partition has the exact same areas of exposure that the information does today on systems without LT. If the application designer wants or needs protections, they will have to use some component that resides in the protected partition. The next section, "Protected Partition," explains how to design an application that takes advantage of the protected partition.

Operating System

The OS is any standard operating system like Windows[†] XP, Linux, or a home-grown OS. The specification places no restrictions on the type of OS that runs in the standard partition. If the user runs a particular OS today on their platform based on Intel architecture, the OS would still run in the standard partition. Certainly, if the OS in question is very old, its ability to run using new hardware may be questionable, but not due to LT. The OS probably would not understand the newer hardware.

The OS does not need any knowledge of the MVMM. Certainly if one were to run DOS 3.1, the OS would have no knowledge of the MVMM. DOS 3.1 would run correctly, but a direct knowledge of the MVMM would be impossible.

The OS can be aware that the MVMM and protected partitions are operating and available. A new OS can understand the hardware nature of an LT platform and provide the new services that the hardware allows.

Application

In the standard partition, you can run a normal application such as Quicken[†] or a user-written application. The application makes use of the OS services and executes without any knowledge of the MVMM or the protected partition.

For applications running on an OS that has no knowledge of the MVMM or protected partition, the application's ability to use the protected partition is limited. Unless the protected partition provides a communication mechanism that is publicly available and discoverable by the application, the application is unable to use any services of the protected partition.

If the OS is aware of the MVMM and protected partition, then the OS can expose to applications the services exposed by the MVMM and protected partition.

Protected Partition

All software in the protected partition receives protection from software attack, with no difference in the protection whether the application is running at ring 0 or ring 3.

Kernel

The kernel provides the services for applications running at ring 3. No requirement states that a protected partition must use both ring 0 and ring 3. It is entirely possible to create a domain that only uses ring 0.

The kernel can provide a rich set of services or it can provide limited services. When more code is in the kernel, it becomes harder to evaluate the security properties of the kernel. From the standpoint of security, the kernel should be as small as possible. From a service standpoint, the kernel should provide a wide and deep set of services. Since these two views conflict with each other, the kernel designer must weigh these two issues and make the appropriate choice for the use model.

Rich Service Kernel

One way to provide a rich service kernel would be to use a current OS like Linux. While this certainly provides a rich set of services, most existing operating systems are very large and difficult to evaluate. Nothing in the LT architecture prevents someone from using an OS as a kernel in the protected partition. The ability to show the properties of the OS is very difficult.

A rich service kernel is possible and desirable when the use model allows for user-written applets that provide many user services. Carefully creating and adding the necessary services to the kernel can result in a rich kernel with services that enable a rich set of applications.

Limited Services

A limited service kernel can be either general-purpose or designed to support a special application, which would seem to be an oxymoron. However, by providing a controlled set of services, the limited kernel actually provides a better trust boundary. The rich service kernel described earlier provides lots of services that a special purpose application would not need. By providing only the services necessary for the application, the amount of code that requires validation is smaller.

Another way to provide limited services and keep the kernel small would be to select a set of services that the majority of applications relying on the kernel would need. For instance, providing memory management, trusted input, trusted output, and general thread handling could possibly provide services for a wide variety of applications. While the extra special fancy stuff may not be available, the ability to create trustable applications may be greater.

Applet

The term applet is a very specific label. The idea is that applications using ring 3 in the protected partition are not the rich applications that one sees in ring 3 for the standard partition. Protected partition applications are *applets*: small, single purpose, and capable of being evaluated.

Take an application that does online stock transactions. Most of the application could be a ring 3 standard partition application[3]—that is, parts that display the choices, allow the user to determine what to buy, and create the buy order. The only portion of the application that must be in the protected partition is the component that allows the user to verify and digitally sign the order request. This type of requirement defines an applet very well. The applet does four things:

■ Receives XML string

■ Displays XML string using trusted output

■ Receives user OK through trusted input

■ Signs XML string using a digital signing key protected by LT

---

[3] You can see how the term LHS would work so much easier here had not those marketers gotten involved.

The application then uses a simple applet and the applet only requires a limited service kernel. While it is not the only use of an applet and kernel combination, this use does represent a valid combination.

Application

There is no requirement that entities in the protected partition must be applets. Applications are possible also. The difference between an application and applet is that an application is standalone, not requiring any outside help, while the applet is a component of a larger application.

Applications will come in all of the varieties that are available today. Big large applications with thousands of options and abilities and small single-purpose applications that do their job quickly and efficiently are all possibilities.

Partition Communication

No direct communication occurs between any ring 0 or ring 3 process in the standard partition, and any ring 0 or ring 3 process in the protected partition. The communication vector is the MVMM, which has the responsibility to expose interfaces to the standard and protected partitions such that the two partitions can communicate. The MVMM is under no obligation to provide the communication path, and if it does not, the partitions must communicate using some outside path such as a network or files.

If the MVMM does provide a communication path, it can take any form that the MVMM wants to provide, using a standard protocol or creating a special protocol.

Communication between two processes normally occurs as an InterProcess Communication (IPC) or a Remote Procedure Call (RPC). The mechanism that an MVMM could expose is closer to an RPC than an IPC.

IPC

The IPC mechanisms normally take into account the use of internal resources to make the transfer faster. The activity of two processes mingling some internal resources is the exact type of behavior that LT prevents. It is possible for a MVMM to create mechanisms that look like IPC interfaces but that do not mingle process resources. If the MVMM wants to implement pipes, the MVMM could create a system that allowed a partition to establish a pipe to another partition. The actual implementation of the pipe would be a pipe from the establishing partition to the MVMM and then an MVMM-managed pipe from the MVMM to the destination partition. The creation of a direct pipe between two partitions would be illegal. To the pipe's user, the pipe appears to go directly from one partition to another. The underlying connections require the management of the MVMM.

RPC

The RPC provides a communication mechanism that requires some sort of arbitrator in the middle. The RPC mechanism then matches what the MVMM needs to do to provide communication between the partitions. The MVMM may choose any of the numerous RPC mechanisms that are currently available or it may design a new one. If the MVMM is attempting to hide the protected partition, an RPC could be an appropriate communication mechanism.

Other Mechanisms

IPC and RPC are not the only mechanisms that are possible. While many applications today use IPC and RPC, other mechanisms provide good functionality for specific purposes.

One extremely easy method is to simply have a shared buffer between the two partitions.[4] One guest writes to the buffer, the other guest reads from the buffer. The implementation may or may not cause a security concern—only an evaluation of the MVMM would be able to properly alleviate any security concerns.

---

[4] As this is a very easy mechanism, you should expect to see this mechanism in actual use.

The OS, MVMM, and Kernel Interaction

Who must build the various base components? You have five combinations and each has some advantages and disadvantages.

OS, MVMM, and Kernel from Same Vendor

Advantages are:

- When all of the components come from the same vendor, you have some wonderful opportunities for collaboration. The OS and kernel know about each other and can optimize communication. The range of services can be tuned to the services the OS and kernel want to expose.

- The MVMM provides the glue and understands what the OS and kernel require. The communication mechanism can be configured so the normal transfer of information occurs in an efficient manner.

- When the vendor wants to perform an evaluation of the security properties of the system, the combination of all of the components provides an easier base to show what the component can and cannot do. Being able to show the exact duties of a component in a security evaluation makes it easier to make and prove security claims.

Disadvantages are:

- The major disadvantage is that the vendor has to supply two complete operating systems, standard and protected, and the MVMM. The amount of code is large.

- A negative perception could also be that if one vendor does all of the work, the result can lead to security problems.

MVMM and Kernel from Same Vendor

This combination provides the security components from the same vendor but allows any standard OS to execute. This combination could be the same as all three components coming from the same vendor.

Advantages are:

- The MVMM and kernel understand the use models of the OS and provide for the most efficient use of the resources.

- The MVMM and kernel combination would also support the use of an old OS that had no knowledge of the MVMM and kernel. This approach works very well when the communication mechanism is a RPC and both the OS and applications think that the protected partition resides on some other platform.

Disadvantages are:

- Most of the normal application processing occurs in the OS, so you have no way to build efficiencies into the OS-to-kernel communication.

- Also, you could not design the OS to handle itself efficiently because the MVMM design must allow for all operating systems.

OS and MVMM from Same Vendor

This combination is a strange one. The vendor creates the standard OS and the MVMM but does not provide any protected partitions. This situation combines the worst features of all the other combinations. As the MVMM and kernel provide security, any evaluation of the two would be very difficult. In addition, the combination relies on the ability of the MVMM to properly set up communications, and while all combinations do rely on this ability, this setup would assume that the MVMM has no visibility into the kernel, making the communication mechanism difficult. While strange, this combination is not illegal.

OS and Kernel from Same Vendor

This situation is certainly possible. Think of the OS and kernel as being identical. Nothing requires the OS and kernel to be different. Therefore, in this model the MVMM merely starts two instances of the same OS and places security around one of the instances—you really have to think standard and protected partitions now. The beauty of this approach is that the OSs already know how to communicate with each other through some sort of RPC. The MVMM exposes the RPC for use by the two OSs and it all works from the start. The trick here is to consider whether the OS is robust enough to protect information. A simple OS that provides no internal protections does not give the protected partition the kernel support that is necessary to protect the applets.

The MVMM in this case provides an RPC and the normal resource protections. This MVMM could be a generic one that is designed to work with any OS, or it could be one that is written by a separate vendor to support a specific OS. If the MVMM is small enough, it would be easy to evaluate.

All Three Components from Different Vendors

The combination of all three components from different vendors is possible. Any attempt at efficiencies is a very difficult task. Some efficiency would be possible, but largely everything needs to be written to the lowest common denominator, forcing the design to avoid efficiencies and do tasks in a simple manner.

Simple and slow is not always a bad thing. Components that are simple and slow might have simpler designs, and simpler designs equate to easier to evaluate and maintain. Therefore, the simple design could result in a slower use model but one that provides a higher level of security assurance.

Standalone Applications

When creating applications that are single-purpose and that require no help from any outside partition, the end result is potentially three components from different vendors. The assumption that the application vendor is related to the OS and MVMM vendors is not a strong assumption.

A good example of a standalone application would be an Internet firewall. The firewall has a specific purpose and only needs OS support to perform certain operations. In some instances, the firewall could even work in an environment where the firewall itself makes no communication with the outside world, removing the requirement for input and output support. The firewall vendor could build the application on top of a specific OS, or a custom OS, and there would be no relationship whatsoever to the MVMM. The chances that all three vendors were different would be quite high.

Application Design Options

Application design can be unaware of the protected partition, make use of a small component in the protected partition, or be an application totally consumed by the protected partition.

Unaware Applications

With the application unaware of the protected partition, no direct communication occurs with any applets in the protected partition. The application must make use of some library function that is dynamically linked or that is provided by the OS.

The example in Figure 10.2 shows an application that makes use of a service provided by the OS. The application makes a normal system call to obtain the service. Updating the service to run in the protected partition requires an RPC stub in the standard partition and the actual service running in the kernel. The design could have the server run as an applet, but this example does not illustrate that use.

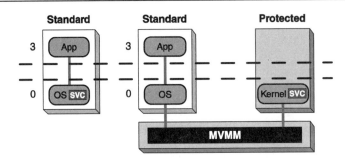

Figure 10.2   Application Unaware of Protected Partition

When the service was in the standard partition, the application made a system call to obtain the service. With the service moved to the protected partition, the application still makes a system call to a service in the standard partition. Instead of performing the actual operation, the service uses the communication mechanism provided by the MVMM and sends the operation request to the protected partition. The protected partition service performs the actual operation and then returns the answer to the application through the MVMM and the OS service.

Protected Component

From a component perspective, the layout is the same as in the previous example with the unaware application. The application does four things:

- The application calls a service.

- The service uses the MVMM to communicate to the protected partition.

- The applet in the protected partition performs an operation.

- The applet sends a response back to the standard partition through the MVMM.

The difference between this situation and the unaware application using a protected component lies in the application being aware of the protected component. With this design, the application can pick the components that need protection. The application can place more of the process in the applet.

Verification Model

The verification model is possible with the protected component option. In this instance, the application can perform whatever operations the application requires and then pass the result of the operation to the protected partition for verification. Figure 10.3 shows an example of a stock market purchasing transaction using the verification model.

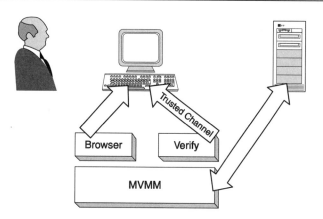

Figure 10.3   Verification Model

The standard partition performs most of the work of the stock transaction. In the standard partition, the user does four things:

1. Browses for possible stock purchases

2. Locates a stock

3. Indicates how many shares to buy at a stated price

4. Creates an XML request to send to stock broker

The sequence is the same for an application without verification, but the verification model adds the following steps:

1. Send the XML request to the protected applet

2. Applet displays request using XML viewer in a trusted output window

3. Applet requests user verification of transaction

4. User OKs transaction using trusted input (mouse or keyboard)

5. Applet performs digital signature on XML transaction

6. Applet returns digitally signed transaction to the standard partition

7. Standard partition sends transaction to broker

The stock broker now receives the transaction, just as they do normally. The difference is that the broker can apply some additional trust to the transaction. The broker knows the following:

■ The platform in use has LT. The proof of the platform claim comes from the attestation the broker performs on this transaction or a previous transaction. The broker can also determine the exact version of the MVMM and applet in use to protect the transaction and display it to the user.

■ The key that signs the transaction requires specific authorization to use it. This proof comes from the keys that are available for use either on the TPM or by the applet. The private portion of the key is always under protection and should not be available to any software process to either steal or misuse.

■ The user saw the transaction. The proof that the user saw the transaction comes from the fact that an LT platform can create a trusted channel to the display adapter, that the applet creates a trusted path to the user, and that the applet uses the trusted window for the XML viewer. If the proof does not include verification of an LT platform, then the broker has no way to be sure that the trusted output was in use. The broker also validates that the XML viewer properly parses an XML string and that the applet requires the use of the XML viewer.

■ The user authorized the transaction. The proof of user authorization comes from the use of the protected input. The user either used the mouse or entered a value from the keyboard and a trusted channel handled either of the inputs.

■ It is now difficult for the user to make a claim that the user did not see what the transaction was or that the user did not explicitly authorize the transaction.

The verification model provides an excellent way to use LT without making major changes to an application. The verification model works on many types of transactions. Applications making use of the verification model can even be unaware that the verification is taking place, by having the verification process take over the normal process of merely transmitting the transaction.

The verification model is not the only model that can use protected components. Many more models are possible, and as the LT architecture becomes available, these models are likely to emerge. It is certainly possible that entirely new models of use could appear.[5]

---

[5] I always liked the verification model because it shows what LT can do but it does not require huge changes to existing applications. In fact, many of us already execute in the verification model. When we do purchases on the Web, we go through the browse and select phase and then the check-out phase. In the LT model, the check-out phase would move to the protected partition.

Contained Application

The contained application lives solely in the protected partition. The actual implementation would normally be an applet, but a service of the kernel is possible. The applet may not even have interfaces available to the standard partition but be solely for the use of the MVMM or other protected partition applets.

A contained applet could be a user agent. Assume a stock agent that the user sets up to buy and sell stock without any interaction once established. The user would set the parameters for what stocks to buy under what conditions. The user would know that the applet would only run in the exact same environment, so any change to the environment, including the parameters, would invalidate the applet and it would no longer run. The design requires the applet to seal the parameters for the MVMM and applet.

The contained applet could be something very different from an agent. The applet could be a firewall or virus engine. The sky is the limit for the design of applets.

Application Use

The previous sections have put the LT building blocks to use. Applications make use of the protected partition with various communication mechanisms. Nothing in this chapter should limit what designers do. They are free to use the LT building blocks and design applications that use both the standard and protected partitions.

This is a really good time to reiterate the comment from the "Actual Use" section. While Chapter 11 uses the terms standard and protected partitions, normal use would be a combination of protected and unprotected physical pages in the guest partition. The mix of protected and unprotected physical pages is a MVMM and guest partition policy decision and not a fixed and unchangeable setting. If the guest partition has a mix of protected and unprotected physical pages, the applications themselves will make use of these protections in interesting ways. No attempt is made to prejudge or define how applications make use of the LT protections.

Chapter 11

Late Launch

A slipping gear in your M203 grenade launcher can cause it to fire when you least expect it. This could make you very unpopular with what is left of your unit.

—Unknown, Army Magazine of Preventive Maintenance

For effective security, knowing what causes the launch of the protected partition is vital. To prevent slipping gears from causing the exposure of protected information, the launch of LaGrande Technology (LT) must ensure that the CPU protection modes receive proper initialization. In general, LT uses the Safer Mode Extensions (SMX) and Virtual Mode Extensions (VMX) as the gears, and controls them through the CPU commands of `GETSEC [SENTER]` and `GETSEC [SEXIT]`. `GETSEC` is the CPU instruction leaf that implements the SMX instructions. To shift these gears smoothly you prepare for `GETSEC [SENTER]` execution, load the MVMM, pass control to the MVMM, and finally remove the MVMM through `GETSEC [SEXIT]`.

Launching the Protected Partition

Figure 11.1 illustrates the typical technical discussion at the "... and magic happens here" point. On the left, you see no protected domain; on the right, the protected partition is executing. Some process changed the state to enable the protected partition. Who waved the proverbial magic wand? What was that process? When did the process occur? [1]

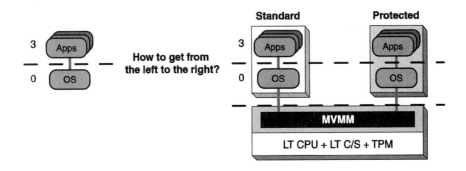

Figure 11.1 The Launch Sequence

The answers to the first set of questions are:

■ *Who?* A platform component will issue GETSEC [SENTER]. The component could be the platform user or the component could be an automatic process.

■ *What?* The GETSEC [SENTER] process.

■ *When?* GETSEC [SENTER] can occur at any time.

Those were the easy questions and the answers merely point to the GETSEC [SENTER] process. Pointing to the GETSEC [SENTER] process slows the hand waving[2] down to a slower speed and bounds the further definitions.

---

[1] "Where" is not forgotten, but the "where" is always platforms with LaGrande Technology.

[2] The realm of hand waving includes the hummingbird effect. The hummingbird effect occurs when the hand waving is so vigorous that the hand waver levitates off the ground and the hands are no longer visible. When discussing LT, and the discussion is at Figure 11.1, the individual leading the discussion would be demonstrating the hummingbird effect.

A History of SENTER

Deciding the properties of the protected partition was the first order of business for the security architects. It was "easy"—well, at the time it was very hard—to specify the protection boundaries of the partition. Many times the team did a hand wave[3] and said, "Let's worry about the initiation of the partition later." Well, later finally came and hand-waving wasn't enough. The time for a definition of the secure entrance into the protected partition was upon the team.

On one difficult day, after many hours of discussion, the team kept coming back to the same simple fact: to have a chain of trust that would ensure the proper launch of the protected partition, you had to have a platform reset. However, the team did not want to require a platform reset because everyone felt that the user experience would be terrible. The team was at an impasse. But, you repeatedly heard the comment that a platform reset was necessary.

The mantra of needing a reboot led the team to ask the question "can we create a reboot without doing a reboot?" Said another way, the question is, could you have a disruptive event that looks like a reboot but does not trigger a complete reset of the CPU internal state? The disruptive event could occur at any time and would not rely on any prior event. The term in use for the disruptive event was a *secure enter*[4] into the protected environment. As all architects want to use abbreviations, secure enter became SENTER. The term *late launch* comes from the ability to issue SENTER at any time.

A disruptive event is the design principle for SENTER: the system must cause one, control the results, and record the software and hardware that participated. The objectives for the disruptive event are:

- Initiate the protections at any time and allow for removal of the partition.

- Make sure that all CPUs participate.

- Detect any tampering with the launch process.

---

[3] These hand waves were so vigorous that the speaker would sometimes pass through the hummingbird effect and initiate the *typhoon phase* of hand waving where *huge* amounts of air are being moved.

[4] As my editor points out, *secure enter* is not grammatically correct, it should be *secure entry*. However, to be historically accurate, the term really was secure enter; the architects were just not concerned about grammatically correct phrases. Heck, we were simply happy to solve the problem.

■ Allow multiple invocations of the protected partition without requiring a platform reboot.

■ Ensure properly configured hardware.

Initiate the Protections at Any Time

Launching the protected partition with a reboot was the initial design. However, the final design uses late launch. The difference lies in the approach to control and measurement.

Launch Control

When people first hear about the protected partition, the assumption is that controlling the process from reboot is the easiest. The idea is attractive . . . but wrong. Directly out of reset, the CPU is a clean slate. The CPU internal state and the settings for the platform all require initialization. The initialization of both areas comes from the BIOS sequence. The code includes BIOS boot block, main BIOS, Option ROMS, Master boot record, and the OS loader.

To provide a secure launch, every line of the boot sequence must be trustable. Option ROMS come from multiple vendors. The master boot record resides on the hard drive with little protection. The OS loader is provided by entities other than the BIOS and Option ROMS, and the BIOS itself is available to update via flashing. The code in some of these entities is years old and the coders did not consider security to be an issue. Requiring the providers of the code to rewrite the entire suite to meet the security requirements is not viable. As a result, the secure launch must not rely on the code in use for reset.

Measurement

Along with controlling the launch process, the design has to meet a requirement to measure the code involved in the launch. In particular, the code that executes as part of the SENTER process must have an accurate measurement. By controlling the launch process, it becomes possible to provide an accurate measurement of the launch code.

Disruptive Event

With SENTER providing the disruptive event for the launch, the process has no tie to platform reset. However, SENTER is a disruptive event that does not need any prior activity to operate. With no prior requirements, SENTER can execute at any time.

Partition Removal

SENTER occurs at any time after platform reset and launches the protected partition. The partition executes until the receipt of a request to remove the partition. If the partition shutdown is complete and leaves no internal state resident in the CPU, then a subsequent SENTER executes correctly. The design allows for multiple invocations of SENTER with different parameters and settings without requiring a reset of the platform.

Many of the same issues that define the launch process are also present in the shutdown process. The name for the shutdown is *secure exit* or SEXIT. GETSEC [SEXIT] is a disruptive event to ensure the complete removal of all CPU state associated with the protected partition.

Trust Framework

SENTER removes all reliance on the reset process for the launch of the protected partition. Use of a disruptive event provides the framework for both trust and security. The SENTER and GETSEC [SEXIT] provide the mechanism that controls and measures the launch process and the subsequent protected partition.

Ensure that All CPUs Participate

Chapter 9 provided a definition of protected execution and showed that one of the main protection mechanisms was the internal CPU protection of physical pages. When one looks at a platform, what is the definition of a CPU? Multi-core packages and Hyper-Threading Technology makes a CPU definition very important.

CPU Definition

Chapter 12 is going to use a definition of CPU as a computing thread. A device that implements Hyper-Threading Technology (HT Technology) would have two CPUs. LaGrande Technology (LT) treats the device with the two CPU threads as two entirely different devices.

If the platform includes two or more packages (and think of packages as the actual physical device one places on the motherboard), then the number of CPUs is the total of all CPU threads. If the device did not implement HT Technology, and there were two packages on the platform, the count of CPU threads would be two. If the devices did implement HT Technology, and there were two packages on the platform, the count of CPU threads would be four. The four coming from two CPU threads on each package and there being two packages.

Multi-core packages add an additional dimension to the CPU thread count. A multi-core package provides complete CPU cores in a single package. Assuming that the multi-core package has two cores and both cores implement HT Technology, the CPU thread count for the package would be four. A platform with two packages, both packages with two cores and all cores HT Technology-enabled, would have a CPU thread count of eight.

The current limiter to the number of packages supported by LT is the chipset. An LT platform only operates with a single chipset.[5]

CPU Synchronization

One can ask, "Why the focus on how many CPUs are present?" The answer[6] involves the GETSEC [SENTER] disruptive event which has a main goal of gaining control of the page tables. What happens with multiple CPUs if the page tables and protections do not match? If one CPU says protect page 22 and the other CPU says page 22 has no protection, you face a very real possibility that software could expose data that is supposedly under protection. The physical pages are just the tip of the iceberg; unsynchronized CPUs could expose numerous items.

The goal of GETSEC [SENTER] is to force a mechanism, like reset, that requires all of the CPUs to have a consistent view of the platform. The mechanism must contemplate the addition or removal of a CPU from the platform.

---

[5] Chapter 15 talks about the future of LT and possible extensions.

[6] Another answer might be that we know what is good for the system. But that answer is so short, one might not be motivated to purchase this book.

Be Sure that the Launch Can Detect Any Tampering

In addition to the hardware mechanisms for GETSEC [SENTER], the launch process has software components that are susceptible to tampering during the launch process. The GETSEC [SENTER] process does not protect the software components from tampering. Instead, the process ensures that the measurement process detects any tampering of the software. In addition to detecting tampering, the measurement process provides the building block for the next objective: knowing the identity of the protected partition.

Knowing the Identity of the Launched Environment

What does identity mean in relation to the protected partition? LT defines identity to be the software that is in use during the protected partition launch. Identity corresponds to the protected partition environment. To provide the identity value, the launch process obtains the digital hash of the code. An inherent property of a hash algorithm is that a single bit change in the input should result in at least 50 percent of the output bits changing. If the hash output represents the identity of the launched environment, and it does, then the single bit change, and the resulting new hash output value, represents a new identity. The new identity based on a single bit change is the exact property desired of the launching and measuring process.

Ensure Properly Configured Hardware

Just as the software identity is important, so is the configuration of the hardware. Some hardware configurations can cause the protected partition to assume that certain protections are in place when the hardware is unable to actually provide the protection. Chapter 12 describes these concerns in detail. Part of the configuration verification uses the secure initialization (SINIT) module. Chapter 11 discusses the loading and execution of the SINIT module. Chapter 12 covers what the SINIT module validates.

The GETSEC [SENTER] Sequence

To accomplish the launch of the MVMM, the GETSEC [SENTER] process follows a set sequence. Figure 11.2 illustrates the SENTER sequence.

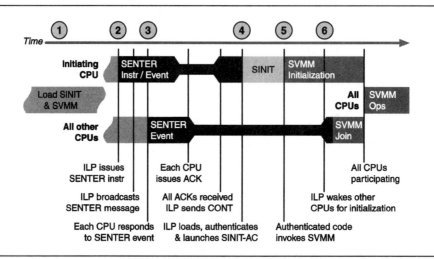

Figure 11.2   The SENTER Sequence

To understand the sequence, you should be familiar with the following definitions:

■ The definition of CPU thread as defined earlier in this chapter.

■ A processor is a CPU thread; a processor is not a package. While the equivalence of processor and thread can create some ambiguity, both terms have been in use for many years. Both terms are used to describe a CPU thread.[7]

■ Initiating Logical Processor (ILP) is the processor that starts the GETSEC [SENTER] sequence. The ILP must be the same processor as the Bootstrap Processor (BSP).

■ Responding Logical Processor (RLP) is any other processor on the platform other than the ILP. The "responding" aspect reflects the fact that all other processors must respond to the messages from the ILP.

---

[7] I understand fully the possible confusion between thread and processor. My early background was in software and thread has a very specific meaning there.

■ Broadcast is the mechanism whereby the ILP sends information to all of the other processors.

■ Sleep is where the processor is performing no operations other than looking for a wakeup message.

Figure 11.2 illustrates the GETSEC [SENTER] process. The numbers refer to points in time and where specific actions take place. The following sections describe each step and the rationale behind it.

Loading the Modules

Before actually executing the GETSEC [SENTER] instruction, the entity currently controlling the CPU must locate the SINIT and MVMM and load them into memory. The controlling entity could be an operating system or the BIOS. The type of controlling entity makes no difference to the GETSEC [SENTER] process. Any software that has control of ring 0 can initiate the GETSEC [SENTER] process.

The controlling entity loads the SINIT module and the MVMM into memory. Neither the SINIT module nor the MVMM has any protection against modification at this time. The design of LT does not require any protection to the modules, and if modification does occur, the GETSEC [SENTER] process detects the tampering.

The SINIT module must reside in a contiguous section of memory. The MVMM uses a page table to indicate the physical pages that contain the MVMM.

SINIT Module Size Requirements

The SINIT module's address and size are parameters of the GETSEC [SENTER] command. The ILP evaluates the address to be sure that the address is on a modulo-4,096 boundary, and the size is 0 modulo-64. Furthermore, the size must be larger than the minimum and smaller than the maximum. The minimum and maximum are processor type-specific. Any errors result in a general protection violation.

MVMM Layout Requirements

The MVMM uses physical pages and a page table to indicate the location of the MVMM. The page table must follow the rules for page tables on the current platform.

Executing GETSEC [SENTER]

With the SINIT and MVMM in memory, the stage is set to start the sequence. The ILP issues the GETSEC [SENTER] instruction. GETSEC is the new instruction that implements all of the VMX commands.

It is important to differentiate between the GETSEC [SENTER] *process* and the SENTER *message*. The GETSEC [SENTER] process is part of the GETSEC instruction. The SENTER message is a result of the GETSEC [SENTER] process.

Before invoking GETSEC [SENTER], the following conditions must be present:

■ The processor must be executing in Ring 0.

■ The processor cache must be available.

■ A LT-enabled chipset must be present.

■ The Trusted Platform Module (TPM) must be present.

■ No MVMM can be executing, therefore only one MVMM can execute at any one moment in time.[8]

■ The processor cannot be in authenticated code mode.

■ The process cannot be in VMX mode.

■ The ILP must be the boot-strap processor (BSP).

■ No outstanding machine-check error conditions exist.

If any of these conditions are not true, the GETSEC [SENTER] process signals a general protection violation. After validating all of the preceding conditions, the ILP issues the SENTER-ACK message.

With the preceding group of requirements and the fact that the GETSEC [SENTER] process takes time, it is a requirement on the invoking entity, OS or BIOS, to ensure the proper environment. The invoking entity should ensure, with all reasonable checks that the GETSEC [SENTER] process will succeed.

---

[8] Do not confuse the restriction on concurrent MVMM execution with sequential MVMM execution. It is possible and desirable to execute one MVMM, terminate the MVMM, and then execute a separate MVMM.

Issuing SENTER-ACK

The issuing of the SENTER-ACK message starts the disruption that the architects designed into LT. Before the SENTER-ACK message is sent, errors would result in a general protection violation. After issuing the SENTER-ACK message, errors result in an LT-shutdown. You can find the complete details of the LT-shutdown later in this chapter.

The ILP issues the SENTER-ACK message on the front-side bus. All other processors, such as the RLPs, must respond to the SENTER-ACK message. The RLPs respond to the SENTER-ACK on the next instruction boundary, so the time before all RLPs respond is variable.

Enumerating the RLP

The ILP needs a mechanism for collating all of the responses from the RLPs. Putting the mechanism in the CPU requires entirely new logic in the CPU. The chipset already has a mechanism that keeps track of individual processors in the system, the bus-agent ID. The chipset assigns to each processor a bus-agent ID and uses the ID to route messages on the front-side bus.

When the chipset receives the SENTER-ACK message, the chipset requires a response from every previously identified bus-agent ID. When a response is present from each RLP, the chipset sets a flag to indicate that all RLPs received and responded to the SENTER-ACK. The ILP polls the flag and waits until the flag is set. Failure to set the flag within a time-out period results in an LT-shutdown.

Each RLP upon receipt of the SENTER-ACK, issues the response to indicate to the chipset the acceptance of the GETSEC [SENTER] processing. The RLP only indicates acceptance of the SENTER-ACK on the next instruction boundary. Only responding at instruction boundaries allows the RLP to treat the SENTER-ACK as an interrupt. This approach simplifies the new code necessary to handle the SENTER-ACK.

RLP Sleep

After responding to the SENTER-ACK, the RLP moves into an SMX sleep state. The sleep state places the RLP into a mode where the RLP waits for the ILP to indicate the successful completion of the ILP GETSEC [SENTER] process.

The SMX sleep state is an important piece of the GETSEC [SENTER] puzzle. By placing the RLP into SMX sleep, the RLP is not executing any instructions. With the RLP not executing, the RLP makes no attempts to access any platform resources. The most important resource the RLP does not access is physical memory.

Ensuring Processor Participation

A major result of the SENTER-ACK and the RLP sleep is the assurance that all processors are participating in the GETSEC [SENTER] process. With all RLPs responding to the SENTER-ACK, the design provides a hardware mechanism that ensures GETSEC [SENTER] participation of all platform processors.

ILP Processing

When the chipset indicates to the ILP the receipt of the acknowledgement from all of the RLPs, the ILP continues the GETSEC [SENTER] process.

Inhibit External Events

Issuing the SENTER-ACK causes the ILP to mask external events. The RLPs mask external events upon receipt of the SENTER-ACK. The events masked include INIT, A20M, NMI, and SMI. Under normal conditions, event handlers process the event. The secure environment needs specific handlers that ensure handling of the event does not leak secrets. Once the secure environment establishes handlers for these events, the events are unmasked. The A20M event remains masked during the entire duration of the protected partition.

Validate Chipset and TPM

The ILP now validates that no outstanding valid uncorrectable machine-check error conditions are present. Prior to issuing the SENTER-ACK, the ILP did the same validation. The second check ensures that no error occurred in any of the RLPs while the RLPs responded to the SENTER-ACK message. The response to the machine-check being present is not a general protection violation, but the more serious LT-shutdown. Here's the reason: after sending the SENTER-ACK message and having all of the RLPs in a sleep state, no execution environment is available.

Verify Power Management Settings

The ILP verifies that the current power management settings are appropriate. The ILP determines appropriateness by looking at the current voltage ID and the bus ratio values held in the GV3 model-specific register (MSR).[9] If the values are not appropriate, the ILP attempts to change the values. If the attempt fails, the ILP issues an LT-shutdown.

Power settings are important to the protected partition because a processor running at power settings that are on the edge of the power envelope could execute unpredictably. Unpredictable execution could lead to an exposure of memory under control of the protected partition. Once the MVMM has control of the system, the MVMM could decide to allow power settings other than the defaults set by the GETSEC [SENTER] process. This change to the settings is permissible as the MVMM can report what the MVMM allows or rejects.

Lock the Chipset to the ILP

A major security tenet is that of defense in depth. Depth of defense means that the design should contemplate more than one attack. The only devices on the front-side bus are CPUs. Every CPU other than the ILP is an RLP. All of the RLPs are in the SMX sleep state. No accesses should be occurring from these processors. To ensure that this is true, the ILP locks the chipset so that only accesses from the ILP are valid. The ILP uses the ILP bus-agent ID to indicate to the chipset that only accesses with the specified ID are permissible.

The lock remains in effect until the ILP specifically releases the lock. The ILP keeps the lock on until the MVMM needs to activate the RLPs.

---

[9] The majority of the power settings are in the GV3 MSR, however specific devices and platforms may have additional MSRs that the SINIT code needs to check. The inclusion of device-specific checks is one advantage of the SINIT ACM.

SINIT Processing

The ILP has assurance that the RLP are sleeping, that only the ILP can communicate with the chipset, and that external events are masked. The ILP now needs to validate various hardware settings. The ILP performs these validations using the SINIT module. The ILP must locate the SINIT module, load it, validate it, and then execute it. SINIT is an Authenticated Code Module (ACM), as described in Chapter 7.

SINIT Load

The SINIT code, loaded by the OS or BIOS, still resides in the same physical memory location. Nothing in GETSEC [SENTER] or the SENTER-ACK processing made any changes to the SINIT code. Up to this point, the hardware provides no protection to the SINIT code. Any RLP, prior to the SENTER-ACK response, or any DMA device could manipulate the SINIT code. SINIT is an ACM to mitigate the vulnerabilities that unprotected code enables.

The GETSEC [SENTER] instruction, takes as one parameter, the location of the SINIT module. The ILP now uses that location to load SINIT into the ACM execution area.

The ACM area provides protection from external bus snoops and the memory type must be WriteBack (WB). If the ILP finds that the WB condition is not present, the ILP forces an LT-shutdown.

Once SINIT is in the ACM execution area, the ILP ensures that the ILP executes in a mode where internal and external events do not disrupt the execution of SINIT. The protections are an inherent feature of ACM, but they have a direct security benefit: the SINIT code executes without any interference. Knowing that the SINIT code runs without interference allows the SINIT code to validate portions of the current hardware configuration. Chapter 13 discusses the platform issues under review by SINIT.

Authenticate the SINIT Module

The SINIT module is a normal ACM module, and ACM modules require a specific format. Chapter 7 discusses the format in detail, but to reiterate, the module has three main sections:

■ Module header

■ Internal working scratch space

■ User code and data

Module Header

The module header contains information necessary to allow the ACM authenticated code processing to validate the SINIT module. The chipset manufacturer is the entity that must vouch for the SINIT module and perform a digital signature on the module. The chipset contains the hash of the public key that can validate the module. An improperly formed SINIT header results in the ILP issuing LT-shutdown.

The ILP obtains the hash of the signing key, from the chipset, using special LT front-side bus cycles. The module header includes the public key that signed the module. The ILP then calculates the SHA-1 hash of the public key in the module header. The ILP compares the hash from the chipset with the calculated hash and if they match, SINIT load continues. A mismatch results in an LT-shutdown.

Validating the Module

With the public key validated, the ILP can now validate that the SINIT is the proper module. Chapter 7 describes the format of those parts of the AC module that the digital signature covers. The ILP calculates a SHA-1 of the appropriate area and then performs a digital signature validation of the module.

The digital signature validation fails with a change to a single bit. Since the SINIT module was attackable until loaded into the ACM execution area, this signature validation is critical. It proves that the SINIT module has no modifications. Any attempt to modify the SINIT code results in the digital signature validation failing. The digital signature validation failure results in an LT-shutdown.

As SINIT is an authenticated code module, an attacker cannot modify the SINIT code in a manner that allows the SINIT code to pass the digital signature validation. The validation detects any tampering with the SINIT module, thus meeting the requirement for tamper detection.[10] The LT hardware enforces the validation and provides assurance that the SINIT code does validate the hardware settings properly. Using the hardware to perform the digital signature validation enforces a model that allows only SINIT code from the chipset vendor to execute.

After validating the signature, the ILP places the 20-byte SINIT module hash in the first 20 bytes of the scratch space. The ILP does not save the 20-byte hash of the signature key.

---

[10] The requirement is not to stop tampering, just detect the tampering.

Storing SINIT Measurement

Attestation requires an accurate measurement and the proper storage of that measurement. The ILP just completed an accurate measurement of the SINIT module. The result of that measurement is the 20-byte hash value in the scratch space. The TPM is the attestation device on the platform, so the ILP needs to send the 20 bytes to the TPM without any interference.

TPM Bus Considerations

The ILP needs to move the SINIT measurement from the currently executing GETSEC [SENTER] instruction to the TPM. The measurement has to travel from the CPU to the MCH over the FSB, from the MCH to the ICH over the hublink, and from the ICH to the TPM over the LPC bus.

It was tempting to consider using a bus like USB, but these busses present some major problems. The first problem is that the processors are masking all events. Therefore, any bus requiring an interrupt cannot work. The only executing processor is the ILP; and the ILP is executing AC code, which has a size limit of around 32 kilobytes. A USB handler and the code to perform the hardware validation would not fit in that size. The bus cannot be a complex bus requiring software handling. The next issue with the bus is the ability to indicate to the TPM that the GETSEC [SENTER] microcode has control of the CPU. A bus like USB does not have the ability to ensure that no other device can generate the signal.

With the USB bus ruled out, and like busses also, the requirement remains of moving the measurement from the CPU to the TPM. The bus of choice is the LPC bus. The LPC bus is available at all times and does not require any interrupts. Another nice feature of the LPC bus is that addressing is available with memory maps. When and how LT uses the features of the LPC bus is revealed in the rest of the GETSEC [SENTER] process.

Setting the PCR

The ILP needs to send the SINIT measurement to the TPM via the indicated busses. The ILP uses TPM commands and special addresses to indicate the CPU control. Figure 11.3 provides the illustration of the process for storing the measurement in the TPM.

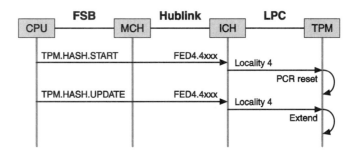

Figure 11.3 TPM.HASH.START Process

The ILP issues a `TPM.HASH.START` command by issuing a single-byte write to the `TPM.HASH.START` port. The definition for the `TPM.HASH.START` command is in the *TCG PC Specific Specification-TPM Interface Specification* (TIS). The `TPM.HASH.START` port is a memory mapped address at location `0xFED4_4xxx`. The ICH reserves the `0xFED4` range for TPM access. Locality 4 access occurs in the `4xxx` range. The ICH blocks all access to `0xFED4_4xxx` unless the CPU indicates that the `GETSEC [SENTER]` microcode is executing.

The ILP uses special FSB cycles to indicate the execution of the `GETSEC [SENTER]` microcode. When receiving the command, the special FSB cycle sends the command to the ICH using special cycles on the Hublink. The ICH accepts the command and writes the command to the TPM on the LPC bus using the `0xFED4_4xxx` address.

The TPM only accepts the `TPM.HASH.START` command on the `0xFED4_4xxx` address range. Using any other address for sending the command to the TPM results in an error condition in the TPM. The combination of the ICH enforcing the protection on the address and the TPM only accepting the command on the address produces an assurance that the `TPM.HASH.START` command only arrives at the TPM during the `GETSEC [SENTER]` process.

TPM Response to TPM.HASH.START

Upon receipt of the `TPM.HASH.START` command, the TPM performs two critical operations: resetting of the dynamic PCR and setting the mode of the TPM to accept any measurements.

Resetting the dynamic PCR involves the TPM setting the PCR to their default values. The TIS specifies that the default value is `0x00` for all bytes in the PCR. The PCRs that are reset using `TPM.HASH.START` are PCRs 17 through 20.

The TPM sets the internal state of the TPM such that the TPM is ready to accept the bytes of the measurement. The TPM clears the TPM input buffer and locks the TPM such that only commands from locality 4 are acceptable.

ILP Measurement Transmission

The PCRs are at the default values and the TPM is awaiting further locality 4 commands. The ILP sends the 20-byte hash value stored in the scratch space by looping through each of the 20 bytes, starting with the least significant byte of the hash. The ILP uses the TPM.HASH.DATA port to perform the writes.

The ILP then performs four single-byte writes of the contents of EDX to the TPM using the TPM.HASH.DATA port. The contents of EDX provide a proof of the parameters set when invoking the GETSEC [SENTER] command. The parameters provide an indication of the level of functionality enabled for use by the protected partition.

The ILP terminates the SINIT measurement by performing a single-byte write of a 0x00 to the TPM.HASH.END port. Upon receipt of the TPM.HASH.END command, the TPM takes the information in the TPM input buffer, which is the SINIT hash value, and the contents of EDX, and performs a TPM_Extend operation to PCR 17. The TPM now contains the SINIT measurement. The TPM provides the protection on PCR 17.

The TPM.HASH.xxx commands bypass the normal LPC bus communication protocols. The bypass allows for ILP microcode that is simpler and smaller.

Initialize ILP State

With the SINIT measurement safely reported to the TPM, the ILP can now make ready to pass control to the SINIT. The ILP needs to initialize the ILP internal state to allow the execution of the SINIT module. A complete resetting of the ILP state is not needed, but certain registers and tables need initialization. The information as to how to set the registers and tables comes from the SINIT module header. A partial list of the items set is:

■ Global Descriptor Table Register (GDTR)

■ Registers CS, DS, SS, and ES

Unlocking the Chipset

The chipset locked down various areas upon receipt of the SENTER-ACK message. The ILP now needs to start opening the locked down areas of the chipset. The ILP issues the LT.CMD.OPEN-PRIVATE message. The message informs the chipset that the SINIT begins executing soon and the SINIT needs access to chipset resources. The ILP issues the LT.CMD.OPEN-PRIVATE message to the chipset using special FSB cycles. The cycles ensure that only the ILP can properly issue the message.

In addition to unlocking the chipset LT private space, the ILP also unlocks the chipset locality 3 TPM address of 0xFED4_3xxx. This space is available to the SINIT module and allows the SINIT module to identify itself to the TPM.

GETSEC [SENTER] Completion

At this point, the GETSEC [SENTER] instruction is complete. The ILP has loaded and authenticated the SINIT module, and it has set the ILP internal state such that SINIT execution is possible.

The ILP and RLPs that were once active now assert an indication that the processor is executing in SMX mode for all bus memory read transactions. This assertion continues until the execution of GETSEC [SEXIT]. The mechanism in place to make the assertion is to use signals on the FSB on all bus memory transactions. Failure to assert the signal when attempting a bus memory transaction results in the chipset issuing an LT-shutdown.

SINIT Execution

The ILP passes control to the SINIT module now. The SINIT code has the following main objectives:

- Test for proper hardware configurations (See Chapter 13 for a detailed explanation of the test)
- Initialize the SMM handling
- Enable the NoDMA handling
- Load and measure the MVMM
- Store the MVMM measurement in the TPM
- Pass control to the MVMM

Initialize SMM Handling

The MVMM has a peer monitor that manages System Management Interrupts (SMI). This peer monitor is the SMI Transfer Monitor (STM). Chapter 7 discusses the SMI handling model. The STM has some configuration options that the SINIT module must validate to ensure proper connection to the MVMM. If the processor MSEG MSR indicates the enabling of the STM, the SINIT code validates the following actions:

1. Read the chipset `LT MSEG.BASE` and `SIZE` registers.

2. Compare the processor MSEG MSR address field to the chipset `MSEG.BASE`. Addresses that are different indicate a configuration error with the STM. In that case, the ILP issues an `LT-shutdown`.

3. Read the STM header, which is located at the base of the MSEG. Extract the STM image size from the header.

4. Beginning from the base of the MSEG, read the STM image up to the size specified in the header. Add each byte of the image to a SHA-1 hash.

5. Starting from the end of the STM image size, write zeros into the remainder of the MSEG region. Writing in these zeros prevents attacks where non-STM code was present in the scratch or data areas of the STM, which later allows some attack mechanism to be invoked by the code.

6. Complete the SHA-1 operation and obtain the 20-byte hash value.

7. Using `0xFED4_3xxx`, locality 3, issue a `TPM_Extend`[11] operation to PCR 17 with the hash value that was created in the previous step. PCR 17 now contains the values of both the SINIT and STM.

---

[11] While we attempted to minimize the TPM-specific code in the microcode during the storage of the SINIT measurement, the SINIT code itself can use the normal TPM commands.

STM and NoDMA

The MSEG area is part of protected memory just like the MVMM. The MSEG area does not require the setting of any NoDMA bits. The chipset automatically blocks all inbound access to SMRAM, and SMRAM includes the MSEG. To make writing the MVMM easier, and for simplicity, the NoDMA table may contain the MSEG pages. The reason for simplicity here is that the MVMM might undergo evaluation. Not having special paths in the code for the STM makes the code smaller and easier to evaluate.

Enable NoDMA

With the ILP CPU memory protections turned on, the SINIT code needs to enable the chipset protections against DMA accesses. Enabling the chipset to provide DMA access protection allows the use of main system memory for protected operations.

While the CPUs—that term includes the ILP and all RLPs—are quiet, DMA devices have no such restriction. A DMA-capable device could initiate a DMA access during the GETSEC [SENTER] process. The chipset is responsible for handling any race conditions where the chipset receives indication to add the page to the NoDMA table and receives a DMA request to access the page. The chipset can automatically protect the NoDMA table, but since the table resides at a known offset from the base address, nothing requires the chipset to add the address of the NoDMA table itself to the NoDMA table.

The chipset may support caches or manually created hash tables. These changes could result in better performance. If the chipset supports the improvements, the SINIT code is responsible for setting the controls correctly.

SCLEAN Validation

Chapter 12 discusses the issues of ensuring proper cleanup after resets or other events. One of the mechanisms performs a "scrub" of memory. Scrubbing involves writing a zero to every byte of memory. SCLEAN is the authenticated code module that performs the scrub.

SINIT needs to validate the installation of the correct SCLEAN module. The TPM holds the module identity in either a PCR or a NV storage location. SINIT loads the SCLEAN module identity and then validates that the SCLEAN is an appropriate module. If the validation fails, SINIT terminates with an LT-shutdown.

MVMM Loading

The SINIT now loads and measures the MVMM. The basic process is to protect a page, read the page and then measure the page.

The first item to find is the MVMM heap. The chipset holds the information in the LT.HEAP.BASE and SIZE registers. The MVMM then adds these pages to the NoDMA table. With the heap protected, the SINIT can now load the MVMM page table.

The SINIT page table is at a specific offset in the MVMM heap. The SINIT verifies that the MVMM page table follows some basic rules. The rules may be processor-specific, but generically they are:

■ Page table entries go from low memory addresses to higher addresses.

■ The page table entry type is fixed for all entries in the table. The actual type is processor-specific.

If the page table does not follow the rules, the SINIT initiates an LT-shutdown. SINIT now performs the following actions for each page in the MVMM page table:

1. Add the page to the NoDMA table. Adding the page to the NoDMA table also invalidates any cache entries for the page, ensuring that the next read of the page, which occurs in the next step, actually reads the physical page.

2. Read the page.

3. Add the page contents to a SHA-1 hash.

After protecting, reading, and hashing all of the MVMM pages, the SINIT module completes the SHA-1 hash. The resulting hash value is the measurement of the MVMM. The TPM needs to receive the MVMM measurement. The SINIT extends PCR [18] using the TPM locality 3 port. Locality 4 is not available to the SINIT module.

The MVMM digest value is in a different PCR than the SINIT identity. This separation is not an issue as when using the TPM. The sealing entity can specify both PCR and ensure that the entire environment—SINIT, SCLEAN, STM, and MVMM—are identical.

Passing Control to the MVMM

The NoDMA table is protecting all of the MVMM pages; the TPM holds the MVMM identity so the last action of the SINIT module is to pass control to the MVMM. The MVMM entry point is part of the MVMM header structure. The SINIT extracts the MVMM entry point and then far-jumps to the entry point. The SINIT uses the `GETSEC [EXITAC]` instruction to perform the jump.

The `GETSEC [EXITAC]` instruction automatically changes the paging mode, sets `CS:EIP` and `SS:ESP` and returns the processor cache to normal operation.

MVMM Execution

The MVMM now has control of the ILP and needs to complete the `GETSEC [SENTER]` process.[12] The initialization process, while complete from the `GETSEC [SENTER]` standpoint, is still a long ways from being able to execute user code. The MVMM has to re-enable interrupts, enable the SMI Transfer Monitor, and rendezvous the RLP. After accomplishing the rendezvous, the MVMM can then perform any additional MVMM initialization.

Enabling Interrupts

Interrupts disabled during the activities of the `GETSEC [SENTER]` instruction now need enabling. The MVMM establishes an IDT entry and enables the ILP to take interrupts. Having the MVMM allow interrupts implies that the MVMM is sufficiently initialized to handle the interrupts when they occur. The MVMM does not enable the RLP to take interrupts at this time. The only process able to take interrupts is the ILP.

The MVMM interrupt handler must be able to accept and handle all interrupts properly.

---

[12] The MVMM initialization steps are all MVMM-specific. While Intel proposes that the MVMM properly perform the steps, it is the responsibility of the MVMM to actually complete a valid initialization.

Enabling SMI

With normal interrupts enabled, the MVMM now needs to start accepting SMI. The timing of acceptance of SMI is very important. SMI comes in three main flavors: system, device, and platform.

System SMI

System SMI deals with information relative to system operation, like cooling and processor speed. The architects knew of one disaster scenario that needed a very complete solution: the case where the system was in a thermal event, where the CPU was too hot, and where the various sensors generated SMI to turn the cooling fans on. Ignoring those events for too long of a period could result in damage to the system.

Execution of `GETSEC [SENTER]` was complete upon passing control to the MVMM. The MVMM has two main roles: bring the RLPs into the MVMM environment and perform MVMM-specific initialization.

Secure Launch Recap

On numerous occasions when teaching this concept, I have teased audiences that seem to be slightly confused:

> I do not understand why you are confused. I have been working on this for many years and I just do not understand why you cannot pick it up in an hour or so.

Anyway, maybe a short recap is in order. The secure launch performed the following steps and operations:

- ■ *Rendezvous all processors, physical and logical*. The rendezvous ensures that all processors are aware of the `GETSEC [SENTER]` process and all processors will enter the MVMM environment.

- ■ *Select the ILP and put to sleep the RLP*. The ILP is the only processor executing and the sleeping RLP ensures that no extra transactions occur on any bus.

- ■ *Protect against outside events*. Outside events, like interrupts, could disrupt the ability of SINIT to properly determine the state of the platform and discover potential hardware misconfiguration.

■ *Load and verify the SINIT module.* The SINIT comes from the chipset manufacturer, is specific to the current platform hardware components, and no tampering of the SINIT code occurred.

■ *Store the SINIT measurement in the TPM.* The SINIT identity, stored in the TPM, allows for both SEAL operations to protect long-term secrets and the attestation of the SINIT code executed.

■ *Establish the NoDMA table.* Protect the MVMM from software attacks launched by entities other than a CPU.

■ *Protect and measure the MVMM.* Protecting each MVMM page allows the MVMM to protect itself. The MVMM measurement, in conjunction with the SINIT measurement, provides the exact MVMM environment that is executing.

■ *Store the MVMM measurement in the TPM.* The stored MVMM measurement enables both SEAL and attestation of the MVMM environment.

■ *Launch the MVMM.* The MVMM can now control the platform.

GETSEC [SEXIT] Processing

The late launch premise is that the protected environment can successfully terminate without requiring a reboot of the platform. The operand for this command is GETSET [SEXIT]. The GETSEC [SEXIT] command works as the reverse of GETSEC [SENTER].

Just as GETSEC [SENTER] needs all processors to rendezvous and have a consistent view of the protections, GETSEC [SEXIT] needs all processors to rendezvous and release all protections. Having one processor still believe that memory has protection results in the exposure of protected information.

GETSEC [SEXIT] does not have the complication that GETSEC [SENTER] does, in that no validation of the hardware configuration is needed. Also, you have no need to bootstrap a protected environment as the protected environment is already running. Without these needs, running an authenticated module during GETSEC [SEXIT] is unnecessary.[13]

---

[13] While the current implementation does not support the GETSEC [SEXIT] SINIT parallel ACM, Chapter 15 does discuss what the future may hold.

GETSEC [SEXIT] Initiation

To start the protected environment, any ring 0 code can call GETSEC [SENTER], as shown in Figure 11.4. The reverse is not true for GETSEC [SEXIT]. The MVMM controls the issuing of GETSEC [SEXIT] and the MVMM can block issuing of the command. The MVMM is the only entity on the platform that can issue GETSEC [SEXIT].

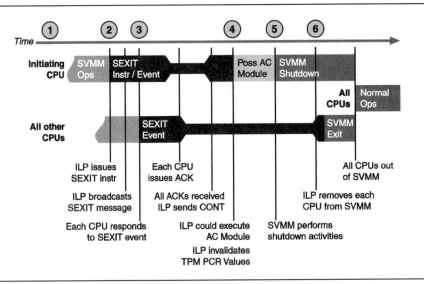

Figure 11.4   The GETSEC [SEXIT] Sequence

Once the MVMM issues the GETSEC [SEXIT] command, the following sequence occurs:

1.   Validate that the MVMM issued the command.

2.   Broadcast a message to rendezvous the processors.

3.   Ensure that all processors respond to the broadcast.

4.   Shut down the MVMM.

5.   Remove all protections and allow normal operations.

GETSEC [SEXIT] Validation

The processor receiving the GETSEC [SEXIT] must be the BSP, which becomes the ILP for the GETSEC [SEXIT] process. The ILP validates the GETSEC [SEXIT] command came from an executing MVMM. The various flags and modes must be present to continue GETSEC [SEXIT] processing. If the MVMM did not issue the GETSEC [SEXIT], the ILP issues a general protection violation.

GETSEC [SEXIT] Rendezvous

Just as the ILP issues the SENTER-ACK for GETSEC [SENTER], the ILP issues the SEXIT-ACK message for GETSEC [SEXIT]. The mechanism is the same for GETSEC [SENTER] and GETSEC [SEXIT]. After the ILP issues the SEXIT-ACK, each of the RLP responds to the message such that the chipset knows that all processors responded.

The same restrictions apply for GETSEC [SEXIT]: the bus-agent ID identifies the processor, and the chipset matches responses to known IDs and failure to have all processors respond results in an LT-shutdown.

After the rendezvous, the GETSEC [SENTER] starts and executes an authenticated code module. The GETSEC [SEXIT], being already in a protected environment, needs no authenticated module.

MVMM Shutdown

The MVMM has ultimate control of the platform. While requests to start the MVMM can occur from any ring-0 process, termination of the MVMM environment is under control of the MVMM itself.

Outside entities can make requests to the MVMM to terminate, but the MVMM has the final say to actually execute the GETSEC [SEXIT] command. The MVMM, when requested to terminate, can refuse the request and continue operations. The MVMM can accept the termination request, but prior to the termination; perform other operations prior to the MVMM termination.

After all protected environments are shut down, the ILP sends the SEXIT-CONTINUE message to each RLP. The RLP accepts the command, removes all protections in the platform, and moves to execute the next instruction. The next instruction was designated as the instruction to execute upon receipt of the SEXIT-ACK. The setting of the next instruction is one reason that the MVMM must control when the GETSEC [SEXIT] operation is valid. The best practice would be to put the RLP into some sort of sleep state. After the GETSEC [SEXIT] execution, then the operating system would wake up the processors.

LT-Shutdown

Many times in this chapter, the issuing of the LT-shutdown is the response to an error. LT-shutdown is a special error that makes sure that the error condition does not result in the exposure of protected information.

LT-shutdown first writes to the chipset's LT.CRASH register the LT-shutdown error code. The error code indicates the type of LT-shutdown that is occurring.

The processor then writes to the LT.CMD.SYS-RESET register, the system issues an LT special cycle to initiate a platform reset. All processors, in response to the special cycle, enter a shutdown sleep state. The sleep state masks:

- External pin events
- LT bus events or error events
- Machine check signaling
- Other internal states

Only the assertion of a platform reset takes the processor out of the sleep state. The reset does not clear the LT.CRASH register, so the cause of the LT-shutdown is available after the reset.

The LT-shutdown can occur as part of most of the GETSEC leaf functions when recovery from the error would not result in a reliable state. Reliable state would include the inability to complete the GETSEC [SENTER] process.

Legacy IA-32 triple-fault shutdown conditions convert to an LT-shutdown. This conversion generally occurs in the state between GETSEC [SENTER] and GETSEC [SEXIT]. If the processor is in VMX mode, and the triple-fault causes a guest to exit back to the MVMM, the exit to the guest supersedes conversion to an LT-shutdown. If the triple-fault occurs in the MVMM, the conversion does occur.

Chapter 12

Configuration Concerns

Where large sums of money are concerned, it is advisable to trust nobody.

— Agatha Christie (1890–1976)

One could instantly trust the hardware of a platform with LaGrande Technology (LT), but is it possible that troubles could lurk in the hardware? The answer is yes; some hardware configurations make it difficult for the hardware to mitigate threats to a protected partition. The configurations that can cause these problems are discoverable, and during the protected partition launch, the launch process verifies the state of the hardware.

LT works in the Ronald Reagan mode of "Trust but verify." Various components on the platform set up the hardware to operate properly. The configuration of the devices occurs when a protected environment is not available. The protected environment assumes a proper hardware configuration and attempts to verify the current settings.

LT Chipset

An LT platform requires the presence of an LT-capable chipset. The CPU and chipset work in concert for numerous operations, and if the chipset is not capable of supporting LT, the CPU must not start the protected environment.

The GETSEC [SENTER] operation validates the existence of an LT-capable chipset. The validation occurs at the very start of the GETSEC [SENTER] operation. If GETSEC [SENTER] determines that no LT chipset is present, the GETSEC [SENTER] process terminates with a general protection fault. The error does not cause an LT-shutdown because the chipset check occurs prior to any broadcast messages by the Initiating Logical Processor ILP.

The ILP checks an internal CPU register for the existence of the LT chipset. The CPU reset process sets the register. The check occurs on each reset and cold boot. The CPU interrogates the chipset, and if the chipset responds appropriately, the CPU indicates the presence of an LT-capable chipset.

LT chipset support requires the chipset to accept the various LT special cycles, include the LT public and private spaces, and fully support a version 1.2 TPM.

Memory Folding

The CPU gains access to system memory through the Graphics/Memory Controller Hub (G/MCH). The physical memory attaches to the G/MCH. The actual memory package allows configuration options which are settable by software.

One of the largest security concerns is memory *folding*. When two bus addresses point to the same physical location, folding occurs. Figure 12.1 illustrates the concept of folding, two addresses pointing to the same physical location.

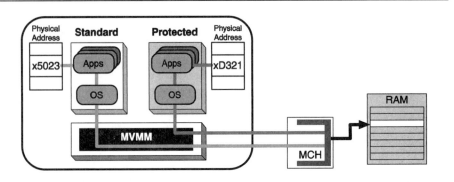

Figure 12.1   Memory Folding

Having two memory locations point at the same physical location leads to an easy attack in which one address is in the protected partition and the other address is not in the protected partition. It is possible to determine the presence of the folded memory configuration. The protected partition launch mechanism must test for and ensure that the folding is not occurring.

Trusting Memory

First, you have to deal with the possibility that folding can occur in system memory and there is no way to use a single byte of the system memory to execute any programs. The system needs some area where code can execute. The solution here is the use of *authenticated code* (AC) modules. An AC module runs without the use of any system memory. One major reason for the design of AC modules is to specifically mitigate memory aliasing threats.

SINIT is the AC module that performs the configuration checks. Chapter 12 shows all of the SINIT functions except the memory check. By using the AC module, not one byte of system memory requires protection prior to the protected partition launch.[1]

Chipset-Specific

The mechanisms to configure the physical memory packages are chipset-specific. The checks necessary to determine that aliasing is occurring are also chipset-specific. Adding chipset-specific code to the CPU is not a good idea, so the SINIT design also provides a way to load and execute chipset-specific code.

The first security idea was to place the memory-fold check in the CPU. Having the check in the CPU results in very good security properties; it does not work well in practice. The CPU works with numerous chipsets. The CPU would need to contain lots of extra code that would never be in use. Using the SINIT places the code execution in the CPU and allows for chipset-specific code. The SINIT module is from the chipset manufacturer and does not need to contain code for other chipsets.

---

[1] What a happy day that was when the LT development team came to the realization that AC mode was the mitigation for memory aliasing.

Locking the Memory Configuration

The SINIT code, prior to any memory authentication, locks the configuration. The rationale behind locking and then verifying is to avoid any chance that, after verification but before the lock, the configuration undergoes some change. The chances for changing the configuration are low, but it is possible, so the design attempts to mitigate the possibility.

The lock mechanism is a combination of actions. The SINIT code issues the LT.CMD.LOCK-MEMCONFIG command to the chipset. The chipset, upon receipt of the command, locks the memory configuration. The lock remains in place until the execution of the GETSEC [SEXIT] operand.

Testing the Configuration

The code necessary to perform the actual test for memory folding is chipset-specific. Those needing to write the code need to understand the nitty-gritty details of the chipset in question. Any failures in the configuration result in the SINIT code issuing an LT-shutdown.

GART/Graphics Aliasing

The SINIT code went to a lot of trouble to verify that two logical addresses do not point to the same physical page. The Graphics Address Relocation Table (GART) provides a mechanism to change the address of a request. The GART allows the page frames for a graphics device to be in a different location then the graphics buffer. The result is a translation that occurs when moving information from one location to the other. Attempts to manipulate an address have a translation that directs the request to the correct physical page.

Figure 12.2 illustrates the translations that the GART performs. Addresses in the graphics aperture undergo a translation to a physical address.

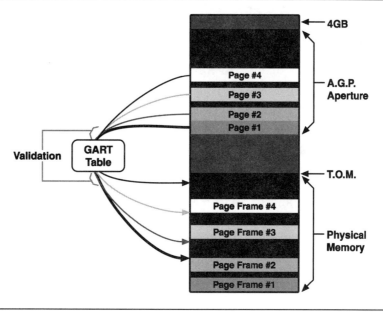

Figure 12.2   Graphics Address Relocation Table (GART) Aliasing

After working so hard to locate and avoid the memory folding, automatically adding it back again is difficult to do.

LT cannot remove the GART translation; too much code and design already take advantage of the GART. The trick is to ensure that no secrets leak when using the GART.

Ensure GART Properties

Leaving the GART in the design requires a modification to the actual translation. The LT GART processing allows the translation but ensures no change in protection mode.

If the first address requires protection, the translated address must require protection after GART processing. If the first address has no protection, the translated address also requires no protection. The chipset enforces the validation on each GART translation when protections are in place.

System Memory Overlap

Another potential problem arises when GART addresses overlap the system aperture. The overlap represents a serious vulnerability and one that must not occur. The SINIT code must validate that the aperture does not overlap with GART addresses. If the SINIT discovers such an overlap, the SINIT issues an `LT-shutdown`.

Power and Frequency

A few years ago, the only consideration for a processor was how fast the processor could execute. Then laptops became popular and speed was not the only consideration; heat and battery life became important.

Heat

A slight detour here for a discussion of the author's background. Looking at my biography on the back cover, you will see lots of software experience and little hardware experience. When I started at Intel, some of the hardware concepts went right over my head. One of the concepts, while blindingly obvious to everyone else, was that a lot of heat builds up inside a PC platform, and platform designers need to spend lots of effort working on airflow, heat sinks, and the like. A corollary to all of the platform heat equations is that the speed you want to go relates directly to the heat in the platform. I thought that all one had to do was put another fan on the platform and all of the problems went away. Boy is that wrong! Proper heat sinks and moving the air from the inside to the outside and around the heat sinks is a difficult job. My group taught me that with modern platforms one gets better cooling with the cover on, as the platform design assumes the cover is present and uses the cover to properly move air and provide cooling. The purpose of the detour is to drive home the fact that correct operation of the platform requires proper configuration of the cooling system. In addition to cooling, there are other platform configuration options that require oversight and proper setup.

Overclocking

The question one may be asking right now is what does heat and cooling and frequencies have to do with security? The answer is surprising: lots. Platforms, and especially CPUs, have specific design points for power, frequency, and heat. Run the CPU too hot or too fast and the CPU might not execute correctly.

A thriving industry takes CPUs and attempts to overclock, or run the CPU faster than recommended by the manufacturer. Overclocking involves adding additional power to the CPU, causing it to run faster and also to run much hotter. Overclockers understand very well that when overclocking, additional cooling is necessary, and this issue is critical—at some speed the CPU will not function correctly. What does "not function correctly" mean? It means that the CPU will attempt to add 1 + 1 and not get 2. As the overclocking goes even higher, other operations cease to work properly, finally ending in the CPU becoming so confused that the CPU refuses to execute any more instructions.

Many of the overclocking configurations are available through software commands, and if software can manipulate a configuration to cause errors, it represents a security concern. Imagine a configuration that caused the CPU to improperly use the page table. If the attacker can reliably cause the improper page table to be used, the attacker might be able to read supposedly protected pages. One very important item to remember is that getting the same error to occur each time when overclocking is most likely not going to happen. However, the possibility does remain that overclocking represents a configuration that may not provide adequate protections.

While overclocking is an attempt to push the CPU to perform more tasks through faster execution, underclocking is merely an attempt to force bad things to happen. Underclocking involves not sending enough power to meet the listed operating frequency and can result in the same operational issues. Heat is not an issue with underclocking.

SINIT needs to ensure that, on startup, all CPU threads are operating inside of the normal range of power and frequency. SINIT performs the checks by ensuring that the CPU is either at the low end or the high end of the allowable frequency scale. The frequency scale is processor-specific and SINIT will know the valid ranges. After SINIT validates the frequency and power, SINIT locks the frequency setting. Once the MVMM has control of the platform, the MVMM can unlock the frequency settings and more finely tune the use of power and frequency.

SCHECK

Here's a minor piece of additional information—well, hopefully you'll feel it is minor. The actual implementation of SINIT could split some of the functionality into two modules. The rationale behind the split is timing. Performing all of the checks during the `GETSEC [SENTER]` process could result in a launch time that is too long. Some of the checks that SINIT performs can be one-time checks. To ensure these one-time checks occur only once, instead of each `GETSEC [SENTER]`, LT allows for the SCHECK AC module.

The SCHECK module performs the same functions as SINIT but the execution of the SCHECK occurs during platform startup. SCHECK only runs once per platform boot. When SCHECK executes, the module performs the configuration checks and locks the configuration. In addition to locking the configuration, upon successful completion of the SCHECK review, SCHECK sets a flag in the chipset indicating that the configuration is valid. SINIT, in the very first check after digital signature validation, checks that the chipset flag is set and then SINIT knows that the configuration is valid.

SCHECK is an Authenticated Code Module (ACM) and as such has all of the normal ACM protections. The module runs in Cache as RAM (CRAM) mode, has a digital signature, and runs without interruption due to the CRAM features.

Additional Platform Configurations

The areas listed so far do not represent the entirety of the platform configuration items that a MVMM must manage. Many of the additional areas are processor-specific, and SINIT checks those configuration settings. For those areas that are not processor-specific, the MVMM must understand the platform, understand the controls necessary to control the platform, and properly manage those controls.

New Issues

It is a very real possibility that a configuration option on a platform will be found, long after the writing of the SINIT code, to represent a security concern. A big advantage of having the SINIT module is that new concerns can be met by issuing a new SINIT module that validates that the configuration option is properly set.

Chapter 13

Hardware Attacks

I always cheer up immensely if an attack is particularly wounding because I think, well, if they attack one personally, it means they have not a single political argument left.

—Margaret Thatcher

If the LT system is protecting against software attacks, the attackers have no choice but to mount hardware attacks. The protection and attack matrix from Chapter 6 comes into play here. If the LT design has successfully pushed the attackers from using software attacks to attempting hardware attacks, can LT provide some protection from classes of hardware attacks?

When considering hardware attacks, a critical piece of information to remember is that the attacker needs to have physical possession of the machine. If the attacker is launching an attack from a remote location, the only way to execute the attack is with software. While it might be possible to have remote robots launch attacks in the future, this is a very remote possibility today. The hardware attacker must have physical contact, which means that the attacker can only attack one platform at a time.[1]

Many of the attacks in this chapter use front-side bus (FSB) mechanisms to mitigate the vulnerabilities. If platforms change from the FSB to some other bus, the new bus will support the same type of mitigations.

---

[1] Do not lose sight of the BORE attack potential. If the attacker can use a hardware attack on one platform, obtain the software secret, and then launch the remote software attacks, the system is not that robust. The design point is to ensure that all attacks using the same mechanism must be hardware attacks.

Rogue CPU

In a system with multiple CPUs, can an attacker manipulate a single CPU to avoid participation[2] in the protected environment? If the attacker can manipulate a CPU in this manner, the attacker would be able to access memory bypassing the VMX protections. Figure 13.1 shows how a rogue CPU attack might be mounted and defended against.

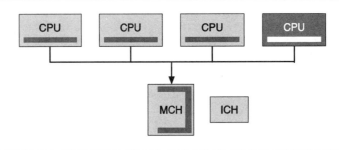

Figure 13.1   Rogue CPU

Not Joining the Protected Environment

The attacker could attempt to hold an RLP in some suspended state, and then after the establishment of the protected environment, take the RLP out of the suspended state. The GETSEC [SENTER] process detects this attack directly by ensuring that all bus agent IDs respond to the SENTER-ACK message. If the CPU ever sends a message on the FSB, the chipset assigns a bus-agent ID and requires a response from the CPU to indicate the receipt of the SENTER-ACK.

The attacker could attempt to suspend the CPU from the time of reset of the platform. The suspension of the CPU results in no traffic on the FSB and hence no assigned bus-agent ID. Without the bus-agent ID, the chipset would not fail the GETSEC [SENTER] process waiting for the CPU. To handle this type of attack, the chipset issues an LT-shutdown, if a CPU without a known bus-agent ID attempts to issue a message on the FSB while the protected environment is executing. The addition of any CPU in the system, while the protected environment is executing, results in an LT-shutdown.

---

[2] Participation is any operation that uses a resource external to the CPU package.

Not Exiting the Protected Environment

So you might ask: "with the join covered, can the attacker attempt to keep a CPU in the protected environment while all other CPUs exit the environment?" The answer is that the GETSEC [SEXIT] process ensures that all CPUs exit the environment. The ILP sends the SEXIT-ACK message, and all bus-agent IDs must respond. If the attacker attempts to hold the RLP in VMX mode, the chipset times out awaiting the response and causes an LT-shutdown.

The attack of holding the RLP from reset does not matter here. With the attacker waiting until the VMX environment goes away, no protected memory is available. The attacker gains no advantage waiting until the system has no secure environment because the chipset always registers the new bus-agent ID. When the platform attempts to launch another protected environment, the new RLP must respond.

Results of Suspending the CPU

The chipset detects attempts to suspend a CPU through the GETSEC [SENTER] process and to add a CPU after the GETSEC [SENTER] launch. The chipset detects attempts to hold a CPU in the protected environment through GETSEC [SEXIT]. The LT system therefore provides protection from a rogue CPU.

RESET Protection

The protections on memory require the graceful shutdown of GETSEC [SEXIT]. What happens if the graceful shutdown does not occur and the platform performs a reset? Would that expose protected memory?

Reset Definition

The first order of business is to define a reset. The system programming guide states:

> Following power-up or an assertion of the RESET# pin, each processor on the system bus performs a hardware initialization of the processor (known as hardware reset) and an optional built-in self-test (BIST). A hardware reset sets each processor's registers to a known state and places the processor in real-address mode. It also invalidates the internal caches, translation look-aside buffers (TLBs) and the branch target buffer (BTB). (Intel 2003)

Either by powering the system or by asserting the RESET# pin, initialization of the CPU internal state occurs. For our purposes, we make no distinction between the RESET# pin and power-up when looking at reset attacks. For the rest of this chapter "RESET" means RESET# pin or power-up cycling.

System Memory Properties

The rationale behind treating power-up and RESET the same comes from the properties of system memory. Everyone knows that system memory loses the values inside of the memory when power is lost to the physical device. However, the real question is about how fast the physical memory information degrades. The LT architects at first thought that a way to handle RESET was to require the power to remain off for a few milliseconds and the physical memory would lose information. While this solution is tempting, it turns out that memory can retain information for longer than milliseconds. In fact, it may remain intact for several seconds or longer. Having the memory retain information for seconds could allow an attack. The bottom line is that LT must handle a power-up exactly as it does a RESET.

What to Protect?

The reset clears out the state maintained by the CPU and chipset. The system memory could retain information, so LT needs to protect that system memory until the system can determine that system memory contains no "secrets." It is impossible for LT to determine what was or was not a secret. The LT designers adopted this definition of secret: any memory page that is assigned to a protected partition. The content of the page makes no difference. Once assigned to a protected partition, LT treats the page as one containing a secret.

Who Determines Prior State?

Here's the question the LT system needs to answer after a reset: were any secrets in the system memory prior to the reset? The platform needs to provide some area for the various components to ask the question and receive a reliable answer upon reset.

First, we can eliminate two places for the question-answer activity:

■ *The CPU has no persistence areas*, and upon reset, it loses all internal state. Trying to add this capability to the CPU would greatly add to the cost of a CPU. As an aside, this persistence question is one place where the author was severely beaten about the head and shoulders by the internal CPU architects for suggesting the addition of some sort of flag that could be maintained across the reset.

■ *The MCH has no persistence areas*, and upon reset, it too loses all internal state. Cost issues are the same as those for the CPU. And after the CPU architects' beating on me, I didn't try to add the persistence here.

So what component determines prior state? The ICH does have persistence. The ICH is where the platform keeps track of the date and time and other such values. The ICH maintains this information in the "power well," which maintains values even when the platform is not plugged into the wall or the mobile battery is flat. The power comes from the small motherboard battery.[3]

---

[3] The power well also goes by the name of RTC well or VCC well.

Protection Sequence

When the platform starts after a reset, the immediate task is to determine whether or not secrets were in memory. While the platform makes the determination about the previous state, it is possible for some memory access to occur. The easiest way to prevent this vulnerability is to block all access to all system memory. The enforcement of the block occurs in the MCH. Immediately after a reset, the MCH automatically blocks all access to system memory.

Once the system determines that memory contains no secrets, the BSP unlocks the MCH and allows access to memory. In a normal situation, a read of the ICH determines no secrets were in memory, and a message is sent to the MCH to unlock memory and allow the rest of the reset processing to occur.

The flow chart of the sequence is in Figure 13.2.

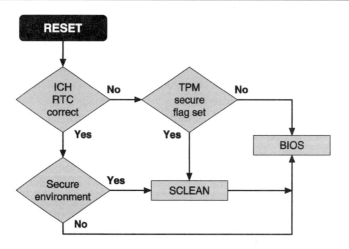

Figure 13.2   Reset Protection

The platform keeps the evidence of a previously running protected environment in two locations: the ICH and the TPM.

Setting the ICH Flag

The ICH maintains the LT.HADSECRETS flag. The MVMM sets the LT.HADSECRETS to TRUE using the LT.CMD.SECRETS command. The flag remains TRUE until the MVMM executes the LT.CMD.NOSECRETS command.

The MCH checks the ICH and the status of the LT.HADSECRETS flag. If the flag is TRUE, then the MCH continues to block memory until after execution of the SCLEAN module. The SCLEAN module has the ability to set the LT.HADSECRETS flag to FALSE.

The LT.HADSECRETS flag is held by the ICH in the power well. The power well provides the ability for the ICH to maintain information when no platform power is present. Platform power comes from the wall via a power cord or from the main battery on a mobile system. Platform power is likely go away if the plug is pulled from the wall or if the main battery goes flat. The ICH power well does not rely on these sources of power. Instead, the power well has a dedicated battery. If you have ever opened a PC and looked at the motherboard, you probably have noticed a small dime-sized battery. This battery supplies the power well.

You have no guarantee that the ICH power well battery would maintain power forever. In fact, nothing prevents someone from removing the battery. If the battery goes away, what happens to the power well? On a loss of power, the ICH losses all information held in the power well, such as the current date and time. The ICH has an indicator that is set when power is not sufficient to maintain the information in the power well. Once the low power bit is set, the ICH requires a re-initialization of the ICH information, like resetting the clock.

The obvious attack is for the attacker to remove power from the wall and then pull the battery. The ICH no longer has valid information and the chipset does not know whether blocking should or should not occur after a reset. If the attacker performs this attack fast enough, secrets could be in memory where they are vulnerable.

Adding the TPM

You cannot defend the battery from this type of attack, so a location on the platform must keep safe the information regarding the existence of secrets in memory across such loss of power events. The TPM provides that type of area. The issue here is that normal non-volatile storage has a write limit on it, and the designers would not want to limit the platform to only a certain number of protected environment launches.

The solution is for the TPM to keep track only of the LT.HADSECRETS flag. If there *ever* is a secured environment, it's not the environment present immediately before the reset. The chipset only needs to check the TPM when the power well is invalid, and that event should be a very rare occurrence.

The TPM sets the SECRETS.ESTABLISHED flag to TRUE upon receipt of the TPM_HASHSTART command. If the bit is already TRUE, the TPM does not perform any action on the flag. The TPM maintains the SECRETS.ESTABLISHED flag across all power cycles and system events. The SCLEAN module has the ability to reset the flag.

State Table

Table 13.1 shows the state of the RTC and TPM flags, and the resulting action upon reset.

Table 13.1   Normal Flag Settings

Event	RTC Secrets	RTC BatteryFail	TPM Secrets	Result if Reset occurs
First boot	FALSE	FALSE	FALSE	Normal processing
TPM_HASHSTART	FALSE	FALSE	TRUE[1]	Normal processing
LT.CMD.SECRETS	TRUE	FALSE	TRUE[2]	SCLEAN required
LT.CMD.NOSECRETS	FALSE	FALSE	TRUE	Normal processing
RTC battery fail[3]	?	TRUE	TRUE	SCLEAN required
SCLEAN[4]	FALSE	FALSE	FALSE	Normal processing

[1] It is possible to execute GETSEC [SENTER] without having the MVMM use the LT.CMD.SECRETS command. If this event occurs, then the RTC SECRETS flag is not set.

[2] The LT.CMD.SECRETS command is only available to MVMM code, hence the TPM_HASH_START command must execute prior to LT.CMD.SECRETS command.

[3] The battery failure could occur at any time but the RTC BatteryFail flag is only checked during the reset.

[4] The assumption is that a new RTC battery is available. If not, the system sets RTC BatteryFail to TRUE again.

SCLEAN AC Module

When secrets appear to be in memory, the SCLEAN module provides a way to remove the secrets. After a reset, the chipset can request the startup code to locate, load, and cause the execution of the SCLEAN module. The module is an authenticated code (AC) module that is specific to each chipset.

Being an AC Module allows SCLEAN to operate in the authenticated code space where it has no reliance on any area of system memory. SCLEAN is attempting to clean up memory and cannot rely on system memory for execution. The only space meeting these requirements is the AC Module execution area.

Running SCLEAN

When the chipset makes the determination that secrets *were* in memory, the chipset blocks access to all of system memory. The block is absolute and extends from address 0 to the top of physical memory.

SCLEAN Location

The BIOS must be able to locate the SCLEAN module in the BIOS flash.[4] Having the SCLEAN module in flash memory allows access to the code without any reliance on system memory.

SCLEAN Loading

After locating the module, the BIOS executes the GETSEC [ENTERACCS] command. The command takes as input the location of the SCLEAN module. The ENTERACCS command then performs the normal AC Module digital signature validation of the code using the public key from the chipset.

SCLEAN Execution

As an AC Module, SCLEAN has access to all of memory. An AC Module can bypass the system memory block that was set by the chipset. The bypass is only available to AC Modules, and only signed code is eligible to be an AC Module. This restriction prevents an attacker from loading an incorrect SCLEAN module and gaining access to system memory.

SCLEAN configures the memory controller with a default configuration that permits read and write access to all possible memory locations. This configuration does not take advantage of any memory controller enhancements for speed or efficiency.

SCLEAN then writes a data pattern to each byte of memory. SCLEAN reads each byte to ensure that the write functioned as expected. The pattern may be any value from 0x00 to 0xFF.

---

[4] While it is possible to put SCLEAN in something other than the flash memory, the other area must be addressable and available without reliance on any memory accesses. While an area with these requirements might be found, it is much more likely that the platform will use the flash memory.

Setting the Flags

After writing to all memory locations, the SCLEAN module needs to reset the flags so that the chipset unblocks system memory access. The first flag to clear is the RTC HADSECRETS flag. Setting this flag to FALSE allows the chipset to unlock memory and continue normal reset processing.

The SCLEAN does not manipulate the RTC BatteryFail flag. The flag has specific rules as to when and how the flag is set, and SCLEAN does not affect those rules.

The SCLEAN module can reset the TPM SECRETS.ESTABLISHED flag. The assumption is that the RTC BatteryFail flag is now FALSE and the chipset has no need to communicate with the TPM. That assumption could be incorrect, and having SCLEAN reset the SECRETS.ESTABLISHED flag removes the loop where the platform performs a scrub on every reset. While modern platforms do not operate very well with a dead RTC battery, having SCLEAN reset the TPM flag does avoid the possibility of unnecessary scrubs.

Continuing Execution

The BIOS can continue execution in two ways. First; it can execute the next instruction in the boot process. This action is tempting, since the user has been sitting watching the machine do nothing for some time. I recommend that you avoid this temptation. Causing a reset at this time ensures that the BIOS understands completely the current state of the platform.[5] During AC Module execution, interrupts are off and various events could occur. For example, suppose that devices other than the chipset and CPU were performing initialization and attempts to communicate with the chipset and CPU resulted in no response. So, the safest path would be to cause a reset and start the process all over again. All devices, including the CPU and chipset, receive the request to reset and restart their initialization process. The CPU and chipset then respond normally to events during the reset process, and the BIOS handles them without a special delay.

---

[5] Understanding the platform state allows the BIOS to properly set up the platform. After the termination of SCLEAN, the platform does not guarantee any specific platform state.

Speeding SCLEAN Up

To speed SCLEAN processing up, the chipset can include the ability to lock the memory configuration registers and maintain the contents of the registers across an `INIT` operation. The information is lost when power is lost. In this context, power means main system power; not the power to the RTC. If this information is available, the SCLEAN operation can use information relative to the chipset to perform faster verification of the memory configuration and use better methods to access memory.

Registering SCLEAN

SCLEAN is an AC Module that is embedded in the BIOS. It performs a vital function, ensuring that secrets held in the protected environment do not leak when errors cause an immediate shutdown of that protected environment. The MVMM must understand which SCLEAN version is in use. The MVMM might require special processing or a special version of the SCLEAN. A registration process for the SCLEAN operation should make it possible for the MVMM to validate the SCLEAN module that performs the scrub.

A really unique attack would be to launch a protected environment, load in a bad SCLEAN, force the reset—just unplug the power cord!—and then take advantage of the bad SCLEAN. The definition of bad is an SCLEAN that does not scrub all of memory. Clearly, this version would be unacceptable.

The only way to measure SCLEAN acceptability is to use the hash from the digital signature. Other than loading SCLEAN, you have no way to be sure that the measurement is occurring on the actual SCLEAN module. Loading the SCLEAN and having the SCLEAN register itself on each `GETSEC [SENTER]` would add too much overhead to the launch. Loading SCLEAN after each reset also adds way too much overhead to the reset processing.

TPM Registration

What the SCLEAN registration needs is a value, set by the SCLEAN, readable by the MVMM, and not changeable by any other entity. The TPM provides non-volatile storage with access control. The location must allow for reads by any entity; but for writes, only by locality three or an AC Module. The system defines a location, naming it SCLEAN, and the system sets the access to be writeable by locality three and readable by any locality.

SCLEAN Flow

The SCLEAN execution flow has two main branches, a scrub flow and a registration flow. The pseudocode in Figure 13.3 shows the basic code flow.

SCLEAN Module Flow

```
1    registeredDigest := read (TPM "SCLEAN" buffer)
2
3    IF (NOT memory-blocked) THEN
4      // This branch is taken if memory is not blocked
5      // It registers the SCLEAN version if necessary
6      IF (myDigest == registeredDigest)
7        exit with status code (already registered)
8      ENDIF
9      write (TPM "SCLEAN" buffer, myDigest)
10     exit with status code (registered)
11   ENDIF
12   // This branch when memory blocked, and must be scrubbed
13   IF (myDigest != registeredDigest) THEN
14     exit with error (Wrong version, memory remains blocked)
15   ENDIF
16   scrub memory
17   IF (scrub NOT successful) THEN
18       exit with error code (scrub failed)
19   ENDIF
20   remove memory-block
21   exit with status code (memory scrubbed)⁶
```

Figure 13.3 SCLEAN Execution Flow

The self-check in line 13 is critical to the success of SCLEAN. If the attacker ran GETSEC [SENTER], changed the SCLEAN code, and then pulled the plug, the SCLEAN-registered value would not match the value calculated on execution. The check prevents the attack and ensures that the MVMM knows the identity of the SCLEAN to execute in case of any shutdowns or resets. Since the SCLEAN code is an AC Module that comes from the chipset manufacturer, it is reasonable to require inclusion of line 13 in every SCLEAN module.

---

⁶ Please, no comments from the "peanut gallery" regarding the quality of this code snippet. I was a good coder when I wrote code. Mind you, the last section of code that I wrote was on punch tape—not really, but it sure sounds good.

The TPM SCLEAN buffer definition requires that only locality three has access to the area. The only entities able to assert locality three are AC modules. All AC Modules are under control of the chipset manufacturer and again, it is reasonable to assert that only the SCLEAN module can manipulate the TPM SCLEAN buffer.

The BIOS runs SCLEAN whenever the chipset blocks memory. The BIOS also runs SCLEAN whenever the SCLEAN module changes. This requirement allows the SCLEAN to run the registration flow and properly store the SCLEAN identity in the TPM.

Validating the SCLEAN Identity

The TPM contains the SCLEAN identity. Two obvious control points ensure that the SCLEAN is correct before allowing secrets into memory.

The first control point is for the SINIT to validate the SCLEAN identity. Either the SINIT can have an internal list of known good SCLEAN modules or it could have access to a signed list of good SCLEAN modules. Either way, the SINIT would generate an error if the SCLEAN module was unknown. Having the SINIT perform this validation is difficult because the maintenance of the good list is difficult to manage.

For the second control point, the SINIT could merely place the SCLEAN identity into a PCR register. The identity of a module comes from a measurement of the module; all AC modules are digitally signed and the hash value in use for the digital signature also functions as the module identity. When any entity launches the AC module, the launching process can use the module identity as the value to extend into a TPM PCR register. With the module identity in a PCR register, the user and any other entity can use the TPM SEAL process to identify any changes in the SCLEAN module.

As a third alternative control point, the SINIT could ignore the SCLEAN and allow the MVMM to perform the same types of validation. The MVMM is easier code to modify, and passing in signed lists is much easier. So, the SCLEAN validation may be a job for the MVMM. The decision as to what component makes these decisions lies with the system because the LT architecture supports a wide range of solutions.[7]

---

[7] I certainly feel that SCLEAN validation by the MVMM is very natural. The other methods are valid, but I think MVMM validation is the most flexible.

INIT Protection

The INIT# pin requires that the device receiving the signal reset itself. Originally, the LT architects were under the impression that broadcasting INIT# enabled all logical processors to receive the signal at the same time. We were wrong. A single logical processor is capable of being the target of an INIT# message. Having one CPU drop out of the protected environment is just as bad as having a logical processor not join in.

The system handles the INIT# by requiring the MVMM to block all INIT# messages. The MVMM can determine that the appropriate response is to broadcast an INIT# message, but the MVMM should have a high assurance that all logical processors would receive the message. Figure 13.4 shows the problem.

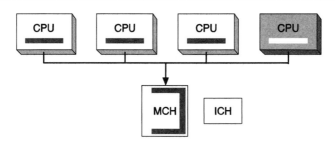

Figure 13.4   INIT Protection

S2/S3/S4 Sleep Protection

The platform has four sleep states: off, on, sleep, and hibernate. The specification for these sleep states is the *Advanced Configuration and Power Interface Specification* (ACPI 2004). The ACPI specification explains how to enter and exit the states, what the CPU and platform do in each state, and what devices should get power.

The specification makes for very fun reading. One of the most interesting points is that various components may respond to the ACPI event by performing a reset. Other devices might not perform a reset in response to the same event. From the standpoint of a protected partition, it is very bad to have one device reset and another device not do so. The S3 state removes power from the CPU but keeps power supplied to memory. The state then causes the CPU to loose track of the details of the protected partition while leaving the protected memory available, which is especially bad for trustworthiness.

The whole point of the ACPI states is to save power and battery life. Ignoring the ACPI events could reduce the platform's available use time drastically. Accepting the ACPI events could expose protected information. These two options cannot co-exist.

When notified that an ACPI transition is pending, the MVMM makes a decision regarding how to respond. The MVMM can encrypt the protected partition information and execute a `GETSEC [SEXIT]` command, which removes the protected partition. The MVMM could ignore the ACPI event and not allow the CPU and other devices to operate on the ACPI event.

The generic response to an ACPI event from the MVMM standpoint is:

1. Encrypt the protected partition.

2. Exit from the protected partition using the `GETSEC [SEXIT]` operation.

3. Change the ACPI state so the system goes to sleep or hibernates.

4. Return to normal operations.

5. Execute `GETSEC [SENTER]` operation.

6. Decrypt the protected partition.

The most interesting event scenario is: an ACPI sleep event occurs when the protected partition is active. When it receives the ACPI sleep event, the chipset treats the event as an attack. Since this event should not occur, the existence of the event must be an attempt to reset the processors and read memory. The chipset responds with an `LT-shutdown`, which in turn causes a complete platform reset. With the `LT.HADSECRETS` flag set to TRUE, the platform performs an SCLEAN to remove any secrets in memory. The interesting aspect of this scenario is the reliance on the MVMM to ensure that the chipset never receives a sleep request while the MVMM is active. As soon as the chipset receives the request with the MVMM active, the `LT-shutdown` sequence will start.

SMI Handling

System Management Mode (SMM) and the System Management Interrupt (SMI) are really interesting in conjunction with security. SMM handles platform events without notifying or using the operating system. A simple example of an SMI is when the user pushes the volume button on a mobile PC. Usually, this action causes a picture of the current volume level to pop up on the bottom of the screen. The button press does the following:

- First, it generates an SMI event.

- The SMM handler wakes upon receipt of the SMI event. Waking up the handler causes other processes to wait.

- The SMM code changes the volume. The change requires intimate knowledge of the platform and is platform-specific. Normal SMM-handling code is OEM-specific.

- The volume level is displayed and the display requires knowledge of the frame buffer and other display characteristics.

- Control is returned to the normal executing code.

The SMM code runs in Big Real mode, in which no paging is allowed. No paging means that the page tables are inactive. No page table means that all of physical memory is available to the SMM code. Having all of physical memory available to the SMM code means that the handler must have the same trust level as the MVMM. Since SMM code tends to be both old and new, it is quite likely that the writers of some SMM code did not consider protection of secrets when they were writing that code.

Removing SMM from the platform is impossible. Numerous entities use SMM to handle device faults, special features, and incompatibilities. If SMM went away, some new mode would have to replace SMM. Instead of eliminating SMM, one needs to find a way to protect SMM by making it unable to access protected resources. The way to accomplish that is to run the SMM code in a protected partition dedicated to SMM.

SMM Transfer Module

The SMM Transfer Module (STM) provides a mechanism to accept the SMI, invoke the SMM, and ensure no leakage of information to the SMM. Figure 13.5 shows the potential for attack during SMI handling activities.

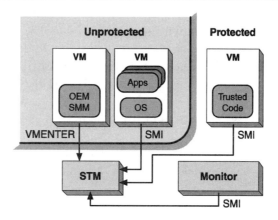

Figure 13.5   SMI Handling

The STM runs as a peer to the MVMM. The interaction between the MVMM and STM is open to negotiation. Both the STM and MVMM can decline the policies set by the other, but the result of a failed negotiation is that the protected environment does not launch.

The STM is part of the trust chain for the platform. It must be possible for an entity requesting the current platform configuration to be able to evaluate the current STM, just as it can evaluate the MVMM. Therefore, the STM must have the following characteristics:

- An accurate measurement
- Reliable storage of the measurement
- Verifiable reporting of the measurement

The solution to this problem on an LT platform is to find a way to measure the code and then report the measurement to the TPM.

SMM Loading

The BIOS holds the SMM code, which is normally placed within the Firmware Hub and loaded during the initialization of the platform. As part of the SMM, the STM needs to load at the same time, but loading the STM at this time divorces the STM load from the GETSEC [SENTER] process. Therefore, the measurement technique in use for the SINIT and MVMM will not work with the STM.

The current SMM code loads using three addresses: the HSEG, TSEG, and CSEG. The HSEG and CSEG do not affect the STM. The current TSEG splits to include a new MSEG area. The STM resides in the MSEG area. When the BIOS loads the SMM code, it also loads the STM into the MSEG area. The BIOS also sets the LT.MSEG.BASE, LT.MSEG.SIZE, and MSEG_MSR.BASE registers. The remainder of the SMM code loads into the TSEG area. Figure 13.6 shows that the HSEG and CSEG are in different areas and that the MSEG and TSEG are in a contiguous area.

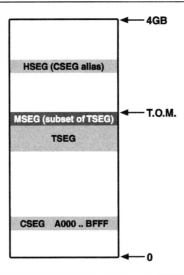

Figure 13.6   STM SMRAM

SMI ACPI Extensions

The BIOS manipulates the registers using ACPI extensions to the SMI_CMD port. The new commands to use are:

- GetMsegStatusCmd provides information if the MSEG area is set.
- UpdateMsegSizeCmd allows the BIOS to change the size of the MSEG area.
- LoadStmCmd loads the STM code into the MSEG area.
- UnloadStmCmd unloads the STM and clears the MSEG area.
- GetVendorSmiGuidCmd returns the identifier of the SMM developer.

STM Loading

The STM can load at two separate points of time. The first takes place during POST, the second upon request of the OS.

When loading during the POST processing, the BIOS locates the STM, which is most likely part of the SMM, and loads the SMM and STM. The BIOS uses the LoadStmCmd to perform the actual load. The command ensures that if the load is successful, the MSR_MSEG.VALID flag is set to TRUE. The BIOS must have access to the STM image to load the STM. The typical platform implementation would be to put the STM in the FWH.

The OS can request a load of a different STM at any time. The BIOS has the opportunity to accept or reject the request to load the STM. If the BIOS accepts the request, the OS needs to provide the STM image and the BIOS would then load the STM using the LoadStmCmd.

The STM must be present in the MSEG prior to execution of the GETSEC [SENTER] command. Failure to set the MSEG results in the GETSEC [SENTER] processing failing. GETSEC [SENTER] checks the status of MSR_MSEG.VALID, and if FALSE, aborts the GETSEC [SENTER] process. The MSR_MSEG.VALID flag is only writable by SMM code, so the loading process ensures that the SMM code sets the flag to TRUE.

STM Measurement

The SINIT code must measure the STM. The SINIT code has access to the MSEG region. SINIT measures the area specified by the `LT.MSEG.BASE` and `LT.MSEG.SIZE` parameters. To maintain an accurate identity, the STM must not modify any of the data that resides in the area specified by the base and size registers. If the STM does modify these areas, the measurement would result in two different values and cause problems with SEALed data and attestation evaluations.

After `GETSEC [SENTER]`, the MVMM has the opportunity to evaluate the identity of the STM and determine whether the STM provides adequate services that do not conflict with the goals of the MVMM. If the MVMM does not approve of the STM, the MVMM can cause an immediate SEXIT and stop the launch of the protected environment.

STM MVMM Negotiation

With the STM and MVMM loaded, the two entities need to negotiate what the STM can and cannot do. The MVMM requires protection from SMM code that touches registers or other internal CPU state. The STM ensures that the SMM code does not access protected pages or devices that could access protected pages.

After approving of the STM identity, the MVMM needs to inform the STM of the policy that the MVMM needs the STM to enforce. The policy would include what MSRs to protect, where the MVMM page table is, and other information that the STM needs to ensure the enforcement of the proper protection boundary. The STM is free to reject the requests of the MVMM, but the likely result of a failure to agree on a policy would be the aborted launch of the protected environment.

Bus Attacks

When the attacker has physical access to the machine, they can remove the cover and attach probes to the various busses on the platform. The information gathered by the attacker may allow the attacker access to information under protection of LT.

The type of bus directly affects the ability and expertise necessary for the attacker to read the information. Fast busses require special equipment and special software. Slower busses are readable using equipment found in a college or high school computer lab.

The LT design point is to provide protection from software attack, so the fact that attackers can succeed using hardware is not a surprise. Future versions might address these busses in different ways.

Front Side Bus

The FSB provides the connection between the CPU and the MCH. The FSB is a fast bus with speeds of 1,066 MHz, in 2005. Watching the bus is possible, and if the attacker has the expertise and equipment, the information is readable.

The information passing on the FSB includes reads and writes to system memory through the MCH. The information includes keys, code, and data. An attacker who is able to read this information can obtain all information under LT protection. The attack exposes information sent from the TPM to the protected environment, but the attack does not break the TPM protections. The difference is that the TPM still provides the correct protections, but the protected environment does not.

Hublink

The hublink provides the connection between the MCH and ICH. The hublink is a fast bus. Watching the bus is possible, and if the attacker has the expertise and equipment, the information is readable.

The security information passing on the hublink is only information in transit from the TPM to the CPU. The normal reads and writes of system memory do not travel down the hublink.

An attacker is certainly capable of watching this bus, but the work is not worth the effort given the difference between the hublink and the LPC bus.

Low Pin Count Bus

The LPC bus provides the connection between the ICH and the TPM. The LPC bus is slow and very simple, due to the low number of pins required for the bus. The LPC bus is very easy to watch and interpret.

With the LPC bus being so easy to watch, the system must add some protection to the data. Version 1.2 TPMs have the ability to create transport sessions. TPM transport sessions provide confidentiality of the information traveling between the TPM and the CPU by encrypting the data.

The most crucial informational items traveling on the LPC bus are keys that were UNSEALed on the TPM and the resulting plain text sent to the CPU. Encrypting the transaction removes the ability of attackers to watch the LPC bus to obtain the data. The transport sessions only provide protection for the data as it travels between the TPM and the CPU. When the CPU stores information in system memory, the data travels over the FSB to the physical memory and the TPM transport sessions provide no protection for data in system memory. The attacker could still watch the FSB and obtain the data. The difference lies in the resources and expertise needed by the attacker. The LPC bus requires low-cost equipment and little expertise, the FSB requires expensive equipment and high expertise.

Part V

The Bottom Line

I do not participate in a sport with ambulances at the bottom of the hill.

—Erma Bombeck (1927–1996)

Part V is the bottom of the hill for this book. I hope that if you arrive here, you do not need an ambulance. By now, an understanding of LaGrande Technology should lead one to anticipate the types of attacks that LaGrande Technology mitigates. Part V reviews some of the previously described attacks and then tries to do some crystal ball gazing.

Chapter 14: Defending the Platform Against Attacks

Chapter 4 was all about describing an application and the attacks on the application. Chapter 14 describes how LaGrande Technology mitigates those attacks. From accessing memory to manipulating input and output, Chapter 14 uses the LaGrande Technology features and shows how the attackers do not gain access to protected information.

Chapter 15: The Future

Chapter 15 is for gazing into the future. A product that provides security is never complete. Attackers learn new techniques, users require new protections, and LaGrande Technology must respond to these events and change over time. One obvious change would be for the LaGrande Technology objectives to change regarding hardware attacks.

Chapter 14

Defending the Platform Against Attacks

So in war, the way is to avoid what is strong and to strike at what is weak.

—Sun Tzu, *The Art of War*

This same Sun Tzu quote applied to Chapter 4, too. In that chapter, the discussion centered on successful software attacks on platform designs available in the 2004 timeframe. Chapter 14 shows how the design and architecture of LaGrande Technology (LT) mitigates these attacks. If the design is successful, attackers need to move from software attacks to hardware attacks. To allow only hardware attacks is a large step forward because the hardware attacks require physical access to the platform.

Vulnerabilities

The goal in Chapter 5 was to examine how the attack finds and exploits a vulnerability. The goal in this chapter is to show how the LT design mitigates those same vulnerabilities.

The BORE attack revolved around having the same information on every platform. Discovery of the information on one platform allowed the attacker to use the information on all other platforms. The design of LT does not use keys or other information that is the same on each platform. If it requires an encryption key, the MVMM can generate a random number, SEAL the random number to the SINIT and SENTER identities, and only allow use of the key in the correct configuration. A MVMM of this design has a unique key on every platform so that any exposure of the key only affects an individual platform and not all LT platforms.

While an MVMM could use the same value on every platform, this design of the MVMM would be incorrect. A review of the MVMM by an independent reviewer would see this problem, and entities wanting to rely on the platform would not trust the platform that has an incorrect MVMM executing.

From a design standpoint, LT does not provide the repeatable value necessary for a BORE attack. Applications using LT could use repeatable values but that is an application decision and not part of the LT design.

The Example Application

The application program from Chapter 4 performs some operations on a special number. The operations are:

■ Display the special number

■ Update the special number

■ Encrypt the special number

■ Enter and process the user's password

The Chapter 14 version of the application makes use of LT and performs all of the operations of the application in the protected partition. To distinguish between the versions of the application, "V4" refers to the Chapter 4 version and "V14" identifies the Chapter 14 version.

The Attacker's Goal

The goal of the attacker does not change: discover the special number or find a way to alter the special number. The same restriction is in place. To accomplish the goal, the attacker can use software attacks but not hardware attacks.

Application Functionality

The application functions that were present in V4 remain in V14. The following list provides a break-down of the functionality into components:

- Display window that requests password
- Mechanism to read the keystrokes that provide the password
- Mechanism to process the password[1]
- Decision to display the special number
- Display window that shows the special number
- Process to update the number

Application Design

While the functionality of V14 mimics V4 and parts of the program remain exactly the same, other parts of the program require modifications. The application developer can make numerous tradeoffs between ease of development and deployment, and complete use of the LT protection capabilities.

A design characteristic that the V14 architect[2] was following, was an attempt to keep as much of the V4 code in use as possible. Other designs are possible and sometimes desirable, but for V14 code, reuse has the highest priority.

---

[1] Our application is severely limited in functionality; there is no way to change the password. Real applications would provide mechanisms to change the password. The change mechanism requires the same protections as the special number change mechanism.

[2] The architect is the author and the purpose of V14 is to only illustrate some points, not be a perfect application. Real life applications will make very different choices depending on the needs of the application.

Figure 14.1 illustrates the basic V14 architecture. The code runs in a separate partition from any other application. The V14 code makes use of both the trusted input and trusted output channels. Long-term secret protection comes from the SEAL property of the TPM.

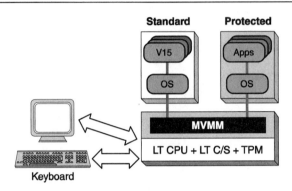

Figure 14.1   Preferred V14 Architecture

V14 Unchanged Program Components

The functionality that does not change in the V14 version includes:

■ *Mechanism to process the password.* The code in V4 takes the input, processes the input (normally a cryptographic hash), and then makes the resulting processed password available to other sections of the application. V14 needs to make no modifications to this section of code. While protections are in place on how to obtain the password, the actual processing can be the same code.

■ *Decision to display the special number.* The code in V4 makes a programming decision, based on various inputs, to display the special number. The same decisions are available in V14 without modification.

■ *Process to update the special number.* The code in V4 obtains the new special number and then processes the input and creates the new special number. V14 uses the same process.

V14 Changed Program Components

The V14 code has the following additions to take advantage of the LT protections:

- ■ *Trusted output channel.* Both the display window for the user-id and password and the display window that shows the special number require a trusted channel. The V14 code creates the channel to the display adapter, discrete or integrated, and the channel ensures that what the application creates is what the display actually shows.

- ■ *Trusted input channel.* The V4 code accepts keystrokes directly from the keyboard driver. The V14 code accepts keystrokes from the trusted input channel.

- ■ *Trusted path indicator.* To ensure for the user that the trusted output channel is present and operational, the V14 code places a "border" around the display windows. The border is a tartan pattern that appears only when the trusted display is active. The V14 code keeps the tartan pattern secure by encrypting the data. The V14 code provides long-term protection of the tartan pattern by using the TPM SEAL property to ensure that the tartan border is only available when the correct MVMM environment is present.

Vulnerabilities

The V4 code has specific vulnerabilities that Chapter 5 enumerated. The V14 code mitigates those vulnerabilities.

Display Window That Requests Password

In the V4 program, the display window had two major vulnerabilities: access to the frame buffer and the ability of an attacker to mimic the window. In the V14 program, the frame buffer obtains protection using the trusted channel between the protected partition and the display adapter. As a result, the attacker does not have access to the buffer and cannot see the buffer or change any data in the buffer, mitigating the V4 vulnerability.

The LT design, using the trusted display and the SEAL[3] operation, can create a mechanism that allows the user to know that the display is present. The attacker's ability to mimic the window is gone and the vulnerabilities present in V4 are not present in V14. The application designer has mechanisms in place that allow the designer to mitigate the vulnerabilities on the platform.

Mechanism to Read the Keystrokes That Provide the Password

In the V4 code, the attacker accessed system memory to read the keystrokes or install a password sniffer. In V14, access to system memory is not available to the attacker. The MVMM protects the physical memory where the MVMM itself resides. The MVMM also ensures that partitions are properly isolated. The measurement of the MVMM allows those wishing to rely on the platform the assurance that the proper components are present and are active.

The V14 version of the application uses the trusted input channel to send the information from the keyboard to the protected partition in a secure way. The protections block the attempts by a keyboard sniffer to obtain the information from the sending of keystrokes from the keyboard to the protected partition. V14 does not prevent the introduction of a sniffer onto the platform, but V14 does prevent the sniffer from obtaining information under protection of the protected partition. V14 has mitigations for both of the vulnerabilities in V4, memory and sniffers. The attackers need to look elsewhere to succeed.

Mechanism to Process the Password

The V4 vulnerability to password processing lay in the ability for attack code to run in ring 0. In V14, with the application running in the protected partition, the attacker cannot install code in ring 0. If the MVMM did allow new code to execute in ring 0, the application can still protect itself by using the SEAL operation's properties and ensuring that the application runs only in environments that provide protection.

---

[3] Remember that SEAL uses the measurement values of the SINIT and MVMM; hence, the system can provide long-term protection for the trusted display trusted path indicator.

Decision to Display the Value

In V4, the decision to display the value was vulnerable to ring 0 code, and in V14, the same protections on password processing apply to the display decision.

Display Window that Shows the Value

In V4, the display window was vulnerable to the same frame buffer attacks as the password window. The V14 program's use of the trusted display mitigates these attacks.

Process to Update the Value

In V4, the value update process was susceptible to a ring 0 attack, and V14 mitigates ring 0 attacks.

Underlying V4 Vulnerabilities

The exploits in V4 revolved around the following vulnerabilities:

- Memory access
- Driver manipulation
- Uncontrolled program access

The LT design mitigates these underlying vulnerabilities by restricting memory access, preventing driver manipulation, and denying uncontrolled program access.

Memory Access

The protected partition provides excellent memory access protection. Any process outside of the protected partition cannot access memory pages protected by the MVMM.

All of the physical memory associated with the MVMM is kept separate from operating systems at ring 0 and applications at ring 3. Applications running in ring 3 of a protected partition have complete separation from any other ring 3 process. The separations protect information by making deliberate or unintentional access to the memory impossible. The V4 code attacker had a goal of obtaining access to a ring 0 process. The attacker who gains access to ring 0 in any partition has no access rights to any memory in ring 3 protected partitions. The basic mechanism of obtaining information in V4 is mitigated by the protected partition. The combination of the ring structure and the protected partition removes the attacker's ability to access memory.

DMA Access

In the V4 code, the attacker could also access memory through DMA devices. The V14 code allowed no DMA access to protected pages, preventing it with the NoDMA table, which blocks all access attempts using DMA. The attacker again has to look for another vulnerability to exploit.

Driver Manipulation

In the V4 code, the attacker could change a driver on the system. Driver manipulation is a mechanism to gain access to ring 0, but as in the case of keyboard sniffers, the new driver could be malicious in and of itself. In V14 code, the location of the driver determines whether manipulation is possible.

If the driver executes in the standard partition, the protections and vulnerabilities present in V4 are still present. LT does not provide protection for code running in the standard partition. The attacker can manipulate the driver and gain access to ring 0. However, the attacker does not gain an advantage, as ring 0 in the standard partition provides no access to any memory in the protected environment.

If the attacker attempts to change a portion of the code in use for the protected environment—it could change either the MVMM or SINIT—the measurement of these entities registers any changes. If the attacker changes SINIT, the ACM digital signature validation fails and the secure launch is terminated. If the attacker changes the MVMM code, the measurement changes and no data that was SEALed to the previous environment is available to the new environment. The MVMM itself should provide the same type of protections on the code that the MVMM uses to launch code in a ring 0 of the protected partition.

Uncontrolled Program Access

In V4 code, once the attacker obtained knowledge of the encryption key, no available mechanism would prevent access to the data. In V14 code, in addition to encryption, the application can SEAL the data to a specific environment. With this change, even knowledge of the encryption key prevents the attacker from manipulating the value.

What Remains

Reading the above mitigations one could get the opinion that all work is done, all attacks have mitigations, and the attackers will all give up and stop attempting to attack applications. Nothing could be further from the truth. Lots of work remains to be done, there are numerous attacks that still require mitigation, and the attackers will still attempt to gain access to information.

Isolation

The V14 design makes a critical and vital assumption: the code runs in a separate partition. Compare Figure 14.1 and Figure 14.2. Notice that while V14 is present in both, only in Figure 14.1 is V14 isolated from the other application. Critically, notice that in Figure 14.2, V14 and the other application share the same OS. The sharing violates the separation necessary to obtain the full benefit of LT. When applications share the same OS, they are sharing the same ring 0 code, and sharing the same ring 0 code allows for all of the current attacks.

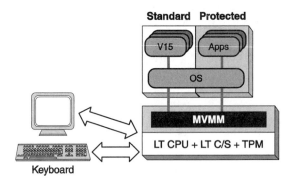

Figure 14.2   Incorrect V14 Architecture

When creating the trusted channels for V14, the OS may provide the basic connection ports for the trusted channels. If the architecture shares the same OS, as Figure 14.2 does, then there is the possibility that the other application can be corrupted and expose V14 information.

Getting to Figure 14.1 requires more effort that Figure 14.2, but the result is a much more robust and trustable architecture.

Hardware Attacks

The V14 architecture is a design that is resistant to software attacks. V14, as is LT, is not resistant to hardware attacks. Attackers wishing to attack V14 using hardware mechanisms may succeed. All of the hardware attacks previously discussed may be successful against the V14 design.

The goal of LT is to force attackers to use hardware mechanisms to attack the platform. The LT design protects from attacks accessing memory, changing drivers, or changing the application. The attacker needs to use hardware to gain access to the protected memory.

A critical point is the discussion about the use of the partition isolation. Without partition isolation the full effect of LT is not available.

Matching Requirements

In Chapter 2, Table 2.1 identified six requirements for a trusted computing platform. Here, near the end of the book, a review of the requirements and the components that provide the features that meet the requirements is in order. To just sum things up, let us look at Table 14.1.

Table 14.1   Requirements and Support

Requirement	Hardware Support	Comments
Isolation of programs	Intel® Virtualization Technology Paging and segmentation	Multiple partitions provide isolation and the partition can enforce the ring 0/ring 3 separation.
Separation of user from supervisor	VMM Ring 0 and Ring 3 separation	The VMM is a supervisor, and virtualization provides automatic separation of user from supervisor and the ability to maintain multiple partitions provides user supervisor separation in individual partitions.
Identification of current configuration	The GETSEC [SENTER] measurement of the VMM	Providing the measurement of the VMM identifies the VMM and enables both long-term storage and reporting.
Long-term protected storage	VMM measurement and TPM	By ensuring that the VMM measurement is properly stored in the TPM, the VMM can use the TPM SEAL capability to have long-term protection of secrets.
Verifiable report of current configuration	TPM	With the VMM measurement in the PCR registers, any observer can use the defined TPM properties to obtain a verifiable report of the PCR register contents.
Hardware basis for protections	Intel® Virtualization Technology LaGrande Technology TPM	The combination of Intel® Virtualization Technology, LT, and TPM provides a hardware base of the features.

Chapter **15**

The Future

Neither a wise man nor a brave man lies down on the tracks of history to wait for the train of the future to run over him.

—Dwight D. Eisenhower

Security requirements do not stand still. What is an appropriate protection today may be inadequate tomorrow. The first version of LaGrande Technology (LT) sets a protection boundary and attempts to mitigate vulnerabilities within that boundary. It is unreasonable to assume that LT never has to respond to additional threats or to a change in the boundary. Future versions will change the protection boundary.

New Attacks

As the author reads his crystal ball, one section is not hazy at all. That section shows those persons wishing to break into our computers and networks still at work attacking vulnerable systems. The ball is hazy on the exact mechanisms the attackers are using, but the attacking is clearly visible. Given the haziness on the exact attack mechanisms, the nature of responses and mitigations are obviously hazy at this time also.

Changing the Protection Boundary

One area of change that will occur over time is the inclusion of mitigations to current threats. The current boundary specifically mitigates some threats and places other threats outside of the protection boundary. Future versions of LT will change the boundary and add mitigations to threats outside the current boundary. Many of these mitigations will be responses to specific hardware attacks.

Devious Attackers

It is imperative to understand that attackers will not only use current mechanisms to launch software and hardware attacks. Attackers can be extremely devious; they thrive on looking at systems and finding new ways to access information.

Attempting to create a protection boundary ensures that attackers will attempt to cross the boundary. Some of the attempts will succeed. The possibility of success will continue to depend on the skill, motivation, resources, and desire of the attacker. Future versions of LT will respond to these attacks by providing new forms of mitigations.

Being Perfect

Providing security is not about providing absolutes. Those who say a product is 100-percent secure are 100-percent wrong! Security is always risk mitigation. Some risks have mitigations, some do not. New threats appear and old threats migrate to access and manipulate new areas. The crystal ball is hazy as to which threats will require mitigation, so attempting to predict what hardware and software changes will occur in the next versions of LT is impossible.

What is certain is that future versions of LT will respond to new attacks. I just have no way to predict the roadmap,[1] the when, and the how of these future responses.

---

[1] I am an architect and not a planner. The meetings I've had with my planning counterpart are always fun meetings that attempt to balance architectural needs and business decisions.

New Features

Just as I see a guarantee of new attacks, I also expect the desire of system developers to extend the protection boundary to other areas of the platform. Providing protections to hard drives or printers or the new finger implants[2] could become a requirement for future versions of LT.

When evaluating what new devices need protection, many choices must be made. The architecture, planning, and marketing teams will meet and evaluate the necessity of protecting one device over another, or for providing some generic protections. As with attacks, the only certainty is that changes are in the future.

Chipset Topologies

The current LT system topology uses a single chipset to control any and all of the CPUs that might be on the system. Future topologies, like Figure 15.1, are possible and desirable in many usage models. The LT mechanism and messages will work in the Figure 15.1 layout, but there are some architectural issues to solve.

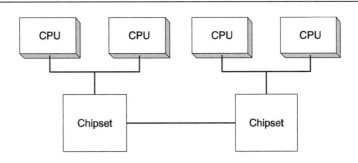

Figure 15.1   Future Topology

---

[2] The finger implants are just a joke.

TPM Location

One issue that the Trusted Computing Group (TCG) is working on is where does the TPM reside in Figure 15.1? There are numerous designs that are possible and the simplest is a single TPM attached to one of the chipsets. All communication to the TPM would then route through the chipset connected to the TPM.

While a single TPM is a simple response, there are many reasons why system designers would desire multiple TPMs. Figure 15.1 is normally a server topology and on servers the addition of multiple components to assist with throughput and reliability is a very common occurrence. Multiple TPMs would increase the reliability, but what about the uniqueness that each TPM carries? How does the system designer use the uniqueness appropriately? The answers to these questions are the tasks currently in front of the TCG Server workgroup.[3]

SEXIT ACM

SINIT is the ACM in use during `GETSEC [SENTER]` but no corresponding ACM for use during `GETSEC [SEXIT]` exists. The rationale behind the lack of a `GETSEC [SEXIT]` ACM is that the `GETSEC [SENTER]` ACM provides a secure execution area and during `GETSEC [SEXIT]` there is already a secure execution area, the MVMM itself. Certainly the rationale feels right at this time but are there circumstances where an exiting ACM would solve some architectural problems? The answer is yes. The infrastructure to invoke an exiting ACM is present, but not currently in use. Future versions could invoke an ACM during `GETSEC [SEXIT]`.

Additional Hardware Protections

The main protection feature of LT is to provide protection from software attacks. Future versions of LT could change that attack model and include some hardware attack protections.

---

[3] One request I always make is to indicate that membership in the TCG allows one to help solve the questions in front of the TCG. Having spent many years working on these issues, the introduction of new points of views and new individuals can certainly be the catalyst for innovative solutions.

Following the Principles

While you could expect new features to respond to new attacks or provide protections to new features, the basic design principles also are guaranteed to drive the future versions of LT. The list in Chapter 6 of the basic security principles will hold true in the future, and the author lists them here again:

- Least privilege

- Economy of mechanism

- Complete mediation

- Open design

- Separation of privilege

- Least common mechanism

- Psychological acceptability

These security principles do not change with attempts to mitigate new threats or to provide protections to new entities; in fact the principles become even more of a driving factor. With the protection boundary set by the first version of LT, subsequent versions should not roll back the boundary. The security principles drive many of the internal architectural decisions. Trying to remove one of the principles or making a fundamental change in the support for the principle undermines all previous versions of LT.

Glossary

Application Code written to perform an operation that the user wants.

Attack An entity taking advantage of some vulnerability. The vulnerability could be either a hardware or software.

Authenticated Code Module (ACM) Code that executes in a special CPU location and that prior to execution requires an internal digital signature validation.

BIOS Basic Input/Output System The built-in software that discovers and configures the hardware available on the platform.

BIOS Boot Block The built-in software that discovers and configures the BIOS such that the BIOS can perform its job.

Boot Strap Processor (BSP) The CPU that is designated to receive control after the platform reboots.

Break Once Run Everywhere (BORE) An attack mounted by a single attacker that, when successful, allows duplication by all other attackers merely with information supplied by the first attacker.

Bus Agent ID Chipset-assigned identifier for each CPU on the platform.

CPU Central Processing Unit.

CR0[1] or Control register 0 The five control registers (CR0 through CR4) determine the operating mode of the processor and the characteristics of the currently executing task. See the "Control Registers" section in Chapter 2 of the *IA-32 Intel® Architecture Software Developer's Manual*, Volume 3.

Digital Signature A guarantee that the information vouched for has not changed. The digital nature of the signature comes from the use of cryptography to create the signature and the ability of the system to validate the signature using software processes.

Direct Memory Access (DMA) A mechanism to allow faster memory access to hardware peripherals. Typically, this mechanism would be something done by a hard drive to allow faster transfer of information from the drive to the platform memory.

Domain manager The application that controls the standard and protected partitions.

Denial of Service (DoS) An attack where the attack consumes all of the resources and denies the user the facilities of the platform.

Endorsement key A Trusted Computing Group term that refers to the cryptographic uniqueness inside of a Trusted Platform Module.

Entropy A measure of the randomness in a system. Cryptographic key generation requires high entropy.

Front Side Bus (FSB) The link between the CPU and MCH. The FSB allows for multiple CPUs to connect to a single MCH.

FirmWare Hub (FWH) Flash device that holds BIOS code.

Graphics Aperture Relocation Table (GART) The mechanism to allow the graphics system to translate buffer addresses to physical page addresses.

Global Descriptor Table Register (GDTR) The control register that provides the base pointer for the paging mechanism.

Graphics Translation Table The mechanism that allows a logical address, in use for displaying graphics, to point to a physical memory page.

Grid Computing Many separate platforms are connected into a coherent whole platform and the larger platform then attempts to solve a problem that requires vast computing resources.

---

[1] This is not the postal code prefix for Cryodon, UK.

Hash The execution of a cryptographic hash algorithm such as SHA-1. The hash algorithm converts a string of arbitrary length into a fixed-size output. The properties of the resulting output are: given a hash value, it is computationally infeasible to construct the input. A second property of the hash algorithm is that the resulting value is order-dependent. That is, hashing A then B results in a different value than when one hashes B then A.

Human Input Device (HID) A device that transmits information from the user to the computer. Typical HIDs include keyboards, mice, and microphones.

HW Shorthand for hardware, where hardware is the physical mechanisms of a computer.

Input/Output Controller Hub (ICH) The device that provides connections to various peripherals including USB devices.

Initiating Logical Processor (ILP) The processor that initiates the MVMM measurement process. The GETSEC [SENTER] instruction is only valid on the ILP.

Interprocess Communication (IPC) A protocol to send information from one execution unit to another execution unit.

I/O Acronym for input and output.

LaGrande Technology Often called LT for short, this technology provides for measurement of a virtual machine monitor and the ability to create protected virtual guest partitions.

Late launch The invocation of the protected environment at a time other than platform reset.

Load Descriptor Table (LDTR) Control register.

Low Pin Count (LPC) A bus available on the PC platform that has a limited number of pins and works at a slow bus speed. Typical devices on the LPC bus include the Firm Ware Hub (FWH) and the Super I/O. The LPC bus connects to the ICH.

LT *see* LaGrande Technology.

Malware Code that is written to perform some operation that harms the information on the platform. This could be a virus, Trojan, worm or other type of code.

Memory Controller Hub (MCH) Device that provides a connection between the CPU and physical memory. The MCH also provides connections to display adapters and the ICH.

Measure To take a hash value of some information.

Multiplexer (MUX) Combines several different signals onto a single communication channel for transmission. While the multiplexing could be done for video, audio, or other communications, the MUX in LaGrande Technology combines the video channels for normal and trusted displays.

NoDMA A chipset feature that prevents DMA devices from accessing physical memory.

Non-Volatile (NV) Storage A type of memory that preserves the value even when no power is available to the memory device. See also "volatile storage."

Option ROM Software on hardware devices that helps the BIOS and the device to properly configure the platform and the device.

Opt-in The process whereby the user decides to turn a feature on as the feature ships initially turned off.

Pass phrase Related to a password but hopefully longer and harder to guess. A password would look like "password1" or "hne76$3". While a pass phrase would look like "this is a t3st phrase!" The idea behind a pass phrase is that it is longer but easier to remember.

PCR Platform Configuration Register.

Physical presence A Trusted Computing Group term to indicate that a human is directly using, i.e. has their hands on, the platform.

Prime number A number that is only divisible by itself and 1. (2, 3, 5, 7 …).

Protected partition A VT guest that has physical pages that have NoDMA protection.

PS2 Connector that allows connection of keyboard and mouse to platform.

Random Number Generator (RNG) The RNG provides a source of numbers that are not related to any previous or subsequent numbers.

Ring 0 through Ring 3 The protection mechanism that isolates user applications from OS components.

Responding Logical Processor (RLP) Any processor that responds to the SENTER message.

Remote procedure call (RPC) A protocol to send information from one platform to another.

Root of Trust for Measurement (RTM) A Trusted Computing Group term to describe the entity that is implicitly trusted to measure platform components.

Root of Trust for Reporting (RTR) A Trusted Computing Group term to describe the entity that has uniqueness capable of validating attestation requests. Normally the RTR is a cryptographic key.

Root of Trust for Storage (RTS) A Trusted Computing Group term to describe the entity that provides the basis for long-term non-volatile protection of data. Normally the RTS is a cryptographic key.

Security Architecture Specification (SAS) The name of the underlying LT security specification and the name of the team and meetings that defined the specification.

Sealed Storage The use of the TPM to encrypt data such that the data will only successfully decrypt when the platform measurements are in a defined state.

SENTER The process to start and measure the MVMM.

SHA-1 Secure Hash Algorithm A cryptographic hash algorithm defined in FIPS 180-1 http://csrc.nist.gov/cryptval/shs.html.

SINIT The authenticated code module that validates the platform is in a valid configuration during the launch of the MVMM.

System Management Interrupt (SMI) An event on the platform that invokes a special event manager.

SMI Transfer Module (STM) Software that receives an SMI event when the MVMM is executing and sends the event on to a SMI handler.

Standard partition A VT guest that has no pages requiring NoDMA protection.

Storage Root Key A Trusted Computing Group term that defines the cryptographic key that forms part of the Root of Trust for Storage.

SW Acronym for software.

Safer Mode Extensions (SMX) The CPU instructions necessary to run LT.

Timing Attack An attack that uses small tidbits of performance information to deduce a cryptographic key.

Trusted Platform Module (TPM) The TPM is the root of trust for both storage and reporting. The TPM uses the version-1.2 definition from the Trusted Computing Group (TCG).

Trusted Graphics Translation Table (TGTT) The mechanism that allows a logical address, in use for displaying trusted graphics, to point to a physical memory page.

Virtual Machine Extensions (VMX) The CPU instructions that enable virtualization, through Intel® Virtualization Technology.

Volatile storage A type of memory that does not preserve the value when power is lost to the memory device. See also "Non-volatile storage."

Wild Attacks that can arrive on an individual platform.

References

Note Intel® Corporation product manuals are generally available from the Intel developer Web site at developer.intel.com.

Bell, D. Elliott, and Leonard La Padula. 1973. *Secure Computer Systems: Mathematical Foundations and Model.* Technical Report M74-244, The MITRE Corporation.

Department of Defense. [1983] 1985. *Trusted Computer System Evaluation Criteria (Orange Book),* DoD 5200.28-STD.

distributed.net. Public source code. http://www.distributed.net/source/.

Jones, A. Russell. Old hacks never die, they just mutate: Passport is convenient, but watch out for fake login screens. *DevX,* January 14, 2002. http://www.devx.com/webdev/article/16881.

Intel. 2003a. *IA-32 Intel® Architecture Software Developer's Manual Volume 1: Basic Architecture.* Santa Clara: Intel Corporation. Order Number 245470-012.

Intel. 2003b. *IA-32 Intel® Architecture Software Developer's Manual Volume 2: Instruction Set Reference Manual.* Santa Clara: Intel Corporation. Order Number 245471-012.

Intel. 2003c. *IA-32 Intel® Architecture Software Developer's Manual Volume 3: System Programming Guide.* Santa Clara: Intel Corporation. Order Number 245472-012.

Kocher, Paul. 1996. Timing attacks on implementations of Diffie-Hellman, RSA, DSS, and other systems. *Advances in Cryptology–CRYPTO '96.* Lecture Notes in Computer Science, N. Koblitz, ed. Springer, 1109 (1996): 104-113.

Krawczyk, Hugo, Mihir Bellare, and Ran Canetti. 1997. RFC 2104–HMAC: Keyed-hashing for message authentication. http://www.faqs.org/rfcs/rfc2104.html.

Lampson, Burt. 1973. A note on the containment problem. *Communications of the ACM* 20, (October): 613-615.

Machrone, Bill. 2001. The evil sniffer. *PCMag.com*, December 4. http://www.pcmag.com/print_article/0,3048,a=19167,00.asp.

RSA Data Security, Inc. 2002. *PKCS #1: RSA Encryption Standard, Version 2.1*

Saltzer, J. H., and M. D. Schroeder. 1975. The protection of information in computer systems. *Proceedings of the IEEE,* 63(9):1278-1308.

Sheehan, Madelyn Diness. 2003. *Fishing in Oregon.* 9th ed. Scappoose, OR: Flying Pencil Publications.

Sullivan, Bob. 2003. E-card trickery now in spyware, too: Fake greeting cards seem to be the ploy of choice lately. *MSNBC.com.* http://msnbc.msn.com/id/3078535/.

Trusted Computing Group. 2005a. *TCG PC Client Specific Implementation Specification for Conventional BIOS.* http://www.trustedcomputinggroup.org

Trusted Computing Group. 2005b. *TPM Main Spec.* Parts 1, 2, and 3. http://www.trustedcomputinggroup.org

Trusted Computing Group. 2005c. *TPM PC Client Specific TPM Interface Specification.* http://www.trustedcomputinggroup.org

Ware, Willis, ed. 1970. Security controls for computer systems: Report of defense science board task force on computer security. Rand Report R609-1, Santa Monica, CA: The RAND Corporation.

Index

A

access to files, ability to control, 19

ACM. *See* authenticated code module (ACM)

addresses, 27

Advanced Configuration and Power Interface Specification (ACPI 2004), 234

AIK. *See* attestation identity key (AIK)

aliasing, GART/graphics, 216

anatomy of attacks, 43

anti-virus (AV) programs, 40

applications. *See also* malware

anti-virus (AV) programs, 40

components of, 47

contained application design options, 184

defined, 263

design options, 180

partition

protection, 175

standard, 172

program decisions and attacks, 49

protected component application design options, 181

protection partition, 175

secrets, 116

standalone, interaction between OS, MVMM and kernel, 179

standard partition, 172

suitability, 72

trusted computing, 39

unaware applications, 180

use, architecture and, 184

version of, 39

arbitration memory, 170

architecture. *See also* partitions

    actual use, 169

    Applet protection partition, 174

    application

        design options, 180

        protection partition, 175

        standard partition, 172

        use, 184

    arbitration, memory, 170

    assignment of resources, 171

    communication channel, MVMM, 171

    communication, partition, 175

    configuration concerns, 213. *See also* configuration concerns

    contained application application design options, 184

    current Intel® architecture security support, 30

    design options, application, 180

    different vendors, OS, MVMM, and kernel interaction, 179

    hardware attacks. *See also* hardware attacks

    IPC, 176

kernel, OS, and MVMM interaction, 177

kernel protection partition, 173

late launch, 185. *See also* late launch

lifecycle of partition, 171

measured virtual machine monitor (MVMM), 170

memory arbitration, MVMM, 170

MVMM and kernel from same vendor, interaction, 177

MVMM, OS, and kernel interaction, 177

operating system, standard partition, 172

options, application design, 180

OS, MVMM, and kernel interaction, 177

protected component application design options, 181

protection partition, 173

RPC, 176

same vendor, OS, MVMM, and kernel interaction, 177

security architecture specification (SAS), 267

standard partition, 172

unaware applications, 180

assignment of resources, MVMM, 171

assumptions, user's, 85

asymmetric encryption, 13

    break once run everywhere (BORE), 41

attack and protection matrix, 66

attackers, 85

    identity of, 60

    resources of, 61

attacks. *See also* protection. *See also*
    hardware attacks
        anatomy of, 43
        applications and, 46
        bus attacks, 241
        components of applications
          and, 47
        definition, 263
        display windows, 48
        DoS. *See* denial of service (DoS)
          attack
        hardware attacks. *See also*
          hardware attacks
        input manipulation by
          malware, 52
        keystrokes, reading, 48
        loss of power, 68
        malware attack points, 50
        manipulation by malware, 50
        matrix of types of attacks, 66
        memory manipulation by
          malware, 50
        mitigation of, 160
        output manipulation by
          malware, 53
        power loss, 68
        present time, 46
        program decisions, 49
        programmer vs attacker, 45
        protection coverage versus
          attack incidents, 10
        reading keystrokes, 48
        software-based attacks, 67
        timing attacks, 68
        types of attacks matrix, 66
attestation, 78, 119
    identity key, TPM, 134
    information, 141
    roots of trust, 119
attestation identity key (AIK), 141

authenticated code module (ACM), 115
    defined, 263
    SCHECK, 220
authentication
    hashed message authentication
      code (HMAC) validation, 128
    SINIT module, 198
authorization
    program code and, 123
    SHA-1 authorization values, 126
    TPM, 134
    user identity, 20
AV. *See* anti-virus (AV) programs

B

backwards compatibility of platform
    as objective, 65
bad platforms, 41
    finding, 42
base page address, 27
basic input/output system (BIOS)
    definition, 263
    holding SMM code, 238
basic questions, 60
Bell-LaPadula, 20
BIOS. *See* basic input/output system
    (BIOS)
BIOS boot block, defined, 263
blue screen of death (BSOD). *See*
    panic blue screen
boot strap processor (BSP),
    defined, 263
boundary
    comparison, 101
    conditions, 118
    protection, 87
    summary, 100
break once run everywhere (BORE),
    41, 45
    defined, 263

BSOD. *See* panic blue screen

buffer overflow issues, 40

burn issues, non-volatile (NV) storage, 125

bus agent ID, defined, 263

bus attacks, 241

busses. *See also* universal serial bus (USB)

    attacks, 241

    FSB. *See* front side bus (FSB)

    late launch, TPM bus considerations, 200

    LPC. *See* low pin count (LPC) bus

    TPM. *See* trusted platform module (TPM) bus

    trusted input, 156

C

central processing unit (CPU)

    connections. *See* memory controller hub (MCH). *See* front side bus (FSB)

    definition, 24, 190, 263

    frequency, 36

    internals and trusted computing, 25

    persistance areas, 225

    synchronization, 190

chaining of keyboard drivers, 52

channels

    communication, MVMM, 171

    trusted, 15, 144

chipsets, 24, 96

    configuration concerns, 213

    future topology, 259

    late launch, unlocking for initialization of ILP state, 203

    locking to ILP, 197

    memory, 215

    secured integrated graphics, 151

    validation, 197

    VMM measurement, 95

cleanup of sensitive data, 19

client, defined, 8

code, TPM, 123

combination cryptography, 14

Common Criteria agreement, 21, 87

common distribution methods and third-party data, 75

communication. *See also* interprocess communication (IPC)

    channel, measured virtual machine monitor (MVMM), 171

    limited inter-VM communication, 112

    partitions, 175

compatibility, backwards, 65

confidentiality of transport session, 138

configuration concerns, 213

    additional platform configurations, 220

    Advanced Configuration and Power Interface Specification (ACPI 2004), 234

    aliasing, GART/graphics, 216

    applications, trusted computing, 39

    chipset, 213

    folding, memory, 214

    frequency, power and, 218

    GART/graphics aliasing, 216

    graphics, GART/graphics aliasing, 216

    identification of current configuration, 5

locking memory
configuration, 216

LT chipset, 213

memory configuration,
locking, 216

memory folding, 214

new issues, 220

operating system, 37, 39

overclocking, 219

power and frequency, 218

properties of GART,
GART/graphics aliasing, 217

SCHECK, 220

system memory overlap,
GART/graphics aliasing, 218

testing configuration,
memory, 216

trusted computing, 42

trusting memory, 215

contained application design
options, 184

control
transport session, 138

trusted USB, 159

control register 3 (CR3), 27

control registers, 97

controllers
trusted mobile keyboard
controller, 161

trusted USB controller, 159

cost, trusted USB, 159

counters in software-based attacks, 67

covert channels, 98

CPU. See central processing unit (CPU)

CR0 (control register 0), defined, 264

cryptographic hash, 46, 47

password processing, 49

cryptography, 13. *See also* keys
enveloping, 14

trusted channels, 147

current hardware
identification of current
configuration, 5

trusted computing, 36

current Intel® architecture security
support, 30

D

data to be protected, 60, 67, 70.
See also specific topics throughout
this index

ability to control file access, 19

cleanup of sensitive data, 19

sealed storage, 136

debuggers, 45

software-based attacks, 67

Defense Department, "Rainbow
Series", 20

defined ordinals, non-volatile (NV)
storage, 124

definitions
applications, 263

authenticated code module
(ACM), 263

basic input/output system
(BIOS), 263

BIOS boot block, 263

boot strap processor (BSP), 263

break once run everywhere
(BORE), 263

bus agent ID, 263

central processing unit (CPU),
24, 190

client, 8

CR0, 264

digital signature, 264
direct memory access (DMA), 264
domain manager, 264
DoS, 264
endorsement key, 264
entropy, 264
firmware hub (FWH), 264
front side bus (FSB), 264
global descriptor table register
    (GDTR), 264
graphics
    translation table, 264
graphics aperture relocation
    table (GART), 264
grid computing, 264
hash, 265
human input device (HID), 265
initiating logical processor
    (ILP), 265
input and output (I/O), 265
input/output controller hub
    (ICH), 265
interprocess communication
    (IPC), 265
LaGrande Technology (LT),
    16, 265
late launch, 265
load descriptor table (LDTR), 265
low pin count (LPC) bus, 265
malware, 265
memory controller hub (MCH),
    24, 266
multiplexer (MUX), 266
NoDMA, 266
non-volatile (NV) storage, 266
operator, 9
opt-in, 266
option ROM, 266
owner, 9

pass phrase, 266
physical presence, 266
platform, 8
platform configuration register
    (PCR), 266
prime number, 266
protection partition, 266
PS2, 266
random number generator
    (RNG), 266
remote procedure call (RPC), 267
reset, hardware attacks, 224
responding logical processor
    (RLP), 267
rings (ring 0 through ring 3), 266
root of trust for measurement
    (RTM), 267
root of trust for reporting
    (RTR), 267
root of trust for storage (RTS), 267
safer mode extension (SMX), 267
sealed storage, 267
secure enter (SENTER), 267
secure hash algorithm 1
    (SHA-1), 267
secure initialization (SINIT)
    module, 267
security architecture
    specification (SAS), 267
SMI transfer module (STM), 267
software (SW), 267
standard partition, 267
storage
    root key, 267
system management interrupt
    (SMI), 267
timing attack, 268

trust, 6

trust decision, 7

trusted graphics translation table
(TGTT), 268

trusted platform module
(TPM), 268

user, 9

virtual machine extensions
(VMX), 268

volatile storage, 268

wild, 268

degradation of content, time value
and, 75

delivery of attacker's software, 61

denial of service (DoS) attack, 54
defined, 264

Department of Defense, "Rainbow
Series", 20

descriptor tables, local, 30

descriptors, protected mode, 30

design
application design options, 180
human interface, 155

device focus, trusted channel, 149

digital signature, defined, 264

DIMM settings, 37

direct memory access (DMA)
application design and, 252
backward compatibility, 65
defined, 264
malware, 51
page protections, 88

directory, 27

display. *See also* panic blue screen
driver, changing, 54
screen scraping, 54

display adapter
page protections, 88
trusted channels, 149
trusted computing, 28

display window, 251
as application components, 46, 47
attacks, 47
passwords, 249

disruptive event, protected partition
protections, 189

distribution mechanism of malware, 40

DMA. *See* direct memory access
(DMA)

domain manager, defined, 264

domain separation, 22, 31. *See also*
rings (ring 0 through ring 3)
Intel® 386 processor, 31
rings, 30
VMM, 112

drivers
applications, 39
backward compatibility, 65
changes in, 38
display driver, changing, 54
endpoint, trusted input, 157
keyboard, 48, 52
manipulation of memory, 50
mitigating attacks, 56
operating system, 38
trusted USB, 158
versions, 38, 39

E

e-mail, protection of, 72

ease of use as objective, 63

economy of mechanism
and security principles, 81
defined, 79

enclave model, 10

encryption. *See also* Cryptography
keys, 45, 47
trusted input, 157

endorsement key, 133
defined, 264

endpoint, trusted input driver, 157

entropy, defined, 264

enumeration, responding logical processor (RLP), 195, 196

enveloping, 14

environment requirements, 84

evaluation, target of evaluation (TOE), 87

event log, PCR, 130

execute-only segment option, 30

execution
    changing execution flow, 122
    engine, TPM, 122
    ICH flag, 230
    protection of, 76, 103
    SCLEAN, 229
    SCLEAN execution flow, 232

exiting ACMs, 260

F

fast busses. *See also* hublink bus attacks. *See also* front side bus (FSB)
    attacks on, 69, 70

features, 76

file access, ability to control, 19

firmware hub (FWH), defined, 264

folding, memory, 214

frequency, 36
    configuration concerns, 218

front side bus (FSB)
    attacks, 241
    defined, 24, 264
    trusted computing, 28

FSB. *See* front side bus (FSB)

future chipset topology, 259

future threats and future versions of LT, 257

FWH. *See* firmware hub (FWH)

G

garbage in, garbage out (GIGO), 145

GART. *See* graphics aperture relocation table (GART)

GART/graphics aliasing, configuration concerns, 216

GDTR. *See* global descriptor table register (GDTR)

GETSEC instruction
    [SENTER] completion, 203
    [SENTER] sequence, 192, 193
    [SEXIT] processing, 209

GIGO. *See* garbage in, garbage out (GIGO)

global descriptor table register (GDTR), defined, 264

graphics
    configuration concerns, GART/graphics aliasing, 216
    connections. *See* memory controller hub (MCH)
    MCH (GMCH). *See* memory controller hub (MCH)
    protection, 78
    secured discrete graphics, 150
    secured integrated graphics, 151
    translation table, defined, 264

graphics aperture relocation table (GART)
    configuration concerns, GART/graphics aliasing, 216
    defined, 264

grid computing, defined, 264

GTT. *See* graphics translation table (GTT)

guest-state area, VMCS, 106

H

hardware

   attacker's resources, 61

   attacks. *See* hardware attacks

   changes in, 160

   chipset, 96

   current hardware, trusted
      computing, 36

   defined, 265

   DIMM settings, 37

   late launch, hardware
      configuration, 191

   mainframe computers, 21

   mitigation of attacks, 56

   protections basis, 5

   task-switching, 30

   trusted channels, 147

hardware attacks, 221

   addition of TPM, RESET
      protection, 227

   attacker's resources, 61

   bus attacks, 241

   CPU, rogue, 222

   defined, 44

   determination of prior state,
      RESET protection, 225

   flag, setting ICH flag, 227

   front side bus attacks, 241

   Hublink bus attacks, 241

   ICH flag, setting, 227

   INIT protection, 234

   memory properties, system,
      RESET protection, 224

   mitigation of attacks, 56

   MVMM, STM MVMM
      negotiation, 240

   open case attacks, 69

   prior state, determination of, 225

protected environment

   rogue CPU not exiting, 223

   rogue CPU not joining
      the, 222

protection sequence, RESET
   protection, 226

registering SCLEAN, 231

remote hardware attacks, 61

reset definition, 224

reset protection, 223

results of suspending rogue
   CPU, 223

rogue CPU, 222

running SCLEAN, 229

S2/S3/S4 sleep protection, 234

sequence, RESET protection, 226

setting ICH flag, RESET
   protection, 227

simple hardware attacks, 62

SMI handling, 236

SMM loading, 238

SMM transfer module, 237

sophisticated local hardware
   attacks, 70

state table, RESET protection, 228

STM MVMM negotiation, 240

suspension of rogue CPU, 223

system memory properties,
   RESET protection, 224

TPM addition, RESET
   protection, 227

trusted USB, 160

hash. *See also* secure hash algorithm
1 (SHA-1)

   cryptographic hash, 14

   defined, 265

   TPM response to
      `TPM.HASH.START`, 201

hashed message authentication code
(HMAC) validation, 128

heat, affecting power and
frequency, 218

HID. *See* human input device (HID)

high-level requirements, 84

history of SENTER, 187

host-state area, VMCS, 106

hublink bus attacks, 241

human input device (HID), 155.
See also mouse. *See also* keyboard
defined, 265

human interface design, 155

HW. *See* hardware

I

I/O. *See* input and output (I/O)

IA-32 Intel® Architecture Software
Developers Manual, Volume 3:
System Programming Guide
(Intel®, 2003), 26

ICH. *See* input/output controller hub
(ICH)

identification of current
configuration, 5

identification of users, 20
user-ID, 53

identity
attackers, 60
description of measurement
and, 94
key, attestation, 134, 141
launched environment, late
launch, 191
SCLEAN identity, 233

ILP. *See* initiating logical processor
(ILP)

infection mechanism of malware, 40

initialization (INIT). *See also* secure
initialization (SINIT) module
protection, 234
trusted mobile keyboard
controller (TMKBC), 163

initiating logical processor (ILP)
defined, 265
late launch
measurement
transmission, 202
processing, 196
state, 202
measurement transmission, late
launch, 202
unlocking the chipset for
initialization, late launch, 203

input and output (I/O), 98. *See also*
trusted I/O. *See also* periphcrals
defined, 265
human input device (HID), 265
manipulation of input by
malware, 52
manipulation of output by
malware, 53
ports, 97
protection of, 77, 143
TPM, 121

input manipulation by malware, 52

input/output controller hub (ICH)
defined, 24, 265
hardware attacks, ICH flag,
227, 230
trusted computing, 29

input/output controller hub (ICH)
flag, hardware attacks, 227, 230

installation of applications, trusted
computing, 39

Intel® Virtualization Technology, 80,
81, 94, 97, 104, 169, 170, 255

intentions of user, 70

interaction between OS, MVMM and kernel, 177

internal TPM values, non-volatile (NV) storage, 124

internet transactions, protection of, 73

interprocess communication (IPC), 176
  defined, 265

interrupt system and unanticipated conditions, 18

interrupts, enabling, MVMM execution, late launch, 207

IPC. *See* interprocess communication (IPC)

isolation of programs, 5

K

KBC. *See* keyboard controller (KBC)

kernel
  interaction between OS, MVMM and kernel, 177
  interaction of MVMM and kernel from same vendor, 177
  interaction of OS and kernel from same vendor, 178
  interaction of OS, MVMM, and kernel from different vendors, 179
  limited services, 174
  protection partition, 173
  rich service kernel, 173

keyboard, 98
  and scan code, 48
  client, defined, 8
  controller (KBC), 161
  drivers, 48, 52
  sniffers, 53
  trusted computing, 29
  trusted mobile keyboard controller, 161
  trusted USB, 158

keyboard controller (KBC), 161

keyboard sniffers, 53

keys. *See also* passwords
  asymmetric encryption, 13
  attestation identity, 134
  distribution, trusted USB, 160
  exchange, 148
  symmetric encryption, 13
  TPM key generation, 132
  unique, 46

keystrokes
  attacks, reading keystrokes, 48
  reading, 47, 250
  receiving keystroke entity, 53

L

LaGrande Technology (LT)
  attack and protection matrix, 66
  Basic Questions, 60
  boundary, protection, 87
  chipset configuration concerns, 213
  configuration concerns, 213
  defined, 16
  design principles, 79
  ease of use, 63
  execution, protection of, 76, 103
  late launch, 185
  matrix, protection and attack, 66
  need for trusted channel, 145
  objectives, 59
  principles of LaGrande Technology design, 79
  protected execution, 76
  protection and attack matrix, 66
  protection boundary, 87
  requirements, 84, 101
  shutdown, late launch, 212
  suitability of application, 72

LaGrande Technology (LT). *See also* specific topics throughout this index. *See also* trusted computing
  defined, 265
  late launch. *See also* late launch
language processors, 19
late launch, 185. *See also* measured virtual machine monitor (MVMM)
  assurance of participation of all CPU's, 189
  assurance that launch can detect any tampering, 191
  chipset, unlocking for initialization of ILP state, 203
  configuration of hardware, 191
  defined, 265
  detection of tampering, 191
  enabling interrupts, MVMM execution, 207
  enabling SMI, MVMM execution, 208
  execution of GETSEC [SENTER], 194
  execution of MVMM, 207
  execution of SINIT, 203
  GETSEC [SENTER] completion, 203
  GETSEC [SENTER] sequence, 192, 193
  GETSEC [SEXIT] processing, 209
  hardware configuration, 191
  history of SENTER, 187
  identity of launched environment, 191
  ILP measurement transmission, 202
  ILP processing, 196
  ILP state, initialization of, 202
  initialization of ILP state, 202
  initialization of SMM handling, 204
  initiation of GETSEC [SEXIT], 210

initiation of protections at any time, 188
interrupts, enabling, MVMM execution, 207
issuing SENTER-ACK, 195, 196
launching the protected partition, 186
measurement, ILP measurement transmission, 202
NoDMA, SINIT execution, 205
participation of all CPU's, assurance of, 189
passing control to MVMM, SINIT execution, 207
PCR, setting the, 200
protected partition, launching, 186
recap, secure launch, 208
rendezvous, GETSEC [SEXIT], 211
SCLEAN validation, SINIT execution, 205
secure launch recap, 208
SENTER-ACK, issuing, 195, 196
SENTER, history of, 187
setting the PCR, 200
shutdown, 212
  MVMM, GETSEC [SEXIT] processing, 211
SINIT
  execution, 203
  load, 198
  measurement, storing, 200
  processing, 198
SMI enabling, MVMM execution, 208
SMM handling, initialization of, 204
storing SINIT measurement, 200
tampering, detection of, 191
time of protection initiation, 188

TPM bus considerations, 200

TPM response to
TPM.HASH.START, 201

unlocking the chipset for
initialization of ILP state, 203

validation of
GETSEC [SEXIT], 211

launching. *See also* late launch
protected partition, 186
VMM, 115

least common mechanism, 79, 83

least privilege
and security principles, 80
defined, 79

left-hand side (LHS). *See* standard
partition

lifecycle of partition, measured
virtual machine monitor
(MVMM), 171

linear address, 27

load descriptor table (LDTR), 30
defined, 265

loading SCLEAN, 229

local hardware attacks, 70

locality, TPM, 139

location
SCLEAN, 229
trusted platform module
(TPM), 260

logical address, 27

long-term protected storage, 5

loss of power attacks, 68

low pin count (LPC) bus
attacks, 69, 242
defined, 265
trusted computing, 29

LPC. *See* low pin count (LPC) bus

M

machine specific register (MSR), 97

mainframe computers, 21

malware, 40, 44
attack points, 47, 50
BORE. *See* break once run
everywhere (BORE)
changes in program, 51
components, 40
defined, 265
display driver, changing, 54
distribution mechanism, 40
DMA access, 51
infection mechanism, 40
payload, 41
screen scraping, 54

malware attack points, 50

manageability as objective, 63

manipulation by malware, 50

matrix, protection and attack, 66

MCH. *See* memory controller hub
(MCH)

measured virtual machine monitor
(MVMM), 95, 168, 170
hardware attacks, STM MVMM
negotiation, 240
interaction between OS, MVMM
and kernel, 177
interaction of MVMM and kernel
from same vendor, 177
interaction of OS and MVMM
from same vendor, 178
interaction of OS, MVMM, and
kernel from different
vendors, 179

late launch
  execution, 207
  GETSEC [SEXIT]
    processing, shutdown, 211
  loading, SINIT execution, 206
  passing control, SINIT
    execution, 207
  passing control to, SINIT
    execution, 207
  shutdown,
    GETSEC [SEXIT]
    processing, 211
page protections, 88, 89
shutdown, late launch,
  GETSEC [SEXIT]
  processing, 211
measurement
  agent, attesting to
    information, 142
  current platform configuration, 42
  definition of measure, 266
  description of, 94
  ILP measurement
    transmission, 202
  late launch, storing SINIT
    measurement, 200
  of VMM, 94, 113
  protected partition
    protections, 188
  root of trust for measurement
    (RTM), 119
  STM, 240
memory. *See also* system memory.
  See also memory controller hub
  (MCH)
  arbitration, measured virtual
    machine monitor (MVMM), 170
  chipset specific, 215

folding, configuration
  concerns, 214
hardware attacks, system
  memory properties, RESET
  protection, 224
locking memory
  configuration, 216
management and trusted
  computing, 26
manipulation by malware, 50
pages, protection of, 77
random access memory (RAM), 24
size, protected mode, 30
testing configuration, 216
trusted computing, 28
trusting memory, configuration
  concerns, 215
memory controller hub (MCH)
  connections. *See* front side bus
    (FSB)
  defined, 24, 266
  persistance areas, 225
  trusted computing, 28
mitigation of attacks, 56
mobile keyboard controller,
  trusted, 161
mouse, 98. *See also* keyboard
  trusted USB, 158
multi-partition environment, 107
multiple CPU systems
  FSB connections, 24
  trusted computing, 28
multiplexer (MUX)
  defined, 266
  secured integrated graphics, 153
MUX. *See* multiplexer (MUX)
MVMM. *See* measured virtual
  machine monitor (MVMM)

N

1970 task force on trusted computing, 18

NoDMA, 91
   defined, 266
   SINIT execution, late launch, 205
   STM and, 205
   table, page protections, 89

non-requirements, 86

non-volatile (NV) storage
   burn issues, 125
   defined, 266
   defined ordinals, 124
   internal TPM values, 124
   TPM, 124

nonces, 131

"North Bridge". *See* memory controller hub (MCH)

O

obfuscation, 45

offset, 27

open case attacks, 69

open design
   and security principles, 82
   definition, 79

operating system (OS)
   ease of use, 63
   interaction between OS, MVMM and kernel, 177
   interaction of OS and kernel from same vendor, 178
   interaction of OS and MVMM from same vendor, 178
   interaction of OS, MVMM, and kernel from different vendors, 179
   mainframe computers, 21
   partition, standard, 172
   standard partition, 172
   trusted computing, current OS, 37

operations, trusted mobile keyboard controller (TMKBC), 163

operator, defined, 9

opt-in
   defined, 266
   TPM, 133

option ROM, defined, 266

"Orange Book" (Department of Defense, 1985), 20

OS. *See* operating system (OS)

oscilloscopes and open case attacks, 69

output. *See* input and output (I/O)

overclocking, configuration concerns, 219

overlap, system memory overlap, configuration concerns, GART/graphics aliasing, 218

overt channels, 98

owner, defined, 9

P

page protections, 88

page swapping, 27

paging, 26
   control, 27
   mechanism, 89, 90
   page protections, 89
   trusted computing, 31

panic blue screen, 154

panic mode implementation, 154

partitions. *See also* protection partition. *See also* protected partition
   Applet protection, 174
   communication, 175. *See also* remote procedure call (RPC). *See also* interprocess communication (IPC)
   creation of multi-partition environment, 107

kernel protection partition, 173

lifecycle, MVMM, 171

protected partition, late launch, 186

protection, 173

removal, 189

standard, 172

pass phrase, defined, 266

passwords, 46

    application design, 248

    attacks, password processing, 49

    display window requesting, 249

    keystroke reading, 250

    processing, 47

path, trusted, 15, 144

payload, malware, 41

PCR. *See* platform configuration register (PCR)

performance counters in software-based attacks, 67

performance level as objective, 64

peripherals. *See also* universal serial bus (USB). *See also* direct memory access (DMA)

    trusted input, 156

    trusted USB peripheral, 157

personal computers

    basic components, 24

    trusted computing, 23

phishing, 53

physical address, 27

    paging and, 31

physical page protections, 89

physical presence, defined, 266

platform. *See also* operating system (OS). *See also* hardware. *See also* configuration. *See also* applications "bad" platforms. *See* bad platforms

    current platforms, 36

    defined, 8

    finding bad platforms, 42

    identity, verifiable report of, 5

    trusted computing, 36

    unique values, 63

platform configuration register (PCR)

    defined, 266

    event log, 130

    late launch, 200

    reporting current value, 130

    resetting, 130

    TPM, 129

ports, input and output (I/O), 97. *See also* universal serial bus (USB)

power

    Advanced Configuration and Power Interface Specification (ACPI 2004), 234

    configuration concerns, 218

    managment settings, 197

previous platform objectives, 62

prime numbers

    defined, 266

    key generation, use in, 132

prior state, hardware attacks, determination of prior state, RESET protection, 225

privacy as objective, 63

privilege

    levels. *See* rings (ring 0 through ring 3)

    separation, security principles, 82

program code, TPM, 123

protected component application
  design options, 181

protected environment
    hardware attacks, rogue CPUs,
      222, 223
    rogue CPUs, 222, 223

protected partition, 167, 168.
  See also protection partition
    launch control, 188
    launching, 186

protected storage, long-term, 5

protection. *See also* attacks
    attack incidents, protection
      coverage versus, 10
    boundary, 87
    execution, 76, 103
    graphics, 78
    input and output, 77, 143
    matrix, protection and attack, 66
    memory pages, 77
    page, 88
    requirements, 86
    reset protection, 226
    secrets, 116
    supervisors, 18
    virtual machines, 109

protection mode
    CPU internals, 25

protection partition, 173
    defined, 266
    late launch, 186

PS2, defined, 266

psychological acceptability
    and security principles, 83
    definition, 79

R

The Rainbow Series, 20

RAM. *See* random access memory
  (RAM)

random access memory (RAM), 24

random number generator (RNG)
    defined, 266
    TPM, 131

read-only segment option, 30

reboot, launching the protected
    partition, 188

receiving keystroke entity, 53

registers in software-based attacks, 67
    control register 3 (CR3), 27
    control registers, 97

registration
    SCLEAN, 231
    TMP registration, 231

remote hardware attacks, 61

remote procedure call (RPC), 176
    defined, 267

removal of partitions, 189

rendezvous, late launch,
    GETSEC [SEXIT], 211

reporting
    current PCR value, 130
    root of trust for reporting
      (RTR), 119

reset definition, hardware attacks, 224

reset protection, hardware attacks, 223

resetting PCR, 130

resource protection, VMM, 112

resources of attacker, 61

responding logical processor (RLP)
    defined, 267
    enumerating, 195, 196
    sleep, 196

response packet, 123

RFC 2104-HMAC:Keyed-hashing for
  Message Authentication (Krawczyk
  1997), 128

rich service kernel, 173

right-hand side (LHS). *See* protected
  partition

rings (ring 0 through ring 3)
    applet, 174
    defined, 25, 266
    mitigating attacks, 56
    protection partition, 173
    trusted computing, 30, 37

risk assessment, security as, 66

RLP. *See* responding logical processor
  (RLP)

rogue CPUs, hardware attacks, 222

root of trust for measurement (RTM);
    defined, 267

root of trust for measurement
  (RTM), 119
    boot of platform, 139

root of trust for reporting (RTR), 119
    defined, 267

root of trust for storage (RTS), 120
    defined, 267

roots of trust, 119

RPC. *See* remote procedure call
  (RPC)

RSA engine, TPM, 131

RTM. *See* root of trust for
  measurement (RTM)

RTR. *See* root of trust for reporting
  (RTR)

RTS. *See* root of trust for storage (RTS)

S

S2/S3/S4 sleep protection, 234

safer mode extension (SMX), 95.
    See also GETSEC instruction
    defined, 267
    measurement instructions, 95

SAS. *See* security architecture
  specification (SAS)

SCHECK, 220

SCLEAN
    AC module, 228
    execution flow, 232
    speeding up, 231
    TMP registration, 231
    validating identity, 233
    validation, SINIT execution, late
      launch, 205

screen scraping, 54

sealed storage, 77
    defined, 267
    TPM, 136
    unsealing of data, 136, 137

secrets
    establishment of, 117
    protection of, 116

secure enter (SENTER)
    defined, 267
    GETSEC [SENTER]
      sequence, 192, 193
    history of, 187

secure exit (SEXIT) shutdown, late
  launch, GETSEC [SEXIT]
  processing, 209

secure hash algorithm 1 (SHA-1)
    authorization values, 126
    binding structures together, 126
    continued use of, 128
    defined, 267
    TPM, 126

secure initialization (SINIT) module
  defined, 267
  execution, 203
  header, 199
  load, 198
  processing, 198
  storing, measurement, 200
  system management interrupt
    (SMI), 204
  validation, 199
secure launch recap, 208
secured discrete graphics, 150
secured integrated graphics, 151
  panic blue screen, 154
  resource management, 152
  trusted sprite model, 151
security architecture specification
  (SAS), defined, 267
security principles, 80
segment
  descriptors, 31
  limit checking, 30
  logical address, 27
  swapping, 30
segmentation, 26, 27
SENTER. *See* secure enter
  (SENTER)
SENTER-ACK, issuing, 194, 195, 196
separation of domains, 22
separation of privilege
  definition, 79
  security principles, 82
separation of user process from
  supervisor processes, 5, 22
sequence of commands in transport
  session, 138
session key creation, verification
  of, 159

SEXIT. *See* secure exit (SEXIT)
  shutdown
SEXIT ACM, 260
SHA-1. *See* secure hash algorithm 1
  (SHA-1)
shutdown. *See also* secure exit
  (SEXIT) shutdown
  late launch, 212
  MVMM, GETSEC [SEXIT]
    processing, 211
  orderly, 19
  SINIT execution and MVMM
    loading, 206
  trusted USB controller or
    peripheral, 161
simple hardware attacks, 62
SINIT. *See* secure initialization
  (SINIT) module
sleep
  Advanced Configuration and
    Power Interface Specification
    (ACPI 2004), 234
  protection, 234
  responding logical processor
    (RLP), 196
SMI. *See* system management
  interrupt (SMI)
SMI transfer module (STM), 93
  defined, 267
  measurement, 240
  MVMM negotiation, hardware
    attacks, 240
  NoDMA and, 205
  page protections, 89
  SINIT execution, 204
  SMRAM, 238

SMM
   handling, late launch, 204
   loading, hardware attacks, 238, 239
   transfer module, hardware attacks, 237
SMX. *See* safer mode extension (SMX)
software (SW). *See also* operating system (OS). *See also* attacks.
   See also applications
   attacker's resources, 61
   attacks, 44, 67. *See also* attacks
   defined, 267
   delivery of attacker's software, 61
"South Bridge". *See* input/output controller hub (ICH)
standalone applications, interaction between OS, MVMM and kernel, 179
standard partition, 167, 168, 172
   defined, 267
startup sequence, 19, 29
state table, hardware attacks, RESET protection, 228
STM. *See* SMI Transfer Module (STM)
storage. *See also* sealed storage.
   See also non-volatile (NV) storage
   long-term protected storage, 5
   root key, defined, 267
   root of trust for storage (RTR), 120
   VMM measurement in TPM, 96
   volatile, 126
stored data, protection of, 72
suitability of application, 72
summary, boundary, 100
supervisor, 18
   programs, 19
   protection, 18
   rings, separation, 30
   separation of user process from supervisor processes, 5, 22

symmetric encryption, 13, 45
   break once run everywhere (BORE), 41
synchronization, central processing unit (CPU), 190
system management interrupt (SMI).
   See also SMI Transfer Module (STM)
   ACPI extensions, 239
   defined, 267
   enabling, MVMM execution, late launch, 208
   handling, 236
   page protections, 88
   SINIT execution, 204
   system SMI, 208
system memory
   attacks and, 48
   connections. *See* memory controller hub (MCH). *See* front side bus (FSB)
   hardware attacks, system memory properties, RESET protection, 224
   malware attack points, 50
   overlap, configuration concerns, GART/graphics aliasing, 218
   password processing, 49
   program decisions, 49
   screen scraping, 54
system SMI, 208

T

table, 27
target of evaluation (TOE), 87
TCG PC Client Specific Implementation Specification for Conventional BIOS (TCG 2005a), 120, 129, 139
   TPM.HASH.START, 201

TCS. *See* trusted configuration space (TCS)

teardown, trusted mobile keyboard controller (TMKBC), 164

test of configuration, memory, 216

TGTT. *See* trusted graphics translation table (TGTT)

third-party data, protection of, 70, 75

thread information in software-based attacks, 67

time of protection initiation, late launch, 188

timing attack, defined, 268

TOE. *See* target of evaluation (TOE)

TPM. *See* trusted platform module (TPM)

TPM Main Specification (TCG 2005b), 120, 129, 139

TPM.HASH.START, TPM response to, 201

transitive trust, TPM, 135

transport session, TPM, 138

trust decision, defined, 7

trust, defined, 6

trusted channel, 15
    and trusted path, 144
    application design, 249
    basics, 146
    cryptographic trusted channels, 147
    device focus, 149
    hardware trusted channels, 147
    key exchange, 148

trusted computer, attributes of, 5

trusted computing, 3. *See also* specific topics throughout this index. *See also* LaGrande Technology (LT)
    applications, 39
    attributes of trusted computer, 5
    background of, 3
    Bell-LaPadula, 20
    break once, run everywhere malware, 41
    configuration, 42
        applications, 39
        operating system, 39
    CPU internals and, 25
    current environment, 35
    current Intel® architecture security support, 30
    display adapter, MCH, 28
    drivers
        applications, 39
        operating system, 38
    early papers, 18
    front-side bus, 28
    future, 22
    hardware, current, 36
    history of, 17
    ICH, 29
    industry response, 21
    installation of applications, 39
    keyboard, 29
    LPC bus, 29
    malware, 40
    memory, 28
    memory management, 26
    multiple CPU systems, 28

1970 task force, 18

operating system, current, 37

paging, 31

personal computers, 23

platforms

    current, 36

    finding bad platforms, 42

present issues, 35

properties, security, 31

protected mode

    CPU internals, 25

    current Intel® architecture
        security support, 30

protection, 12

ring use, 37

rings, 30

security properties, 31

The Rainbow Series, 20

USB, 29

weakest link, 10

trusted computing group (TCG),
  finding bad platforms, 42

trusted configuration space (TCS), 150

trusted graphics translation table
  (TGTT), 92, 153

    defined, 268

    page protections, 89

trusted I/O, 155

    and LT, 164

trusted mobile keyboard controller
  (TMKBC), 161

trusted path, 15, 86

    indicator, application design, 249

    trusted channel and, 144

trusted platform module (TPM)

    basic components, 121

    basic TPM design, 121

    changing execution flow, 122

    defined, 268

    design, 120, 121

    finding bad platforms, 42

    functionality, 135

    hashed message authentication
      code (HMAC) validation, 128

    key generation, 132

    location, 260

    platform privacy, 63

    registration, 231

    roots of trust, 120

    secure hash algorithm 1
      (SHA-1), 128

    TPM Main Specification (TCG
      2005b), 120

    `TPM.HASH.START`, response
      to, 201

    use of, 142

    validation, 197

    VMM measurement, 95

    XOR strings, 128

trusted platform module (TPM) bus

    considerations, 200

    hardware attacks, addition of
      TPM, RESET protection, 227

    late launch, 200, 201

    TPM response to
      `TPM.HASH.START`, 201

trusted sprite model, 151

trusted USB

    controller, 159

    operation, 160

    peripheral, 157

    teardown, 161

trusting memory, configuration
  concerns, 215

U

unanticipated conditions, 18, 22
    protected partition
        protections, 189
unaware applications, 180
universal serial bus (USB). *See also*
   trusted USB
     controller hubs, 29
     peripherals and trusted
       channels, 149
     trusted computing, 29
     trusted input, 156
unsealing of data, 136, 137
upgrade requirements, 86
U.S. Department of Defense,
  "Rainbow Series", 20
USB. *See* universal serial bus (USB)
user
     assumptions, 85
     defined, 9
     identification, 20
     intent, 70
     isolation, 18
     mode, 18, 19
     separation of user process from
       supervisor processes, 5, 22
     user-ID, 53
user-ID, 53
utility routines, 19

V

validation
     chipset, 197
     current settings, 37
     GETSEC [SEXIT], late
       launch, 211
     hashed message authentication
       code (HMAC) validation, 128
     program code and, 123
     SCLEAN identity, 233
     secure initialization (SINIT)
       module, 199
     trusted platform module
       (TPM), 197
vendors
     interaction of OS and kernel
       from same vendor, 178
     interaction of OS and MVMM
       from same vendor, 178
     interaction of OS, MVMM, and
       kernel from different
       vendors, 179
     same vendor OS, MVMM, and
       kernel interaction, 177
     TPM vendors, 120
verification model, protected
  component, 181
verification of session key creation, 159
versatility of platform as objective, 64
version of applications, 39
versions of drivers, 38, 39
virtual machine extensions (VMX)
     defined, 268
     events, 105
     operation, 104

virtual machines (VM)
  control structure, 106
  creation, 107
  entry controls, 106
  execution controls, 106
  exit controls, 106
  life-cycle support, VMM, 112
  limited inter-VM
    communication, 112
  protected, 109
  scheduling, VMM, 112
  secrets, 116
virtual memory management
  (VMM), 93
  chipset hardware
    measurement, 96
  environment models, 111
  identity, obtaining, 94
  launch and VM creation, 107
  measured, 113
  measurement, 94
  obtaining the VMM identity, 94
  protected mode, 30
  secrets, 116
  with kernel features, protected
    virtual machines, 112
  with no services, protected
    virtual machines, 112
VM. *See* virtual machines (VM)
VMM. *See* virtual memory
  management (VMM)
VMX. *See* virtual machine extensions
  (VMX)
volatile storage
  defined, 268
  trusted platform module
    (TPM), 126

W
wild, defined, 268
windows, attacks, display windows, 47

X
XOR strings, 128

66 *As the pace of technology introduction increases, it's difficult to keep up. Intel Press has established an impressive portfolio. The breadth of topics is a reflection of both Intel's diversity as well as our commitment to serve a broad technical community.*

I hope you will take advantage of these products to further your technical education. **99**

Patrick Gelsinger
Senior Vice President
Intel Corporation

**Turn the page to learn about titles
from Intel Press for system developers**

Take full advantage of 64-bit computing on IA-32 processors

Programming with Intel® Extended Memory 64 Technology

Migrating Software for Optimal 64-bit Performance

By Andrew Binstock
ISBN 0-9764832-0-3

Intel® Extended Memory 64 Technology (Intel® EM64T) brings 64-bit processing capabilities to desktops, servers, and workstations while ensuring full compatibility with current 32-bit operating systems and applications. Intel EM64T improves performance by allowing the system to address more than 4 gigabytes of virtual and physical memory. Using this technology, you can enjoy the flexibility to move to 64-bit processing whenever it makes the most sense for your needs.

Learn how to migrate 32-bit code to processors with Intel EM64T and achieve better performance when working with large datasets. This practical guide removes the guesswork, giving you tips on optimization and best known methods to develop flexible, scalable, 64-bit software applications for desktops and general-purpose server/workstation platforms.

Highlights include:

- Description of Intel EM64T and the associated programming changes
- Implications of ILP 64 for data structures and byte alignment
- Tools and techniques for successful migration to 64 bits
- Mixing of 32-bit and 64-bit applications
- Writing code that takes advantage of new instructions
- Effective use of big memory while avoiding the pitfalls
- Examples written in C language

Essential reading for every developer whose code will run on Intel® Architecture Processors with Intel EM64T.

> 66 *This book is really practical and useful. It thoroughly covers depth of the technology and background of portable programming.* 99
>
> *Oleksiy Danikhno,*
> *Director, Application*
> *Development and Architecture,*
> *A4Vision, Inc.*

● *Multi-Core Programming*
Increasing Performance through Software Multi-threading

By Shameem Akhter and Jason Roberts
ISBN 0-9764832-4-6

Software developers can no longer rely on increasing clock speeds alone to speed up single-threaded applications; instead, to gain a competitive advantage, developers must learn how to properly design their applications to run in a threaded environment. This book helps software developers write high-performance multi-threaded code for Intel's multi-core architecture while avoiding the common parallel programming issues associated with multi-threaded programs. This book is a practical, hands-on volume with immediately usable code examples that enable readers to quickly master the necessary programming techniques.

Discover programming techniques for Intel multi-core architecture and Hyper-Threading Technology

● *The Software Optimization Cookbook, Second Edition*
High-Performance Recipes for IA-32 Platforms

By Richard Gerber, Aart J.C. Bik, Kevin B. Smith, and Xinmin Tian
ISBN 0-9764832-1-1

Four Intel experts explain the techniques and tools that you can use to improve the performance of applications for IA-32 processors. Simple explanations and code examples help you to develop software that benefits from Intel® Extended Memory 64 Technology (Intel® EM64T), multi-core processing, Hyper-Threading Technology, OpenMP†, and multimedia extensions. This book guides you through the growing collection of software tools, compiler switches, and coding optimizations, showing you efficient ways to get the best performance from software applications.

❝ *A must-read text for anyone who intends to write performance-critical applications for the Intel processor family.*

—Robert van Engelen, Professor,**❞** Florida State University

- ## *Change-Based Test Management*
  ### *Improving the Software Validation Process*
  By Jon Sistowicz and Ray Arell
  ISBN 0-9717861-2-7

This introduction to Change-based Test Management (CBTM) provides software engineers and test specialists with a detailed explanation of applying this new methodology significantly improves quality while reducing development time. Case studies and author insights help readers visualize CBTM in action.

66 *An essential book for any developer involved with software testing. Extremely practical.* **99**

—*Virginia Aldrich, Senior Software Engineer, Express Imaging Systems*

Special Deals, Special Prices!

To ensure you have all the latest books
and enjoy aggressively priced
discounts, please go to this Web site:

www.intel.com/intelpress/bookbundles.htm

Bundles of our books are available,
selected especially to address the needs
of the developer. The bundles place
important complementary topics at
your fingertips, and the price for a
bundle is substantially less than
buying all the books individually.

About Intel Press

Intel Press is the authoritative source of timely, technical books
to help software and hardware developers speed up their development
process. We collaborate only with leading industry experts to deliver
reliable, first-to-market information about the latest
technologies, processes, and strategies.

Our products are planned with the help of many people in the developer
community and we encourage you to consider becoming a customer advisor.
If you would like to help us and gain additional advance insight to the
latest technologies, we encourage you to consider the Intel Press
Customer Advisor Program. You can register here:

www.intel.com/intelpress/register.htm

For information about bulk orders or corporate sales, please send email to
bulkbooksales@intel.com

Other Developer Resources from Intel

At these Web sites you can also find valuable technical information
and resources for developers:

developer.intel.com	general information for developers
www.intel.com/software	content, tools, training, and the Intel® Early Access Program for software developers
www.intel.com/software/products	programming tools to help you develop high-performance applications
www.intel.com/netcomms	solutions and resources for networking and communications
www.intel.com/technology/itj	Intel Technology Journal
www.intel.com/idf	worldwide technical conference, the Intel Developer Forum

Intel
PRESS

Notes

■ Notes

■ Notes

■ Notes